THE SYNTAX AND SEMANTICS

THE SYNTAX AND SEMANTICS OF THE VERB IN CLASSICAL GREEK

AN INTRODUCTION

ALBERT RIJKSBARON

University of Amsterdam
Department of Classical Philology

Third Edition

THE UNIVERSITY OF CHICAGO PRESS

CHICAGO AND LONDON

The University of Chicago Press, Chicago, 60637
© by A. Rijksbaron, 1984, 1994, 2002
All rights reserved.

The first edition of this book was published in Amsterdam by
J. C. Gieben in 1984.
The third edition was first published in Amsterdam by
J. C. Gieben in 2002.
University of Chicago Press edition 2006
Printed in the United States of America
13 12 11 10 09 08   2 3 4 5

ISBN-13: 978-0-226-71858-3 (paper)
ISBN-10: 0-226-71858-1 (paper)

Library of Congress Cataloging-in-Publication Data
Rijksbaron, Albert.
   The syntax and semantics of the verb in classical Greek : an
introduction / Albert Rijksbaron.—3rd ed.
      p. cm.
   Originally published: 3rd ed. Amsterdam : J. C. Gieben, 2002.
   Includes bibliographical references and index.
   ISBN-13: 978-0-226-71858-3 (pbk. : alk. paper)
   ISBN-10: 0-226-71858-1 (pbk. : alk. paper)   1. Greek
language—Verb.   I. Title.
   PA337.R55   2006
   485′.6—dc22

                                        2006031795

To the Memory of Han Gieben

CONTENTS

CHAPTER III THE USE OF MOODS AND TENSES IN DEPENDENT CLAUSES

Preface to the first edition

Whereas there are many extensive treatments of the syntax and semantics of the verb in ancient Greek, a concise, and yet comprehensive and linguistically up-to-date introduction to this subject is lacking. The present book aims at providing such an introduction, both for University students of Greek and for professional classicists. Whenever this seemed profitable, elements of the earlier treatments have, of course, been included, but the emphasis is on incorporating recent insights, both from general linguistics and from work done in Greek syntax and semantics. As an introductory course, it concentrates on 5th and 4th century Greek.

The book is written within the framework of Dik's Functional Grammar. This, however, mainly concerns the general organization of the book; discussions of a theoretical nature are rare, except in the chapter on voice. The treatment of active, middle and passive profits considerably, I think, from the application of grammatical notions such as Agent, Goal, causativity etc. By its more theoretical nature this chapter may also serve as an introduction to the interesting work which is presently going on concerning both active, middle and passive and the role of semantic and syntactic functions.

The book presupposes a reasonable knowledge of the morphology of classical Greek. Since all examples, however, are provided with a translation, the book may prove useful also for students of general linguistics and of other languages.

My thanks are due to a number of persons and institutions. Irene de Jong and Rik Deinema assisted me in collecting the material. Niek van der Ben, Jan Maarten Bremer, Alwies Cock, Harm Pinkster, Kees Ruijgh and Elseline Vester commented upon whole or part of earlier versions. Hetty de Schepper expertly typed the text. Ester Wouthuysen designed the cover. Hotze Mulder not only translated chapters I - IV from the original Dutch text, but also commented upon its contents. Furthermore, he corrected the English of chapter V and compiled the indexes. The Fondation Hardt at Genève-Vandœuvres enabled me at several occasions to profit from its rich library and excellent working-facilities. The Netherlands Organization for the Advancement of Pure Research (ZWO), finally, subsidized a stay at the Fondation Hardt.

Albert Rijksbaron
Amsterdam, June 1984

Preface to the second edition

While the general structure of the book has been retained, the text has been revised, and partly rewritten. I have added several new subjects. Besides a large number of smaller changes and additions, the main changes relate to: the treatment of aspect; the imperfect of modal verbs; the optative in indirect speech; consecutive clauses; conditional clauses; and the participle. The chapter on the infinitive has been entirely rewritten. The more important additions include: sections on the discourse function of the imperfect, the imperfect of likelihood, the inceptive imperfect; and on periphrastic constructions. As a result, the number of examples illustrating the various constructions has considerably increased. General linguistic notions are used on a slightly larger scale than in the first edition. Finally, the bibliography is still concise, but a number of older publications have now been included, and it includes also, of course, several recent books and articles, with assenting as well as dissenting views. More extensive bibliographies may be found in the recent works of F. Adrados and M. Meier-Brügger.

It is, once more, a pleasure to acknowledge a debt to several friends and colleagues, both inside and outside the Classical Institute of the University of Amsterdam. Gerard Boter, Irene de Jong and especially Anne-Marie Chanet and Gerry Wakker commented on part or whole of the first edition. Ineke Blijleven expertly decoded a scrambled copy of the first edition, and transformed it into a smooth computer text. Nancy Laan and Emilie van Opstall came to the rescue at various moments during the final stage of the correction of text and indexes. Finally, Noor Kegel skilfully manipulated the text so as to give it its present appearance.

Amsterdam, August 1994

Preface to the third edition

The text of this edition is substantially that of the second edition, but a number of sections have been rewritten entirely or in part, notably those on the historic present, the future indicative, and causal clauses. There is a new section on the aorist of performative verbs, which replaces that on the aorist of verbs of emotion. Several notes have been rewritten or added, e.g. on the uses of μέλλω. The part on the oblique optative has been considerably modified. A number of examples have been replaced by more relevant texts, and some twenty new examples have been added. The bibliography has been brought up to date. I should mention here that an extensive bibliography of Greek linguistics, maintained by Michel Buijs of the University of Utrecht, is now available at www.let.uu.nl/hist/goac/bgl/.

Two important changes concern the addition of an Index locorum and of a sixteen-page summary, 'Essentials of *Syntax and Semantics*'. The Index locorum was for the greater part compiled by Jan Ebele van der Veen (The Hague), whose services are gratefully acknowledged here. The summary makes it possible, I hope, to have a quick look at the basic syntactic properties of the Greek verb; at the same time it may serve as a repertory that can be memorized.

I am again indebted to a number of persons for their painstaking accuracy in reading and using the previous edition: Rutger Allan (Amsterdam), Gerard Boter (Amsterdam), Ton Kessels (Nijmegen), Bram Wieringa (Aduard) and, especially, Gerry Wakker (Groningen). Sé Lenssen of the Classical Institute of the University of Amsterdam provided valuable assistance in solving various computer problems.

Finally, my thanks are due to Han Gieben, whose long-standing commitment to publishing studies on Greek and Latin syntax is mentioned here with gratitude.

Albert Rijksbaron
Amsterdam, May 2002

Preface to the American edition

Thanks to the initiative of the University of Chicago Press, for which I am most grateful, *The Syntax and Semantics of the Verb in Classical Greek* is now starting a new life as an American paperback. May the book continue to serve, for a still larger audience, as a succinct introduction to the Greek verb, which combines traditional philological methods with recent insights from general as well as Greek linguistics.

Albert Rijksbaron
Amsterdam, July 2006

A note on text-editions and translations

The text of the Greek examples is usually that of the editions of the Oxford Classical Texts series. The examples from Aristophanes, however, are taken from the edition in the Budé-series. The translations are either borrowed from or based upon the editions in the Loeb-series, with the exception of Jebb's translations of Sophocles. Greek authors and their works are referred to in accordance with Liddell-Scott-Stuart Jones, *A Greek-English Lexicon*.

I INTRODUCTION TO THE MOODS AND TENSES

§ 1   The semantic value of the tense stems

The Greek verbal system has five *tense stems* (or *aspect stems*, see below, Note 1):

– the present stem   (e.g. βουλεύε-σθαι)
– the aorist stem   (e.g. βουλεύσα-σθαι)
– the perfect stem   (e.g. βεβουλεῦ-σθαι)
– the future stem   (e.g. βουλεύσε-σθαι)
– the future perfect stem   (e.g. βεβουλεύσε-σθαι)

Each stem has a *distinct semantic value*, which may be defined as follows:

– the present stem signifies that a state of affairs is being carried out and is, therefore, *not-completed* (imperfective value);
– the aorist stem signifies that a state of affairs is *completed* (confective value);
– the perfect stem signifies both that a state of affairs is completed and that as a result a *state* exists (stative-confective value);
– the future stem signifies that a state of affairs is located *after* a point in time given in context or situation, without indicating whether or not the state of affairs is completed;
– the future perfect stem signifies that a state of affairs is completed and that as a result a *state* exists *after* a point in time given in context or situation.

All verb forms derived from a certain stem are in principle characterized by the fundamental semantic value of that stem. This holds for the *finite* forms: indicative, subjunctive, optative, imperative (also called the *moods* (cp. § 4)), as well as for the *non-finite* forms: infinitive and participle.

In actual usage, the semantic values defined above serve various purposes. An important application is that they may be used to locate a certain state of affairs with respect to other states of affairs, e.g. in historical narrative. Thus, by the value [not-completed], the forms of the present stem characterize a state of affairs as 'open', thereby creating a framework within which other states of affairs may occur. These forms are, therefore, pre-eminently suited to establish a relationship of *simultaneity* between two or more states of affairs. On the other hand, the value [completed] of the aorist stem may serve to express the *anteriority* of one state of affairs to another.

Note 1 In the literature about the Greek verbal system the terms 'tense stem' and 'aspect stem' are in general use. As to the former, it should be borne in mind that the tense stems do not express time in the sense of 'present', 'past', and 'future'. However, they often - the future and future perfect stem always (cp. the definitions) - express temporal *relationships*: simultaneity (present and perfect stem), anteriority (aorist stem), posteriority (future and future perfect stem). On the other hand, it is often stated that Greek had no proper means to express relative time and that the stems are really *aspect stems*, aspect being defined as 'the speaker's view of the internal constituency of the state of affairs'. Thus, the speaker would be free to choose between, for instance, a present stem form and an aorist stem form, a choice simply depending on whether he would view the state of affairs as 'not-completed' or 'completed'. In general, this opinion is untenable. For one thing, an important function of, for instance, the imperfect and aorist indicative in temporal clauses is neglected: they serve to establish the order of events, a function especially significant in historical narrative. In other words, it is not taken into account that 'not-completed' and 'completed' should in principle be understood as 'not-completed' and 'completed' *with regard to a certain point of orientation*. For another, the choice between tense stems is highly determined by the context. Substitution of one form for another usually changes the information and thus influences the way in which a speaker may proceed with, for instance, a narrative. This is not to say that notions like simultaneity etc. are always of primary importance. In certain cases, especially when a point of orientation is lacking and there is, therefore, no use for notions like simultaneity and anteriority, the values [not-completed] and [completed] are solely relevant. This occurs often with imperatives and with infinitives after verbs like 'try', 'order' etc. Thus, an imperative like λέγε, when used in isolation, stresses the course of the state of affairs concerned, while εἰπέ rather calls attention to the completion, the realization-as-a-whole, of the state of affairs. For details see § 16.2 (imperative) and § 33.1 (ii) (infinitive). - For the sake of brevity the term 'tense stem' will be used in the following.

Note 2 A formal indication of the crucial difference, in terms of completion, between the present stem and the aorist stem is the fact that the forms of the present stem, but not those of the aorist stem, can be construed with verbs meaning 'interrupt', 'stop', as in παῦσαι σπεύδων τὰ σπεύδεις ('stop striving after the things that you are striving after', Hdt. 1.206.1). A related phenomenon is that the adverb μεταξύ 'in the middle of' can only modify present stem forms, as in ὁ Μενέξενος ἐκ τῆς αὐλῆς μεταξὺ παίζων εἰσέρχεται ('Menexenos stepped in from the court, in the middle of his game', Pl. *Ly.* 207b). In view of these facts one might describe the difference between present and aorist also as follows: while a present stem state of affairs can be broken off, an aorist state of affairs denotes an indivisible whole.

Note 3 In the case of certain verbs the tense stems are derived from different verb stems, e.g. 'see': present ὁρῶ, aorist εἶδον, perfect ἑόρακα (ὄπωπα), future ὄψομαι. Such verbs are called *suppletive verbs*. Of other verbs not all tense stems actually occur (*defective verbs*), e.g. 'be gone': present οἴχομαι, future οἰχήσομαι.

Note 4 I use the technical term 'state of affairs', instead of 'action', as a cover term for 'that which is expressed by a predication' (= roughly: a verb form and its arguments, e.g. Agent and Patient. The notion 'argument' will be discussed in more detail in § 41.3). 'Action' is now usually restricted to a particular type of states of affairs, cp. e.g. Dik (1997: 114f.).

§ 2   The role of the lexical meaning of the verb

The interpretation of a certain verb form does not only depend on the semantic value of its tense stem, but also on other factors, e.g. the lexical meaning of the verb. Thus, the imperfect of, for instance, βασιλεύω (a so-called *stative, durative* or *unbounded* verb: the state of affairs does not have an inherent end-point) cannot usually be interpreted in the same way as that of verbs like πείθω or δίδωμι (*terminative, bounded,* or *telic* verbs: the state of affairs has an inherent end-point). Often ἔπειθε must be interpreted as 'he tried to convince': the end-point ('convince') is not attained (so-called *conative* use of the imperfect). The imperfect of durative βασιλεύω cannot possibly be used in this way. The interaction of lexical meaning and tense stem value will be dealt with in a number of sections (notably §§ 6.2.2, 6.3.2).

> *Note 1* As a cover term for features like 'durative', 'terminative' etc. the German word *Aktionsart* (lit. 'action character') is often used. Thus, βασιλεύω is said to have a durative Aktionsart, etc. The relationship between aspect and Aktionsart is discussed extensively in Lyons (1977: 705ff.). For Greek, Fanning (1990) is particularly useful, especially Ch. 3 'The effect of inherent meaning and other elements on aspectual function'. In Rijksbaron (1989) I have presented a typology of verb meanings which in a number of respects resembles that of Fanning.

§ 3   The expression of past, present, and future

Of the various finite forms (or moods, cp. § 1) which are derived from the tense stems only the *indicatives* express so-called *absolute time*, i.e. they locate the state of affairs relative to the moment of utterance in the past, present, or future:

- the primary present indicative (commonly: present indicative or simply: present) locates the state of affairs *at* the moment of utterance (the 'present');
- the secondary present indicative (commonly: imperfect) locates the state of affairs at a moment *before* the moment of utterance (the 'past');
- the secondary aorist indicative (often simply: aorist) locates the state of affairs at a moment *before* the moment of utterance (the 'past');
- the primary perfect indicative (commonly: perfect) locates the state *at* the moment of utterance (the 'present');
- the secondary perfect indicative (commonly: pluperfect) locates the state at a moment *before* the moment of utterance (the 'past');
- the future indicative locates the state of affairs at a moment *after* the moment of utterance (the 'future');
- the future perfect indicative locates the state at a moment *after* the moment of utterance (the 'future').

In summary: the *primary* indicatives express 'present' or 'future' and the *secondary* indicatives (or augment-forms) 'past'. It is clear from the definitions given above that - to name the most important tenses - imperfect, aorist indicative, and pluperfect, on the one hand, and present and perfect, on the other, do *not* differ as to their temporal value: the first three all refer to the past, the latter two both refer to the present. The differences are based exclusively on the semantic values of the tense stems, as defined in § 1.

> *Note 1* The primary present indicative does not only serve to describe states of affairs taking place at the moment of utterance, but is also - and, in fact, more often - used in a so-called generic way: (i) in the case of states of affairs located in the 'present' in a much broader sense, without reference to a specific point in time (*habitual* present, mostly used in the description of habits and characteristic qualities), and (ii) in the case of states of affairs

located in no specific time (*universal* or *timeless* present). English examples of (i) are: 'John runs the 100 meters in 14 seconds', 'Nowadays the English drink much more wine than they used to'; of (ii): 'Two and two make four', 'Newton is the discoverer of the law of gravitation'. Notice that in utterances of the latter type temporal adverbs like 'nowadays' cannot be added: *'Two and two nowadays make four'. (The asterisk (*) is used to indicate grammatical incorrectness). For Greek examples see § 5.3.

Note 2 For the so-called historic present see § 7.

Note 3 There is no primary aorist indicative, since the value of the aorist stem is 'completedness', whereas present states of affairs in principle continue through the moment of utterance and are, therefore, necessarily not-completed.

Note 4 The primary indicatives are also called *principal* tenses, the secondary indicatives *historical* tenses.

Note 5 Besides the indicative, the imperative, too, expresses absolute time, since it locates the state of affairs in the future.

The combined effect of the semantic values of the tense stems and the temporal values of the indicatives may be schematized as follows (ex. παιδεύω, active voice):

state of affairs is → located in	completed		not-completed
	+ resulting state	- resulting state	
present	πεπαίδευκα		παιδεύω
past	ἐπεπαιδεύκη	ἐπαίδευσα	ἐπαίδευον
future	πεπαιδευκὼς ἔσομαι	παιδεύσω	

The other moods (with the exception of the imperative, see note 5 above) as well as the infinitive and the participle do not independently locate a state of affairs in time, but 'derive' their temporal value solely from their interaction with other verb forms, especially the indicative. The temporal reference of states of affairs expressed by the subjunctive etc. - i.e. their location in past, present, or future - must, therefore, depend on the temporal reference of the other verb forms. This dependency may be illustrated with some examples of the participle, where it is fully operative:

(1) ἐπείτε δὲ ὁ Κῦρος πορευόμενος ἐπὶ τὴν Βαβυλῶνα ἐγίνετο ἐπὶ
     Γύνδῃ ποταμῷ ('When Cyrus on his way to Babylon came to the
     river Gyndes', Hdt. 1.189.1; πορευόμενος: past state of affairs,
     since it is simultaneous with ἐγίνετο)

(2) πολλοὺς γὰρ ὑμῶν ὁρῶ δικάζοντας ('For I notice that many of
     you are members of the jury', Lys. 1.43; δικάζοντας: state of
     affairs at the moment of utterance, cp. ὁρῶ)

(3) ἐξ ἀρχῆς ἐπιδείξω ... οὐδὲν παραλείπων ('From the very
     beginning I shall show ..., without leaving out anything', Lys. 1.5;
     παραλείπων: future state of affairs, cp. ἐπιδείξω)

> *Note 6* There are certain restrictions in the case of subjunctive and optative:
> a subjunctive is never used to refer to past states of affairs, nor are the
> cupitive optative and the optative + ἄν.

§ 4   The moods in independent sentences

In addition to the five tense stems Greek has four different *finite* verb
forms (the *moods*) and two *non-finite* forms (infinitive and participle). The
moods enable the speaker to 'clothe' his utterances in such a way as to
express his attitude towards their contents, according to the situation in
which he produces the utterance and the nature of the information which
he wants to convey. In the following I give a survey of the main uses of
the moods in independent sentences; a more detailed analysis will follow
in the sections on the single moods (§§ 5-15).

The moods occur in various sentence-types:

(i) *Declarative* sentences (negative οὐ). The moods used are the indicative,
the optative + ἄν, and the secondary indicative + ἄν. The values of the
moods are as follows:

- *indicative*: the speaker presents the state of affairs as a fact (*factual*
  presentation);
- *optative* + ἄν: the speaker presents the realization of the state of affairs
  as possible (*potential* presentation), e.g. ἡ ῥητορικὴ δημηγορία ἂν εἴη
  'rhetoric is possibly (just) popular oratory'; εἴποι τις ἄν 'someone
  might say';

– *secondary indicative* + ἄν: the speaker presents the realization of the state of affairs as no longer possible (*counterfactual* presentation). Usually, the secondary indicative + ἄν is connected with a conditional clause: (if this had happened) ἀπῆλθον ἄν 'I would have left'.

(ii) *Iussive* (or *directive*) sentences (negative μή). The moods used are the imperative and the subjunctive. They have the following values:
– *imperative*: the speaker commands someone to carry out the state of affairs, e.g. ἄπιθι 'go away'; ἀπίτω 'he must go away';
– *subjunctive* (1st person, usually plural): the speaker commands himself (singular forms) or one or more others as well as himself (plural forms) to carry out the state of affairs, e.g. ἀπίω 'let me go away'; ἀπίωμεν 'let us go away' (*(ad)hortative* subjunctive). The 2nd person of the aorist subjunctive replaces the aorist imperative in prohibitions: μὴ ἀπέλθῃς 'don't go away' (*prohibitive* subjunctive).

(iii) *Interrogative* sentences. Two sub-types may be distinguished: *yes-no* questions and *specifying* questions. In both subtypes the indicative, the subjunctive and the optative + ἄν are used. These moods have the following values:

(a) In *yes-no* questions, i.e. questions which seek a positive or negative answer:
– *indicative*: the speaker wants to know whether or not the state of affairs is a fact, e.g. (ἆρ') ἀπῆλθες; 'did you go away?' - For the negative see Note 1 below.
– *subjunctive* (1st person, usually plural): the speaker is uncertain whether or not to carry out the state of affairs, e.g. (ἆρ') ἀπίωμεν; 'should we leave?' Negative μή (*deliberative* or *dubitative* subjunctive).
- *optative* + ἄν: the speaker wants to know whether the realization of the state of affairs is possible, e.g. εἴποις ἂν τὴν ἀλήθειαν; 'would you say the truth?'

(b) In *specifying* questions, i.e. questions introduced by interrogative pronouns or adverbs asking for specification concerning an aspect of the state of affairs unknown to the speaker:

- *indicative*: the speaker seeks further information about a state of affairs which he considers a fact, e.g. τί εἶπες; 'what did you say?' (i.e. you said something and I now ask you what it was); πῶς ἦλθες; 'how did you get here?'
- *subjunctive*: the speaker is in doubt concerning an aspect of a state of affairs to be carried out by him, e.g. τί εἴπω; 'what should I say?' (i.e. I must say something, but I am uncertain what to say); πῇ φεύγωμεν; 'whither should we flee?'(*deliberative* or *dubitative* subjunctive);
- *optative* + ἄν: the speaker seeks further information about a possible state of affairs, e.g. ποῦ εὕροιμ᾽ ἂν αὐτούς; 'Where can I find them?'

(iv) *Wishes* (negative μή). The moods used are the optative and the secondary indicative + ἄν. They have the following values:
- *optative* (without ἄν): the speaker presents the realization of the state of affairs as desirable and possible, e.g. γένοιο εὐτυχής 'may you become happy' (*cupitive* optative);
- *secondary indicative* (introduced by εἴθε or εἰ γάρ): the speaker presents the realization of the state of affairs as desirable but no longer possible, e.g. εἴθε σοι τότε συνεγενόμην 'if only I had met you then' (*unrealizable wish*).

> *Note 1* In *yes-no* questions both οὐ and μή occur as question particles, expressing a certain expectation on the part of the speaker as to the answer. οὐ elicits a positive answer (asks for confirmation), μή elicits a negative answer (asks for denial).
>
> *Note 2* The uses of the subjunctive discussed in this section are often reduced to the same denominator: *voluntative* subjunctive. - For the use of subjunctive and optative in dependent clauses see Ch. III.
>
> *Note 3* As in English and other languages, commands and wishes may be expressed in various ways: cp. English 'go away', 'you have to go', 'you should go' and 'would that they went away', 'if only they went away', 'I should like them to go' etc. The choice between these and similar alternatives mainly depends on *pragmatic* factors (cp. e.g. Dik 1997: Ch. 13).
>
> *Note 4* In English linguistic studies specifying questions are commonly called *wh*-questions because of the large number of interrogative words beginning with *wh*-.

II THE MAIN USES OF THE SINGLE MOODS AND TENSES IN INDEPENDENT SENTENCES

§ 5 Present indicative

5.1 *Temporal location: location at the moment of utterance*

The present indicative signifies that the state of affairs is located at the moment of utterance; the state of affairs continues through the moment of utterance:

(4) τί κάτησθε, ὦ Πέρσαι, ἐνθαῦτα ...; ('Persians, why are you sitting there?', Hdt. 3.151.2)

(5) ὁ δ' ὦμος οὑτοσὶ πιέζεται ('My shoulder here is stuck', Ar. *Ra.* 30)

> *Note 1* In the case of verbs of saying and perception the present indicative may be used even if the state of affairs of 'saying' or 'perceiving' has been completed. Here the present indicative indicates that the state of affairs itself is not referred to but its result in the situation at hand. E.g., κοίῃ δὴ κρίνεις Τέλλον ὀλβιώτατον εἶναι; ('What is the basis of your opinion that Tellos is happiest?', Hdt. 1.30.4): Croesus' question is prompted by Solon's answer 'Tellos' to Croesus' previous question 'Of the people you know, whom do you consider happiest?'. Solon's opinion exists by itself, independent of its being pronounced. - ὦ Λακεδαιμόνιοι ..., ὑμέας ... πυνθάνομαι προεστάναι τῆς Ἑλλάδος ('Spartans, I hear that you are the leaders of Greece', Hdt. 1.69.2). This phenomenon may be observed in the case of other verbs as well, particularly ἥκω ('arrive' → 'have come, be somewhere'); φεύγω ('flee' → 'be a fugitive, live in exile'); νικῶ ('defeat' → 'be victorious'); ἡττῶμαι ('suffer a defeat' → 'be vanquished'); τίκτω ('give birth' → 'be mother/father'). The other forms of the present stem are used in similar ways; cp. § 6.2.4 (imperfect).

5.2 *In questions with iussive force*

In questions the combination of οὐ + present indicative (1st or 2nd person), often preceded by τί, may express an emphatic request or command:

(6)   δεῦρο δή, ἦ δ᾽ ὅς, εὐθὺ ἡμῶν. <u>οὐ παραβάλλεις</u>; ('Hither, he said, straight to us! Won't you come by?', Pl. *Ly.* 203b)

(7)   <u>τί</u> οὖν, ἦ δ᾽ ὅς, <u>οὐκ ἐρωτᾷς</u>; :: ἀλλ᾽ ἐρήσομαι, ἦν δ᾽ ἐγώ. ('Why don't you ask, he said. All right, I'll ask, I said', Pl. *Ly.* 211d)

The speaker observes that a certain situation does not exist, i.e. that his interlocutor is not carrying out a certain state of affairs, and he inquires whether his observation is correct ((6)), or why the situation is such as he observes it to be ((7)).

In pragmatic terms questions of this type function as requests or commands: 'see to it that the state of affairs is carried out as yet'. In cases like (7) we are not dealing with real *why*-questions; this appears from the fact that the answer does not consist of an explanation.

Note 1 Utterances of this type, which serve a (pragmatic) purpose different from the one they seem to serve (question → request/command) are called *indirect* utterances.

5.3   Generic use

In § 3, Note 1 reference was made to the generic use of the present indicative, (i) in descriptions of habits and properties, and (ii) in timeless statements. Some Greek examples of (i):

(8)   <u>συσσιτοῦμεν</u> γὰρ δὴ ἐγώ τε καὶ Μελησίας ὅδε, καὶ ἡμῖν τὰ μειράκια <u>παρασιτεῖ</u> ('Melesias here and I dine together, and the boys dine with us', Pl. *La.* 179b)

and of (ii):

(9)   τῶν δὲ κροκοδείλων φύσις <u>ἐστὶ</u> τοιήδε· ('The nature of the crocodile is as follows:', Hdt. 2.68.1)

It is, of course, not always possible to distinguish between (i) and (ii): the 'nature' of crocodiles could change, in which case (9) would not be a timeless statement. The problems involved here are of a mainly non-linguistic nature, and will not be dealt with here.

Note 1 For an illuminative discussion of these problems see Lyons (1977: 679-682).

Note 2 For the use of the present indicative in narrative texts, alternating with the imperfect and the aorist indicative (so-called 'historic present') see § 7; for the *praesens pro futuro* see § 7.3, Note 5.

§ 6   Imperfect and aorist indicative in narrative texts

6.1   The alternation of imperfect and aorist indicative and its effects

Imperfect and aorist indicative are predominantly used in narrative texts. By locating the various states of affairs in time relative to each other they serve as the most important structuring elements in a story.

Since the *imperfect* characterizes the state of affairs as 'not-completed' it creates a framework within which other states of affairs may occur, while the *aorist indicative* characterizes the state of affairs as 'completed', as a mere event. This difference in value between imperfect and aorist indicative is significant for the way in which a story is told. The imperfect creates a certain expectation on the part of the reader/hearer: what else happened?; the aorist indicative, on the other hand, does not have this effect: the state of affairs has simply occurred.

These values are applied in various ways. Often one or more states of affairs expressed in the aorist indicative are located within a framework given by the imperfect, as illustrated by (10) and (11):

(10)   καὶ ὅτε δὴ ἦν δεκαέτης ὁ παῖς, πρῆγμα ἐς αὐτὸν τοιόνδε γενόμενον ἐξέφηνέ μιν. <u>ἔπαιζε</u> ἐν τῇ κώμῃ ... μετ' ἄλλων ἡλίκων ἐν ὁδῷ. καὶ οἱ παῖδες παίζοντες <u>εἵλοντο</u> ἑωυτῶν βασιλέα εἶναι τοῦτον δὴ τὸν ... παῖδα. ὁ δὲ αὐτῶν <u>διέταξε</u> τοὺς μὲν οἰκίας οἰκοδομέειν ... ('When the boy [who was to be Cyrus] was ten years old, the following occurrence revealed his identity. He was playing in the street of the village ... with some other boys. And during the game the children picked this particular boy as their king. He instructed one group to build houses ...', Hdt. 1.114.1-2)

At the beginning, ἐξέφηνε sums up the event, which is, in the following, related in detail. The story proper begins with ἔπαιζε. In the course of the game (note also παίζοντες) the children choose little 'Cyrus' to be their king. Then 'Cyrus' gives his 'subjects' a number of tasks. Both of these states of affairs, one (εἵλοντο) anterior to the other (διέταξε), are enclosed within the framework given by ἔπαιζε. In other words: the 'παίζειν' continues when the 'ἑλέσθαι' and 'διατάξαι' take place.

Note 1 A summarizing aorist indicative like ἐξέφηνε in (10) is called *complexive.*

(11) ἐπειδὴ δὲ τῶν τε συμμάχων ἤκουσαν οἱ Λακεδαιμόνιοι τὰ
      ἐγκλήματα καὶ τῶν Ἀθηναίων ἃ ἔλεξαν, ... <u>ἐβουλεύοντο</u> ... περὶ
      τῶν παρόντων (...). παρελθὼν δὲ Ἀρχίδαμος ὁ βασιλεὺς αὐτῶν
      ... <u>ἔλεξε</u> τοιάδε (...). καὶ ὁ μὲν Ἀρχίδαμος τοιαῦτα <u>εἶπεν</u>·
      παρελθὼν δὲ Σθενελαΐδας ... <u>ἔλεξεν</u> ὧδε. ('When the Spartans
      had heard the complaints made by their allies against the Athenians
      and the Athenian reply, they discussed the situation. Archidamos,
      their king, came forward and made the following speech: (...). This
      Archidamos said; Sthenelaïdas came forward and spoke as follows',
      Th. 1.79-85)

In the course of the Spartan deliberation (ἐβουλεύοντο) Archidamos makes a speech (ἔλεξε τοιάδε, summed up afterwards by τοιαῦτα εἶπεν). When he has finished, one of the others responds to Archidamos' words (ἔλεξεν). Both speeches are enclosed within the framework of 'ἐβουλεύοντο' (the βουλεύεσθαι continues) and the aorist indicative characterizes the speeches as completed; Archidamos' speech is anterior to Sthenelaïdas', and the latter speech is anterior to the vote (not cited here) taken on the two proposals.

Note 2 The present participle παίζοντες in (10), expressing simultaneity, and the aorist participle παρελθών in (11), expressing anteriority, are not taken into account here. For these uses cp. § 38. For ἐπειδὴ ... ἤκουσαν in (11), expressing anteriority, and for other temporal clauses, see § 26.

We also find series of imperfects, describing a number of more or less simultaneous states of affairs; a 'scene is painted', so to speak:

(12) δμῶες πρὸς ἔργον πάντες <u>ἵεσαν</u> χέρας·
      οἳ μὲν σφαγεῖον <u>ἔφερον</u>, οἳ δ' <u>ἦρον</u> κανᾶ,
      ἄλλοι δὲ πῦρ <u>ἀνῆπτον</u> ἀμφί τ' ἐσχάρας
      λέβητας <u>ὤρθουν</u>· πᾶσα δ' <u>ἐκτύπει</u> στέγη
      ('The slaves put forth their hands to their work. Some brought a
      bowl to catch the blood, others brought baskets, still others

proceeded to light the fire, and set cauldrons upright about the altar. The whole house resounded with activity', E. *El.* 799-802).

On the other hand, sequences of aorist indicatives occur as well, describing a series of successive states of affairs, e.g.

(13)   (῎Αρδυς) οὗτος δὲ Πριηνέας τε <u>εἷλε</u> ἐς Μίλητόν τε <u>ἐσέβαλε</u>, ἐπὶ τούτου τε τυραννεύοντος Σαρδίων Κιμμέριοι ... <u>ἀπίκοντο</u> ἐς τὴν ᾿Ασίην καὶ Σάρδις ... <u>εἷλον</u>. ῎Αρδυος δὲ βασιλεύσαντος ἑνὸς δέοντα πεντήκοντα ἔτεα <u>ἐξεδέξατο</u> Σαδυάττης ὁ ῎Αρδυος, καὶ <u>ἐβασίλευσε</u> ἔτεα δυώδεκα. ('Ardys took Priene and attacked Miletus, and during his reign over Sardis the Cimmerians came to Asia and captured Sardis. When Ardys had reigned forty-nine years Sadyattes, his son, succeeded him and reigned twelve years', Hdt. 1.15-16.1)

Examples (10) and (11) illustrate the functioning of the imperfect at what may be called the 'micro-level', that is, the level of small-scale narrative units, e.g. a deliberation scene, as in (11). However, the imperfect has also an important function at the 'macro-level', the level of large-scale narrative units. The imperfect is, in fact, the tense *par excellence* for creating *discourse cohesion*. A clear example of this function is provided by the following example from Herodotus:

(14)   ... Καμβύσης ... ἐπὶ ... Αἴγυπτον <u>ἐποιέετο στρατηλασίην</u> ('... Cambyses prepared an expedition against Egypt', Hdt. 2.1.2)

As in the examples discussed above, the imperfect ἐποιέετο creates a framework, and makes us expect that, within this framework, other states of affairs will be presented ('what else happened?'). Here, however, this is not the case, for in the next sentence Herodotus begins his lengthy description of Egypt and its inhabitants, and thus interrupts his story about Cambyses. Thereby, the imperfect acquires a new function: it signals that the author has not yet completed his narrative of Cambyses' campaign and will come back to it later. This happens, in fact, at the beginning of Book III, where we read

(15)   ᾿Επὶ τοῦτον δὴ τὸν ῎Αμασιν Καμβύσης ὁ Κύρου <u>ἐστρατεύετο</u> ('It was against this Amasis that Cambyses, son of Cyrus, was preparing an expedition', Hdt. 3.1.1)

Again, however, the expectations raised by the imperfect are not fulfilled, for there follows another digression. Once again, therefore, the imperfect signals that the author will come back to this story. It is only at 3.4.3 that the narrative about Cambyses really gets going:

(16)   ὁρμημένῳ δὲ στρατεύεσθαι Καμβύσῃ ἐπ' Αἴγυπτον καὶ ἀπορέοντι τὴν ἔλασιν, ὅκως τὴν ἄνυδρον διεκπερᾷ, ἐπελθὼν φράζει μὲν ... ἐξηγέεται δὲ ... ('When Cambyses was fully prepared to set forth against Egypt but was in doubt as to his march, how he should cross the waterless desert, he [a certain Phanes] approached him and told ... and expounded ...', Hdt. 3.4.3)

The historic presents φράζει and ἐξηγέεται signal that these events are important for the sequel of the expedition, cp. § 7.2.

6.2   Further uses of the imperfect

6.2.1   Expresses repeated states of affairs

Just as the present indicative (cp. § 3, Note 1 and § 5.3), the imperfect may express iterative (habitual) states of affairs, i.e. states of affairs that are not located at a specific point in time in the past. An iterative modifier may be present, cp. (17).

Some examples:

(17)   ἐτίμησε δέ μιν μεγάλως· καὶ γὰρ δῶρά οἱ ἀνὰ πᾶν ἔτος ἐδίδου ('He conferred great honours upon him, for every year he gave him gifts', Hdt. 3.160.2)

(18)   ἐπειδὴ δὲ τὸ παιδίον ἐγένετο ἡμῖν, ἡ μήτηρ αὐτὸ ἐθήλαζεν ('When our child had been born his mother suckled it', Lys. 1.9)

In the case of (18) the context indicates that a repeated state of affairs, a habit, is concerned. In a different context such an imperfect form could well have a non-habitual interpretation, e.g. after a temporal clause like 'When we returned home'.

Besides lexical iterative modifiers like ἀνὰ πᾶν ἔτος in (17) Greek also has grammatical means at its disposal with which iteration in the past may be explicitly expressed, e.g. the particle ἄν (so-called 'iterative ἄν'):

(19)   ἀναλαμβάνων οὖν αὐτῶν τὰ ποιήματα ... <u>διηρώτων ἂν</u> αὐτούς,
       τί λέγοιεν ('I picked up their works of art and asked them (each
       time), what they intended', Pl. Ap. 22b)

Iterative ἄν also occurs with the aorist indicative, e.g.:

(20)   δραχμὰς <u>ἂν ᾔτησ</u>' εἴκοσιν ('(Every time) he asked for twenty
       drachmes', Ar. Pl. 982)

In Ionic separate iterative forms exist as well, formed with the suffix
-σκε/ο-, e.g.:

(21)   ἡ δὲ γυνὴ τοῦ Ἰνταφρένεος φοιτῶσα ἐπὶ τὰς θύρας τοῦ βασιλέος
       <u>κλαίεσκε ἂν</u> καὶ <u>ὀδυρέσκετο</u> ('Intaphrenes' wife kept going to the
       palace gates, weeping and lamenting', Hdt. 3.119.3)
(22)   οἱ δὲ <u>ἂν</u> Πέρσαι ἐπελθόντες <u>λάβεσκον</u> τὰ πρόβατα καὶ λαβόντες
       ... ('But the Persians kept coming and taking the sheep and then
       ...', Hdt. 4.130)

In these explicit constructions the different semantic values of imperfect
and aorist are apparent: in (21) the imperfect characterizes the states of
affairs as 'not-completed', while λάβεσκον in (22) refers to a completed
state of affairs (cp. also the anaphoric participle λαβόντες).

Note 1 With the -σκε/ο-forms the augment is not used.
Note 2 Other uses of secondary indicatives + ἄν are discussed in § 8.1 and
§ 24.5.

The presence of a *negation* often causes an imperfect to receive an
iterative interpretation; this is especially frequent in temporal-circumstantial
clauses, like:

(23)   ἐλοῦσι δὲ τὸ τεῖχος ὡς <u>οὐκ ἐφαίνετο</u> ἡ Ἑλένη, ἀλλὰ τὸν αὐτὸν
       λόγον τῷ προτέρῳ ἐπυνθάνοντο, οὕτω δὴ πιστεύσαντες ... αὐτὸν
       Μενέλεων ἀποστέλλουσι ('and when Helen did not show up, after
       they had taken the wall, and they kept hearing the same declaration
       as before, then they believed it ... and sent Menelaos himself', Hdt.
       2.118.4)

The imperfect ἐφαίνετο expresses the idea that the 'non-appearance' of
Helen occurred (i.e. was observed) on several occasions, and suggests,
thus, that the Greeks were for some time busy looking for her. Notice also

iterative ἐπυνθάνοντο. A negated aorist, on the other hand, denotes rather a semelfactive state of affairs, compare:

(24)   Μαζάρης ... ὡς οὐκ εὗρε ἔτι ἐόντας τοὺς ἀμφὶ Πακτύην ἐν Σάρδισι, πρῶτα μὲν ... ἠνάγκασε ... ('When Mazares found Paktyas and his followers no longer in Sardis, he first of all compelled ...', Hdt. 1.157.2)

In the preceding passage Herodotus has told us that Paktyas had left for Kyme. The aorist in (24) indicates that Mazares upon his arrival in Sardis at once noticed Paktyas' absence, and did not go around looking for him.

6.2.2   Conative use; imperfect of likelihood

In the case of terminative (telic) verbs, i.e. verbs which denote a state of affairs that is inherently directed towards an end-point, the value [not-completed] of the imperfect often leads to a *conative* interpretation: the state of affairs did not get beyond the stage of an attempt. Usually, the context makes it clear that the state of affairs concerned did, in fact, not come about.

(25)   ἄγγελοι ἔπειθον ἀποτρέπεσθαι· οἱ δ' οὐχ ὑπήκουον ('Messengers tried to persuade them to turn back, but they would not listen', X. *An.* 7.3.7)

(26)   ... ἀλλὰ πόλις τε ἐδίδου καὶ χρυσὸν καὶ στρατόν. (...) ἀλλ' οὐ γὰρ ἔπειθε, διδοῖ τὸ φᾶρος ('... but he offered her cities and gold and an army. (...) Yet, he could not convince her and gave her the cloak', Hdt. 9.109.3)

(27)   πέμψαντες γὰρ οἱ Λακεδαιμόνιοι ἐς Σάρδις χρυσὸν ὠνέοντο ... Κροῖσος δέ σφι ὠνεομένοισι ἔδωκε δωτίνην ('For the Spartans sent a delegation to Sardes and attempted to buy gold ... But Croesus made a free gift of it to them, even though they were willing to buy it', Hdt. 1.69.4)

(28)   ἔπειθον αὐτοὺς καὶ οὓς ἔπεισα τούτους ἔχων ἐπορευόμην ('I tried to persuade them and with those whom I did persuade I continued my expedition', X. *Cyr.* 5.5.22)

Thus often ἐπυνθανόμην 'I tried to find out, inquired' versus ἐπυθόμην 'I found out, learnt'; ἠνάγκαζον 'I put pressure on ...' versus ἠνάγκασα 'I forced' etc.

Note 1 The other forms of the present stem may also receive a conative interpretation, e.g. (present indicative) ταύτην (τὴν δόξαν) ... πείθουσιν ὑμᾶς ἀποβαλεῖν ('They are trying to persuade you to throw away the glory which ...', Isoc. 6.12), (present participle) διδούσης ῞Ηρας μὲν ἁπάσης αὐτῷ τῆς 'Ασίας βασιλεύειν ('when Hera offered him to be ruler of the whole of Asia', Isoc. 10.41), also ὡς ὥρα μὲν πάντα ἄνδρα σβεννύντα τὸ πῦρ, δυναμένους δὲ οὐκέτι καταλαβεῖν ('when he saw all men striving to quench the fire but no longer able to check it ...', Hdt. 1.87.1).

Related to the conative use is the imperfect of *likelihood*. In this use the imperfect signifies that the state of affairs concerned was likely to come about, or threatened to occur, but did not really occur. Some examples are:

(29)   βάρβαρον λέχος / πρὸς γῆρας οὐκ εὔδοξον ἐξέβαινέ σοι ('... your marriage with a foreign woman was likely to end in an inglorious old age', E. *Med.* 591-2)

(30)   μεταρσία ληφθεῖσ' ἐκαινόμην ξίφει· / ἀλλ' ἐξέκλεψεν .../ ῎Αρτεμις ('having been lifted high in the air I was about to be killed by the sword; but Artemis snatched me away', E. *IT* 27-8)

(31)   ἀπηλλάγη τῆς γυναικὸς ὁ Εὐκτήμων, καὶ ἐπεδείξατο ὅτι οὐ παίδων ἕνεκα ἐγάμει ('Euctemon gave up his project of marriage, proving thereby that the object of his threatened marriage was not to procure children', Is. 6.24)

6.2.3 Immediative imperfect

The immediative imperfect (also called 'imperfect of consecutive action') expresses the idea that the state of affairs was realized *straight away* following another state of affairs. Some examples:

(32)   τοιαύτην ἐμοὶ / δέλτον λιπὼν ἔστειχε ('Having left me with such a letter he went', S. *Tr.* 46f.)

(33)   ... τὸ ὑπολειπόμενον ἤρξατο δρόμῳ θεῖν· καὶ ἅμα ἐφθέγξαντο πάντες ... καὶ πάντες δὲ ἔθεον ('... those who were thus left behind began to run; at the same moment they all set up the war-cry ..., and next all alike were running', X. *An.* 1.8.18)

(34)   διαλαβόντες δὲ τὰς οἰκίας ἐβάδιζον ('They apportioned the houses amongst them, and were gone', Lys. 12.8)

This nuance is another effect of the general semantic value of the present stem: 'signifies that a state of affairs is being carried out'. Thus, (34) could be paraphrased by: '(No sooner had they apportioned the houses than) they were on their way'. Similarly with (32): '(No sooner had he left me with the letter than) he was on his way'. We are placed, as it were, right in the middle of the state of affairs.

> *Note 1* Sometimes this use of the imperfect is called 'inceptive' (also in the 1994 edition of this book), but this wrongly suggests that it is especially the initial stage of the state of affairs that is relevant. To be sure, the close union of the imperfect state of affairs with the preceding one often *implies* that the former began immediately after the latter, but to express the 'beginning' of a state of affairs Greek had other means at its disposal, notably the ingressive aorist (see § 6.3.2) and lexical means, cp. ἤρξατο θεῖν in (33).

6.2.4   *Refers to completed states of affairs*

The imperfect of verbs like πείθω (cp. § 6.2.2) usually has a conative value. In some cases, however, the imperfect of such verbs refers to a state of affairs which is, as appears from the context, completed. E.g.:

(35)   ταῦτα λέγων ὁ Μεγάβαζος εὐπετέως ἔπειθε τὸν Δαρεῖον ... μετὰ δὲ πέμψας ἄγγελον ... ('With this speech Megabazus readily persuaded Darius ... Presently he sent a messenger ...', Hdt. 5.24.1)

(36)   Θέογνις ... καὶ Πείσων ἔλεγον ἐν τοῖς τριάκοντα (...). καὶ τοὺς ἀκούοντας οὐ χαλεπῶς ἔπειθον. (...) ἔδοξεν οὖν αὐτοῖς ... ('Theognis and Peison stated before the Thirty ... And they had no difficulty in persuading their hearers. (...) So they decided ...', Lys. 12.6-7)

From εὐπετέως ('readily') and οὐ χαλεπῶς ('without difficulty') it is clear that the 'πείθειν' is successful. In these cases the value [not-completed] of the imperfect serves to direct the attention to the *consequences* of the completion of the state of affairs: what happened as a result of the fact that Darius and the Thirty tyrants, respectively, were persuaded?

> *Note 1* When the aorist indicative ἔπεισε is used, e.g. in Hdt. 3.119.3 (where, incidentally, one group of manuscripts reads ἔπειθε) and 6.35.3, the 'persuasion' is simply presented as completed.

In a way similar to πείθω in (35) and (36) a large number of verbs of saying is used; these verbs have in common that they intend to obtain a reaction from the interlocutor: the speaker wants to get him to do something. Verbs belonging to this category are, for instance: λέγω, αἰτῶ, δέομαι, ἐρωτῶ, καλῶ, κελεύω, ἐντέλλομαι, (ἀπ)ἀγγέλλω. Very often the imperfect of these verbs is used while the state of affairs itself of asking, calling or requesting is completed. (Cp. the similar use of the present indicative of λέγω etc., § 5.1, Note 1). In general the use of the imperfect suggests that the state of affairs and what follows, i.e. the reaction of the person addressed, are closely connected: the message is delivered, the request is made, the command given, but what does the addressee do as a result? When, on the other hand, the aorist indicative is used, this connection is not emphasized: question, request etc. are simply mentioned. Sometimes there cannot possibly be a reaction, because nothing but the request, command etc. is mentioned. In such cases it is implied that the request, etc. is carried out. Some examples:

(37) τήν τε δὴ θάλασσαν <u>ἐνετέλλετο</u> τούτοισι ζημιοῦν καὶ τῶν ἐπεστεώτων τῇ ζεύξι τοῦ Ἑλλεσπόντου ἀποταμεῖν τὰς κεφαλάς. καὶ οἱ μὲν ταῦτα ἐποίεον ... ('Thus he commanded them to punish the sea and to behead those who had been overseers of the bridging of the Hellespont. So this was done ...', Hdt. 7.35.2-36.1)

(38) Δαρεῖος δὲ ... τὴν κεφαλὴν τὴν Ἱστιαίου ... εὖ <u>ἐνετείλατο</u> θάψαι ... τὰ μὲν περὶ Ἱστιαῖον οὕτως ἔσχε ('Darius gave command that Histiaeus' head should be buried with full observance ... Thus it fared with Histiaeus', Hdt. 6.30.2)

(39) ὁ μὲν δή σφι τὰ ἐντεταλμένα <u>ἀπήγγελλε</u>, τοῖσι δὲ ἕαδε μὲν βοηθέειν Ἀθηναίοισι ... ('Thus he gave the message with which he was charged, and they resolved to send help to the Athenians ...', Hdt. 6.106.3)

(40) ταῦτα μὲν ἡ Πυθίη ὑπεκρίνατο τοῖσι Λυδοῖσι, οἱ δὲ ἀνήνεικαν ἐς Σάρδις καὶ <u>ἀπήγγειλαν</u> Κροίσῳ. ὁ δὲ ἀκούσας συνέγνω ... ('Such was the answer of the Pythia to the Lydians; they carried it to Sardis and told it to Croesus; and when he had heard it, he realized ...', Hdt. 1.91.6)

The close connection expressed by the imperfect in (37) and (39) is also apparent in the fact that the addressed person's reaction is important to the person who gives the command/delivers the message: he waits, as it were, for this reaction. This element is absent in (38) and (40); in (38) the reaction is not even stated explicitly, in (40) the messengers simply deliver the message, without being concerned with the addressee's reaction.

6.3   Further uses of the aorist indicative

6.3.1   Past-in-the-past

In narrative texts the aorist indicative is most commonly used to signify that the state of affairs concerned is completed with regard to (is anterior to) a state of affairs mentioned in the ensuing context, cp. (10), (11), and (40). Sometimes, however, the state of affairs expressed by the aorist indicative is completed with regard to (is anterior to) a state of affairs mentioned in the preceding context ('past-in-the-past'). This nuance may be made explicit by means of a modifier like πρότερον 'earlier'; in other cases, we must rely on the context. Some examples:

(41)   συνήνεικε ὥστε ... τὴν ἡμέρην ἐξαπίνης νύκτα γενέσθαι. τὴν δὲ μεταλλαγὴν ταύτην τῆς ἡμέρης Θαλῆς ... <u>προηγόρευσε</u> ἔσεσθαι ('It happened that the day was suddenly turned to night. Thales had predicted this loss of daylight', Hdt. 1.74.2)

(42)   τούς τε Ἱμεραίους ἔπεισαν ... τοῖς ... ναύταις ... ὅπλα παρασχεῖν (τὰς γὰρ ναῦς <u>ἀνείλκυσαν</u> ἐν Ἱμέρᾳ) ('They persuaded the Himeraeans to supply arms for the crews (for their ships they had beached at Himera)', Th. 7.1.3)

Note 1 Cp. also the pluperfect, § 11.

6.3.2   Ingressive use

In the case of verbs which express a state the aorist may indicate the *beginning* of this state (ingressive aorist). The state itself is referred to only implicitly. Some examples:

(43)   μετὰ δὲ ... <u>ἐνόσησε</u> ὁ Ἀλυάττης. μακροτέρης δέ οἱ γινομένης τῆς νούσου ... ('But presently Alyattes fell sick; and, his sickness lasting longer and longer ...', Hdt. 1.19.2)

(44)   ἀνεῖλέ τε δὴ τὸ χρηστήριον καὶ <u>ἐβασίλευσε</u> οὕτω Γύγης ('The oracle did so ordain; and Gyges thus became king', Hdt. 1.13.2)

(45)   ἐνθαῦτα ὁ Ξέρξης ἑωυτὸν ἐμακάρισε, μετὰ δὲ τοῦτο <u>ἐδάκρυσε</u>. μαθὼν δέ μιν Ἀρτάβανος ... δακρύσαντα εἴρετο τάδε· "... ὡς πολλὸν ἀλλήλων κεχωρισμένα ἐργάσαο νῦν τε καὶ ὀλίγῳ πρότερον· μακαρίσας γὰρ σεωυτὸν δακρύεις." ('Then Xerxes declared himself happy, and presently he fell a-weeping. Perceiving

that he had begun to weep Artabanos questioned him saying: "What a distance is there between your acts of this present and a little while ago! Then you declared your happiness, and now you weep'", Hdt. 7.45-46.1)

Notice that in (43) the implicitly expressed state is made explicit in the following participle-construction; similary in (45) the state which follows the 'falling a-weeping' is referred to by δακρύεις. Here too the interpretation is dependent upon the context, for in other cases the aorist stem of verbs of this type may express a 'regular' completed state of affairs. An example with an aorist participle:

(46)   ... Αἰγύπτιοι μετὰ τὸν ἱρέα τοῦ Ἡφαίστου <u>βασιλεύσαντα</u> ... ἐστήσαντο δυώδεκα βασιλέας ('After the reign of the priest of Hephaestus the Egyptians set up twelve kings', Hdt. 2.147.2)

The main state of affairs, ἐστήσαντο, takes place after the reign of the priest of Hephaestus had *ended* rather than after it had *begun*.

Note 1 The ingressive aorist must be distinguished from the immediative imperfect (§ 6.2.3). Although both uses are predominantly found with stative verbs, there is a difference. Whereas the imperfect presents the state of affairs as being carried out, leaving the initial stage implicit (cp. Note 1 with § 6.2.3), the aorist explicitly denotes the initial stage; now, it is the ensuing state of affairs which is referred to implicitly. By the use of a lexical construction (cp. ἤρξατο θεῖν in example (33)) both the beginning and the ensuing state of affairs are made explicit.

Note 2 The ingressive nuance may also appear in the other forms of the aorist stem, cp. δακρύσαντα in ex. (45) and also e.g. οἱ δὲ Αἰγύπτιοι, πρὶν μὲν ἢ Ψαμμήτιχον σφέων <u>βασιλεῦσαι</u>, ἐνόμιζον ἑωυτοὺς πρώτους γενέσθαι πάντων ἀνθρώπων· ἐπειδὴ δὲ Ψαμμήτιχος <u>βασιλεύσας</u> ἠθέλησε εἰδέναι ... ('Now before Psammetichus became king of Egypt, the Egyptians deemed themselves to be the oldest nation on earth. But ever since he desired to learn, on becoming king, ...', Hdt. 2.2.1)

Note 3 The 'completion' interpretation of βασιλεύσαντα in (46) is due to the fact that it is already known from the context *that* the priests of Hephaestus for a long time reigned over Egypt. The ingressive interpretation of ἐβασίλευσε in (44) and of βασιλεῦσαι and βασιλεύσας in Note 2, on the other hand, is connected with the fact that this information is all new. In the latter case the value [completed] of the aorist stem cannot possibly express the idea that the state of being king is completed, simply because there is as yet no such state at all. Rather, the aorist turns βασιλεύω from a stative into a momentaneous state of affairs; thereby the state of being king is 'reduced', so to speak, to its beginnings.

§ 7 Historic present

7.1 Introduction

Besides imperfect and aorist indicative, which, in a narrative text, as it were, 'carry' the story, the present indicative, too, is used in historical narrative (the so-called 'historic present').

Strictly speaking this historic use conflicts with the fundamental value(s) of the present indicative (cp. § 3): unlike the imperfect and aorist indicative, the present indicative is, 'at heart', not suitable for the expression of past states of affairs. As a result of this special status the historic present has a specific effect, or rather, effects, for a number of nuances may be distinguished. It should be noted that in some of these the notion of 'present' may play a part to the extent that a 'pseudo-present' or 'pseudo-moment-of-utterance' is created: the narrator plays the role of an eyewitness. This does not, however, hold for all uses of the historic present.

7.2 Marks decisive states of affairs

When occurring in a narrative, the present 'enables the reader to distinguish between matter that relates to what is the writer's main concern, and other ingredients of the narrative' (Sicking & Stork 1997: 156). In particular, the present marks states of affairs that are of decisive importance for the story.

Some examples:

(47) ἢ δ' ὡς ἐσεῖδε κόσμον, οὐκ ἠνέσχετο,
      ἀλλ' ἤνεσ' ἀνδρὶ πάντα, καὶ ... (...)
      λαβοῦσα πέπλους ποικίλους ἠμπέσχετο,
      χρυσοῦν τε θεῖσα στέφανον ἀμφὶ βοστρύχοις
      λαμπρῷ κατόπτρῳ <u>σχηματίζεται</u> κόμην, (...)
      κἄπειτ' ἀναστᾶσ' ἐκ θρόνων <u>διέρχεται</u> (...)
      τοὐνθένδε μέντοι δεινὸν ἦν θέαμ' ἰδεῖν·
      χροιὰν γὰρ ἀλλάξασα λεχρία πάλιν
      <u>χωρεῖ</u> τρέμουσα κῶλα καὶ ...

      ('When she had seen the raiment, she could not hold out but consented to all her husband asked, and (...) took the many-colored gown and put it on, and setting the gold crown about her locks, she arranged her hair in a bright mirror (...). And getting up from her seat she paraded about the room (...). But then there was a terrible sight to behold. For her color changed, and with legs trembling she staggered back sidelong and ...', E. *Med.* 1156-1169)

In (47), the messenger-speech from the *Medea*, the messenger reports about the effects of the poisoned robe and crown which Medea had sent as gifts to Glauke, her rival. After a series of aorist indicatives the crucial states of affairs are expressed in the historic present: Glauke does up her hair and walks around wearing her new clothes and crown. After an introductory line, (1167), in which the messenger prepares his audience for the terrible events which follow, the decisive change in Glauke's demeanour is again presented in the historic present.

(48)   ... παρῆν καὶ ἡ γυνή· ἐσελθοῦσαν δὲ καὶ τιθεῖσαν τὰ εἵματα ἐθηεῖτο ὁ Γύγης. ὡς δὲ κατὰ νώτου ἐγένετο ἰούσης τῆς γυναικὸς ἐς τὴν κοίτην, ὑπεκδὺς ἐχώρεε ἔξω. καὶ ἡ γυνὴ ἐπορᾷ μιν ἐξιόντα.

(' ... the woman appeared as well. Gyges saw her enter and watched her take off her clothes. Then, as the woman was getting into bed and her back was turned towards him, he slipped away and went out. And the woman sees him leave', Hdt. 1.10.1-2)

In the story about Kandaules and Gyges ἐπορᾷ is one of three historic presents (the others occur at 11.4 (αἱρέεται) and 12.1 (κατακρύπτει)). It marks a decisive turning-point in the sequence of events: when Kandaules' wife sees Gyges leave after he has secretly been watching her, the first step on the road to Kandaules' downfall is taken.

The use of the historic present in messenger-speeches (as in (47)) may rightly be described as an attempt to create an 'eyewitnesseffect' (cp. § 7.1): after all, the messenger has, in fact, witnessed the events which he reports. In historical narrative, such as that of Herodotus and Thucydides, the effect is that of a 'pseudo-eyewitness': the narrator poses as a 'reporter on the spot'.

The historic present is often used to mark significant events in the course of a person's life, such as birth, wedding, and death. A related use is that which is found in e.g. the first sections of Xenophon's *Anabasis*:

(49)   Δαρείου καὶ Παρυσάτιδος <u>γίγνονται</u> παῖδες δύο (-) Κῦρον δὲ
        <u>μεταπέμπεται</u> (-) <u>ἀναβαίνει</u> οὖν ὁ Κῦρος (-) Τισσαφέρνης
        <u>διαβάλλει</u> τὸν Κῦρον πρὸς τὸν ἀδελφὸν (-) ὁ δὲ <u>πείθεται</u> καὶ
        <u>συλλαμβάνει</u> Κῦρον (-) ἡ δὲ μήτηρ ... αὐτὸν <u>ἀποπέμπει</u> (-) ὁ δὲ
        ... <u>βουλεύεται</u> ὅπως ... Παρύσατις μὲν δὴ ... ὑπῆρχε τῷ Κύρῳ
        ('From the marriage of Darius and Parysatis were born two sons (-)
        Cyrus he summoned (-) Cyrus accordingly went up (-) Tissaphernes
        falsely accused Cyrus to his brother (-) The latter believed this and
        arrested Cyrus (-) His mother, however, ... sent him back (-) He set
        about planning how ... Parysatis evidently was on Cyrus' side ...',
        X. *An.* 1.1.1-4)

These eight historic presents mention in short compass those events of
Cyrus' early life and career that are of crucial importance for the story
proper, which starts with ὑπῆρχε. The historic present in such series is
sometimes called *praesens tabulare* or *annalisticum*.

7.3   'Punctuates' a narrative

'Decisiveness' is a less prominent feature in cases like

(49a)   Κῦρος ... ὡρμᾶτο ἀπὸ Σαρδέων· καὶ <u>ἐξελαύνει</u> διὰ τῆς Λυδίας
        ... ('Cyrus was setting forth from Sardis; and he marched through
        Lydia ...', X. *An.* 1.2.5, and *passim*)

The instances of ἐξελαύνει in the first book of the *Anabasis* mark the
various stages of the expedition; they 'punctuate', as it were, the narrative,
dividing it into narrative units.

> *Note 1* The historic present is only found with terminative (telic), not with
> stative (atelic) verbs (cp. § 2). Thus, the present indicative of verbs like
> βασιλεύω, εἰμι, ἔχω, οἶδα, ῥέω is never used as a historic present.
> *Note 2* The 'decisive' use of the historic present is found both in
> independent sentences (cp. the examples (47) and (48)) and in subordinate
> clauses, e.g. ὁ δὲ Καλλίμαχος <u>ὡς ὁρᾷ</u> αὐτὸν παριόντα, ἐπιλαμβάνεται
> αὐτοῦ τῆς ἴτυος· ('Callimachus, however, when he saw him going by,
> seized the rim of his shield', X. *An.* 4.7.12).
> *Note 3* While imperfect and aorist indicative are indispensable in historical
> narrative, the use of the historic present is determined by stylistic preference
> on the part of the author. This may be concluded from the fact that some

historians, e.g. Diodorus Siculus (1st century BC), hardly use the historic present at all.

Note 4 The historic present is not used in the Homeric epics. An explanation might be found in the nature of this genre; it tells of events from a *mythical* past, knowledge of which is granted to the poet solely by the favour of the Muses. In this context it would be inappropriate for the poet to assume the role of an eyewitness.

Note 5 In a way similar to the use of the present in historical narrative, the present indicative may be used to mark decisive moments in the *future*, the so-called *praesens pro futuro*. This occurs notably in the language of oracles, but is also found in non-specialized Greek; in the latter case usually a conditional clause with future reference precedes. Two examples are: (after a series of future indicatives) τότ᾽ ἐλεύθερον Ἑλλάδος ἦμαρ / εὐρύοπα Κρονίδης ἐπάγει καὶ πότνια Νίκη ('But Zeus far-seeing, and hallowed Victory then shall grant that Freedom dawn upon Hellas', oracle *apud* Hdt. 8.77.2); καὶ εἰ αὕτη ἡ πόλις ληφθήσεται, ἔχεται καὶ ἡ πᾶσα Σικελία, καὶ εὐθὺς καὶ ἡ Ἰταλία ('And if this city shall be taken, all Sicily is theirs, and so presently will Italy be also', Th. 6.91.3). The hearer is present, as it were, at the capture of Sicily and Italy. By the use of the present the 'message' of this sentence is made rather urgent: in view of the consequences the loss of Syracuse should at all costs be prevented. Cp. also § 24.2, Note 3.

§ 8   Non-narrative uses of imperfect and aorist indicative

8.1   The imperfect of modal verbs

In direct speech the *imperfect* of impersonal verbs denoting 'necessity', 'obligation', 'appropriateness' + present infinitive may refer to the *present*, opposing a necessary, intended or more appropriate state of affairs to an existing one, as in

(50)   τούσδε γὰρ μὴ ζῆν ἔδει ('They ought not to be alive', S. *Ph.* 418)

(51)   ἃ χρῆν σε μετρίως ... σπουδὴν ἔχειν ('These things you should strive after in a more moderate way', E. *HF* 709)

Note that in (50) and (51) the existing state of affairs ('they are alive', and 'you are not behaving moderately', respectively) is simply presupposed. It may also be made explicit, as in

(52)   εἶεν, τί σιγᾷς; οὐκ ἐχρῆν σιγᾶν, τέκνον ('Why are you silent? You shouldn't be silent, my child', E. *Hipp.* 297)

Note also that, while in (52) the state of affairs denoted by the infinitive
(the 'being silent') does still exist, there is in itself no indication that it
might not stop; in fact, the addressee, Phaedra, eventually puts an end to
her silence. In this case the expression οὐκ ἐχρῆν σιγᾶν may function as
a cautious variant of a more direct expression like χρή σε λέγειν, cp. Engl.
You shouldn't keep silent as against *You must speak.* Mostly, however, the
imperfect not only presupposes that some state of affairs does (not) exist
but also implies that this situation cannot be altered any more. Again, this
can be made explicit, as in (53). In such a case ἔδει etc. + present
infinitive come close to an unrealizable wish; cp. below, example (58) and
§ 8.2.

(53)   ζῆν ἐχρῆν σ', ὅτ' οὐκέτ' εἶ ('You ought to be alive, right now
        when you're no longer around', E. *Or.* 1030)

> *Note 1* A general feature of these expressions is, then, that they have an
> imperfect tense and yet refer to the present. The explanation of this
> phenomenon, which is by no means confined to Greek, is a controversial
> matter. Some scholars hold that the necessity cannot be but located in the
> past, since it is usually doubtful or even impossible that realization of the
> state of affairs at the moment of utterance is feasible. As Kühner-Gerth put
> it (1, 205): '... die Erfüllbarkeit (der) Forderung gehört der Vergangenheit an,
> da bereits über die Nichtverwirklichung entschieden ist'. To this it may be
> objected, however, that although the 'Erfüllbarkeit' does, indeed, belong to
> the past, the necessity does not. Also, in some contexts the (eventual)
> realization of the 'Forderung' is by no means excluded, cp. ex. (52). Others
> believe that the common feature of the past and the modal use is
> 'remoteness', viz. from the moment of utterance (: past) and from reality (:
> modal use). For a critical discussion of a number of proposals to explain the
> relationship between 'modality' and 'tense' and especially that between
> 'unreality' and 'past' see Palmer (1986: 210-213). His conclusion is (p. 211):
> '... the problem remains'. – For the notion 'presupposition' cp. § 18.2, Note
> 1.

Expressions like ἔδει and (ἐ)χρῆν may, of course, also be used with
reference to the past as such. Two separate uses may be distinguished:
(i) the necessity existed, but the necessary state of affairs has not been
realized;
(ii) the necessity existed and the necessary state of affairs has apparently
been realized.
Examples of (i) and (ii) are (54) and (55), respectively:

(54)   ἀλλά, φαίητε ἄν, ἔδει τὰ ἐνέχυρα τότε λαβεῖν ('But, you might say, sureties should have been taken at the time ...', X. *An.* 7.6.23)

(55)   ὁ Κροῖσος ἔπεμπε ἀγγέλους ..., ἐντειλάμενος ... τὰ λέγειν γρῆν. οἱ δὲ ἐλθόντες ἔλεγον ('Croesus sent messengers ..., having told them what they should say. Upon arrival they said ...', Hdt. 1.69.1)

In such cases the interpretation must depend on the context. Note that in (54), while the necessary state of affairs is not realized, the necessity is, in ἔδει, presented as existing. In cases where the necessity itself is presented as not-existing (unreal), the construction with ἄν is used (cp. § 24.5), e.g.

(56)   εἰ προσεχωρήσαμεν πρότερον τῷ Μήδῳ ... οὐδὲν ἂν ἔδει ἔτι ὑμᾶς ... ναυμαχεῖν ('If we had made terms with the Medes earlier, you would no longer have had to fight at sea' - the necessity would not have existed, Th. 1.74.4)

A construction related to the expressions of 'necessity', etc. mentioned above is that of ὤφελον (lit. 'I owed, I ought') + infinitive, expressing an unrealizable wish (cp. also § 8.2). This is often preceded by εἰ γάρ or εἴ θε. The negative is μή, or, more often, μή ποτε. The wish may refer to the past (in which case the aorist infinitive is found more often than the present infinitive) or to the present (present infinitive). Some examples:

(57)   ὀλέσθαι δ' ὤφελον τῇδ' ἡμέρᾳ ('If only I had perished on that day', S. *OT* 1157)

(58)   ἀλλ' ὤφελε μὲν Κῦρος ζῆν· ἐπεὶ δὲ τετελεύτηκεν ... ('Would that Cyrus were alive; but now that he has fallen ...', X. *An.* 2.1.4)

That, in (58), the state of affairs wished for cannot be realized at the moment of utterance is apparent from the context: ἐπεὶ δὲ τετελεύτηκεν.

Note 2 Factors determining the choice between aorist and present infinitive with ἔδει etc. and wishes referring to the past are not dealt with here. Cp. § 33.1.

Note 3 ὤφελον is the imperfect corresponding to the non-attested present indicative ὀφέλω.

8.2   Imperfect and aorist indicative in wishes

Imperfect and aorist indicative are also used in order to express unrealizable wishes. In this case, the verb form is always preceded by the particles εἴθε or εἰ γάρ, so that no confusion with the declarative use of imperfect and aorist indicative can arise. The negative is μή. Unrealizable wishes, too, are opposed to a - presupposed - existing state of affairs, cp. § 8.1.

In wishes referring to the past, the aorist is more common than the imperfect (cp. ὤφελον + aorist infinitive in (57)):

(59)   εἴθε σοι, ὦ Περίκλεῖς, τότε συνεγενόμην ('If only, Pericles, I had met you then', X. *Mem.* 1.2.46; presupposing 'I did not meet you')

while wishes referring to the present are always expressed in the imperfect (cp. ὤφελον + present infinitive in (58)):

(60)   εἰ γάρ τοσαύτην δύναμιν εἶχον ('Would that I had such power ...', E. *Alc.* 1072)

On the location in the past of a wish referring to the present cp. the remarks in Note 1 with § 8.1.

Note 1 For the use of the optative in realizable wishes cp. § 4 and § 14.1.

8.3   Aorist indicative in direct speech

8.3.1   Constative use

The aorist indicative characterizes a state of affairs as completed in the past, as a mere event (cp. § 6.1). In a narrative the state of affairs concerned is usually completed relative to another state of affairs in the context; in direct speech, on the other hand, the aorist indicative usually indicates that the state of affairs is completed relative to *the moment of utterance.*

Some examples:

(61)   διὸ ὑμέας ἐγὼ νῦν συνέλεξα, ἵνα ... ('For this reason I have called you together, to ...', Hdt. 7.8α.2)

(62)   οὔτ' ἐπὶ θεωρίαν πώποτ' ... ἐξῆλθες ... οὔτε ἄλλην ἀποδημίαν ἐποιήσω πώποτε ... ('Neither have you ever left the city to serve as

a legate nor have you ever stayed abroad for any other reason', Pl. *Cri.* 52b)

The distance in time between the state of affairs and the moment of utterance is often not specified: the completion of the state of affairs is simply ascertained (*constative* use of the aorist indicative). As appears from (61), the state of affairs may have been completed only a very short time before the moment of utterance; notice the presence of νῦν.

A constative aorist is also found with cognition verbs like συνίημι 'understand' and γιγνώσκω 'realize'. The use of the aorist indicative implies that the understanding, etc. came about just before the moment of utterance. An example:

(63)   ... καί μ' ἔρημον οἴχεται λιπών.
        :: <u>συνῆκα</u>· ταρβεῖς τοῖς δεδραμένοις πόσιν.
        ('... and he left me all alone.' :: 'I got it: for what you have done you fear your husband', E. *Andr.* 918-9)

Note 1 For the use of the perfect indicative in direct speech and its relation to the aorist indicative cp. § 10.1, Note 2.

8.3.2   The aorist indicative of performative verbs ('tragic aorist')

In drama, when a speaker reacts to somebody else's words, the first person aorist indicative of a number of so-called performative or speech act verbs (cp. Engl. 'I promise', 'I forgive', 'I swear', 'I approve', 'I lament': the act of promising, forgiving etc. consists in saying 'I promise', 'I forgive' etc.), presents the speech act involved as completely realized even as the speaker is performing it. Thereby the aorist, unlike the corresponding present indicative, suggests a certain matter-of-factness on the part of the speaker: he is not dwelling too long upon the speech act. The effect is like that of Engl. *I've already forgiven you*, besides *I forgive you*. In Greek, this use is found with verbs like ὄμνυμι and compounds ('swear'), οἰμώζω ('lament', 'bewail'), ἀποπτύω ('spit on'), (ἐπ)αινῶ ('approve', 'thank'), δέχομαι ('accept'). Some examples are:

(64)   El. ἐγημάμεσθ', ὦ ξεῖνε, θανάσιμον γάμον.
        Or. <u>ᾤμωξ'</u> ἀδελφὸν σόν. Μυκηναίων τίνι;

('I have been married in a deadly marriage. :: I feel a sting of pity
for your brother. What man of Mycenae is your husband?', E. *El.*
248)

(65)   Ag. ἐπῄνεσ᾽, ἀλλὰ στεῖχε δωμάτων ἔσω·
('Thanks, but come on, go into the house', E. *IA* 440, Agamemnon,
thanking the messenger perfunctorily for the, rather unwelcome,
news that Iphigeneia and Clytaemestra have arrived)

This use of ἐπῄνεσα may be compared with e.g.

(66)   Jas. αἰνῶ, γύναι, τάδε, οὐδ᾽ ἐκεῖνα μέμφομαι·
         εἰκὸς γὰρ ...
('I approve this, woman, nor do I blame your earlier resentment. It
is natural for a woman ...', E. *Med.* 908)

Observe that, in (65), the speaker after ἐπῄνεσ᾽ immediately drops the
subject, and passes on to a more urgent matter. In (66), on the other hand,
the present αἰνῶ is followed by five lines in which Jason elaborates upon
his judgment. Again, in (64), where it is the second half of the line that
reacts to the preceding line, the words ᾤμωξ᾽ ἀδελφὸν σόν are almost a
parenthesis. 'The ... aorist ᾤμωξα allows the speaker to express recognition
that something is lamentable in a less direct manner than by actually
groaning', the latter being expressed by οἴμοι (Lloyd 1999: 28). Likewise,
saying ἀπέπτυσα (e.g. E. *Hipp.* 614, *Hec.* 1276) is less direct than 'the
actual act of spitting'.

> *Note 1* The above analysis is substantially that of Lloyd (1999), with some
> modifications. Lloyd convincingly argues against the traditional view of this
> aorist, that was also adopted in the earlier editions of this book. For details
> and for other examples I refer to his article.
> *Note 2* For a lucid introduction to the theory of performatives and speech
> acts see Levinson (1983), especially chapter 5: 'Speech acts'.

8.3.3 τί οὐ + *aorist indicative with iussive force*

Questions with the 1st or 2nd person of the aorist indicative, introduced by τί οὖν οὐ or τί οὐ, often serve, especially in Plato and Xenophon, as *urgent requests*. Cp. the similar use of the present indicative (§ 5.2). The aorist indicative is more emphatic than the present: the speaker observes that a state of affairs which he apparently wants to occur has, in fact, not occurred, and he asks his interlocutor why it has not. Pragmatically speaking the question signifies 'the state of affairs should have been realized long ago' and hence 'the state of affairs cannot be realized quickly enough'. Some examples:

(67)   τί οὖν, ἔφη ὁ Κῦρος, οὐ καὶ τὴν δύναμιν ἔλεξάς μοι ...; :: ἄκουε δή, ἔφη ὁ Κυαξάρης ('Why, Cyrus said, haven't you told me about the forces as well? (... don't you tell me ...) :: Well then, listen to me, Cyaxares said', X. *Cyr.* 2.1.4)

(68)   τί οὖν οὐ καὶ Πρόδικον ἐκαλέσαμεν; ('Why haven't we invited Prodicus as well? (... don't we invite ...)', Pl. *Prt.* 317d)

8.4   *Generic (gnomic) use of the aorist indicative*

It was observed above (§ 3, Note 1 and § 5.3) that the present indicative is used in descriptions of repeated states of affairs which are not located at a specific point in time. The aorist indicative may be used in this way as well: in this case the state of affairs is presented as confective (completed), while the repeatedness of the state of affairs is left out of consideration and is given only implicitly in the context. Used in this way, the secondary aorist indicative does not have 'past' value, but is *generic* (no primary aorist indicative was, of course, available). A further indication that this generic aorist indicative does not function as a past tense is the fact that verbs in temporal and other clauses modifying it are expressed in the *subjunctive* - as in the case of the present indicative - rather than the optative - as in the case of the common aorist indicative.

The generic aorist indicative is found in descriptions of habits, procedures - e.g. in Homeric similes -, in general truths, etc. It is also called *gnomic* aorist (γνώμη = 'proverbially expressed general truth, maxim').

Some examples:

(69) ἐπεὰν ὦν ἀπίκωνται πλέοντες ἐς τὴν Βαβυλῶνα καὶ διαθέωνται
      τὸν φόρτον, νομέας μὲν τοῦ πλοίου καὶ τὴν καλάμην πᾶσαν ἀπ'
      ὦν ἐκήρυξαν, τὰς δὲ διφθέρας ἐπισάξαντες ἐπὶ τοὺς ὄνους
      ἀπελαύνουσι ... ('So when they (: the Assyrians) have sailed down
      to Babylon and have delivered the cargo, they sell the ribs of the
      ship and all the straw (all at once), and after loading the hides on
      the donkey's backs they return overland ...', Hdt. 1.194.4)

(70) ἐς ἔχθεα μεγάλα ἀλλήλοισι ἀπικνέονται, ἐξ ὧν στάσιες
      ἐγγίνονται, ἐκ δὲ τῶν στασίων φόνος, ἐκ δὲ τοῦ φόνου ἀπέβη ἐς
      μουναρχίην ('They get into serious personal quarrels, which lead
      to party-strife; this leads to bloodshed, and that situation
      (inevitably) results in monarchy', Hdt. 3.82.3)

(71) ῥεχθὲν δέ τε νήπιος ἔγνω ('Once a thing has been done, the fool
      sees it (completely)', Il. 17.32)

Notice that both in (69) and in (70) the generic aorist is coordinated by
means of δέ with a generic present indicative (ἀπελαύνουσι and
ἀπικνέονται/ἐγγίνονται, respectively). It must, of course, be asked what
is the difference between aorist indicative and present indicative. In some
cases, the aorist indicative might be said to characterize a certain state of
affairs as anterior to another, within the description of a habit or procedure
as a whole. This may well be the case in (69): the sale of the goods is
completed when they set out on the journey over land. In other cases the
(sudden) completion of a state of affairs may be emphasized, as opposed
to the durative effect caused by the present indicative; thus, for instance,
(70): the state of affairs expressed by ἀπέβη is the culmination of a series
of states of affairs expressed in the present indicative. The aorist in (71),
a real γνώμη, is more difficult to explain. Possibly, here too the
completion of the state of affairs is stressed: only after something has been
done completely, the fool realizes what has happened (as opposed to a
smarter person, who realizes what is happening while the state of affairs
is being carried out).

> Note 1 An aorist indicative can only be interpreted as generic if its subject
> refers to a group or class of people rather than an individual: 'a fool' or 'the
> fool' as a class; ἔγνω in οὗτος ὁ νήπιος ἔγνω could, therefore, never be
> interpreted as a generic aorist.
> Note 2 The origin of the generic use of the aorist indicative is obscure.
> Perhaps cases like (69) are the key to the explanation: there the common
> confective, anterior value of the aorist stem seems to play a part (in Homeric

similes, this type is quite frequent as well). In a way the state of affairs expressed by ἀπ' ... ἐκήρυξαν is located in the past relative to ἀπελαύνουσι. Another factor may be that the other moods of the aorist stem (particularly subjunctive and participle), which, of course, do not have past value, commonly alternate with the moods of the present stem in descriptions of procedures and the like in order to characterize states of affairs as completed and not-completed, respectively.

Note 3 From the gnomic aorist we should distinguish the use of the (constative) aorist indicative for repeated states of affairs in the *past* (so-called *empiric* aorist: it is used in utterances based on experience). This type of aorist is usually modified by words like πολλάκις 'often', ἀεί 'always' and the like. An example: πολλάκις γὰρ καὶ δεσπόται ὀργιζόμενοι μείζω κακὰ ἔπαθον ἢ ἐποίησαν ('For often even masters have, in rage, suffered more damage than they inflicted', X. *HG* 5.3.7). In cases like this it may be implied that the state of affairs is not restricted to the past but that it is generally true. Thus the empiric aorist may have played a role in the development of the generic aorist.

§ 9   Future indicative

Since 'fact' and 'future' are, strictly speaking, incompatible, the future indicative naturally does not have the same factual value as the past and present tenses. Rather, it presents the realization of the state of affairs in some future world as *(virtually) certain*, more certain e.g. than the potential optative + ἄν. Pragmatically speaking, the future indicative serves a number of communicative purposes (just as English forms referring to the future, see the translations below). In an argumentative text it normally expresses a neutral prediction (ex. 72a); in dialogues, especially those of drama, it may express e.g. an announcement (72b), a promise-like intention (72c), a threat (72d), a reassurance (72e), and an order (72f):

(72a) πᾶς ... ἀποκρινόμενος ἐρεῖ θαυμάζοντι ξένῳ ... ('Everybody will say to the stranger who is surprised at ...' Pl. *Lg.* 637c)

(72b) ἀλλ' εἰς ἀγορὰν ἄπειμ' ('But I'm off to the agora', Ar. *Th.* 457)

(72c) ἐγὼ δὲ τὰ τῷ πέλας ἐπιπλήσσω, αὐτὸς κατὰ δύναμιν οὐ ποιήσω ('But, so far as in me lies, I will not myself do that which I account blameworthy in my neighbour', Hdt. 3.142.3)

(72d) οὔτοι <u>καταπροίξει</u> ... τοῦτο δρῶν ('You won't get away with this behaviour', Ar. *V.* 1366)

(72e) <u>ἔσται τάδ'</u>, <u>ἔσται</u>, μὴ τρέσῃς ('It shall be so, fear not, it shall be so', E. *Alc.* 328)

(72f) χρὴ δὲ λέγειν πρὸς τὸν χόρον· πάντως δὲ τοῦτο <u>δράσεις</u> ('You must speak before the choir; and no doubt you shall do so', Ar. *Nu.* 1352)

In questions introduced by οὐ the 2nd and, sometimes, the 3rd person of the future indicative expresses an emphatic command or request (cp. the comparable use of the present indicative (§ 5.2)). The speaker asks 'won't the state of affairs be carried out by you?' which implies 'the state of affairs will surely be carried out?' and this functions, pragmatically speaking, as a command or request: 'carry out the state of affairs!'. An example:

(73) <u>οὐ σκέψῃ</u> καὶ <u>εἰσάξεις</u> Σωκράτη; ('Won't you take a look and show Socrates in?', Pl. *Smp.* 175a)

The negative variant of this construction, introduced by οὐ μή, expresses an emphatic prohibition, e.g.:

(74) τί ποιεῖς; <u>οὐ μὴ καταβήσῃ</u>; ('What are you doing? You are certainly not going to come down, are you?' (= 'Don't you come down here!'), Ar. *V.* 397)

Note 1 For οὐ in questions, eliciting a positive reaction, see also § 19.1 and § 4, Note 1. What happens in (74), then, is that the speaker elicits a positive reaction to the rejection of the state of affairs concerned, literally: 'Won't you *not* come down?'

Note 2 In Plato, the future indicative often occurs in discussions about some hypothetical world. In this use, the future has an *inferential* value, i.e. it expresses that, in the hypothetical world under discussion, the state of affairs in question with near-certainty follows from the preceding line of reasoning. Two examples are οὗτος ... <u>δυνήσεται</u> and τοῦτον οὐδεὶς ... <u>ἀδικήσει</u> at Pl. *Grg.* 510d, that come at the end of a discussion about the question as to who will be able to avoid being wronged. Answer: the friend of the powerful. 'He will have power, this man nobody will harm'. See Bakker (2002) for more examples.

Note 3 Future states of affairs may also be expressed by means of a periphrastic construction consisting of μέλλω + present, aorist or future infinitive. The former two allow the language user to indicate 'aspectual'

distinctions, a feature which the simple future indicative does not possess (for μέλλω + present and aorist infin. see § 33.1 (ii), Note 2, p. 103). The construction with the future infinitive frequently occurs as well, as a more marked variant of the simple future: 'intend, be intended, be going to'. Its general value is: 'expresses future realization of present (or, with ἔμελλον, past, see below) intention or arrangement'. Cp. e.g. ... μέλλω διδάξειν, ὅθεν μοι ἡ διαβολὴ γέγονεν ('I am going to tell you whence the prejudice against me has arisen', Pl. Ap. 21b), τὰ ὕστερον μέλλοντα ῥηθήσεσθαι ('the things that are going to be said later', Pl. Phd. 88c), ὁ μέλλων σοι δώσειν τὸ φάρμακον ('the man who is to (= who is intended to) administer the poison to you', Pl. Phd. 63d). Cp. also examples (181) and (436) below. The imperfect ἔμελλον + future infinitive expresses an intended state of affairs in the past: τὸν ... ἕνα τῶν στρατηγῶν ... ἀπέστειλαν ὀλίγαις ναυσί, Σοφοκλέα δὲ ... ἐπὶ τῶν πλειόνων νεῶν ἀποπέμψειν ἔμελλον ('One of the generals they sent out with a few ships and Sophocles they were going to send out with the main body of the fleet', Th. 3.115.5).
Note 4 For the future indicative with purpose value in relative clauses see § 29.3 (viii).

§ 10 Perfect indicative (perfect)

10.1 Of terminative (telic) verbs

As we have seen above (§ 3 and § 1), the perfect indicative locates the state resulting from the completion of the preceding state of affairs in the 'present'. This stative-confective value of the perfect particularly occurs in the case of terminative (telic) verbs, i.e. verbs which express a state of affairs that is inherently directed towards an end-point (cp. § 2). These are verbs like παιδεύω 'raise, educate', λύω 'unbind', γράφω 'write', ποιῶ 'make, render', κτῶμαι 'acquire', etc. In translating such perfect indicatives we sometimes use a stative verb, e.g. κέκτημαι ('I have acquired' →) 'I possess'. The notion 'state' can be properly understood only if a distinction is made between, on the one hand, the *active* and *passive* uses of the perfect and, on the other, *syntactic* and *semantic* functions. Both the active and the passive perfect express the state of the syntactic *subject* (morphologically marked by the nominative). Nevertheless, there is a difference, which is based on a difference in the semantic function of the subject: in the case of the active perfect the state concerned is that of the person who has carried out the state of affairs underlying the state (semantic function: *Agent*). In the case of the passive perfect, however, the state concerned is that of the entity which has undergone the state of affairs (semantic function: *Patient*). The various effects connected with these distinctions (active: passive and Agent: Patient) are neatly illustrated by the following examples:

(75)   γέγραφε δὲ καὶ ταῦτα ὁ αὐτὸς Θουκυδίδης Ἀθηναῖος ('Of this too the same Thucydides from Athens is the author', Th. 5.26.1)

(76)   ταῦτα δὲ τὰ δέκα ἔτη ὁ πρῶτος πόλεμος ξυνεχῶς γενόμενος γέγραπται ('This completes the account of the first war, which went on without intermission for these ten years', Th. 5.24.2)

In (75), the 'state' of the subject, Thucydides, as a writer, and therefore, as an Agent, is concerned. Thucydides stresses his role as author; other factors indicating this are the placement of γέγραφε at the beginning of the sentence and the emphatic ὁ αὐτός and Ἀθηναῖος. In concrete terms the 'state' of the subject consists in the fact that the author stresses his responsibility for his activity as a historian. This is a frequent application of this type of active perfect. The effect may be brought out by translating: 'Thucydides is the author of ...'. In (76), as in (75), the state of the subject is concerned; yet, the two cases are quite different, for here the subject is not the author (Agent) but ὁ πρῶτος πόλεμος, which has the semantic function Patient (the 'described'). Here the emphasis is not on the writer's authorship but on the completion of a part of the work: the account of this period has been written and, as a result, exists as a finished product. The central position of the work is confirmed by the fact that the author is not even mentioned.

> *Note 1* For the distinction between semantic and syntactic functions see Dik (1997: chapters 5 and 10) and below § 41.3.
> *Note 2* The (constative) aorist indicative (cp. § 8.3.1) merely expresses the completion of the state of affairs and does not call attention to the resulting state: ὤμοσε 'he has sworn an oath', ὀμώμοκε 'he is under oath'; ἀπέκτεινε 'he has killed (someone)', ἀπέκτονε 'he is (someone's) murderer', etc. A particularly nice illustration of the respective values of perfect and aorist is provided by the following example from Sophocles. Kreon: φῄς, ἢ καταρνῇ μὴ δεδρακέναι τάδε; Ant.: καὶ φημὶ δρᾶσαι κοὐκ ἀπαρνοῦμαι τὸ μή. (Kr.: 'Do you admit or deny that you are responsible for these actions?' Ant.: 'I admit that I have done them and do not deny it', S. *Ant.* 442-43). By using the perfect infinitive Kreon indicates that he wants to hear from Antigone: δέδρακα 'I am responsible for these actions'. Antigone, however, by using

the (constative) aorist merely admits that she has done them. The authorities that are really responsible for her conduct are Zeus and Dike: she has only acted on their behalf.

Note 3 Not seldom the perfect has a 'totalizing' value, i.e. it implies that the state is the result of a series of occurrences of the preceding state of affairs. Thus often with verbs of 'wrongdoing', e.g. ἠδίκηκας 'You are the perpetrator of a number of misdeeds'. The aorist ἠδίκησας would rather refer to one single misdeed. The stative-totalizing value of the perfect was already recognized by the grammarian Apollonius Dyscolus (2nd century AD), as appears from his definition of a 'thief': λέγω σε κλέπτην· ὁρίζομαί σε δεδρακέναι τὰ τῆς κλοπῆς ('I call you a thief: I lay it down that you have done the things connected with theft', Ap. Dysc. *Synt.* p. 422 Uhlig); a thief is someone who is responsible for a number of thefts.

Note 4 The active transitive perfect, such as γέγραφα, does not become widely used until relatively late. In Homer we mostly find intransitive and passive perfects, e.g. ὄλωλα 'be dead', ἕστηκα 'stand', πέφηνα 'have appeared', λέλυμαι 'be released, be free', νένιμμαι 'be washed, be clean', etc. This fact has led to the belief that a shift has occurred in the value of the perfect stem: while originally it expressed the state of the subject, it later calls attention to the state of the object. According to this view, in (75) the state of ταῦτα would be emphasized: 'this has now been recorded, this is now on record'. The term used for this alleged use of the perfect is 'object-resultative perfect'. In general, this opinion is untenable. Thus (75) and (76) would convey the same information: in both cases the emphasis would be on the state of ταῦτα. This is, given the availability of two different constructions, a priori improbable. In other words: if Thucydides' intention was to stress the state of ταῦτα, he should not have used (75), a construction with an explicit Agent, but a construction like (76), in which no Agent at all occurs, so that all attention would have been directed towards ταῦτα.

Note 5 Like the present indicative (cp. § 7.3, Note 5), the perfect indicative may have future reference. In such cases a very strong rhetorical effect is produced: although the state of affairs concerned has still to be realized, the perfect suggests that it has already been realized, and with lasting results. Cp.: εἰ δὲ δὴ κατακτενεῖτ᾽ ἐμέ, / ὁ νόμος ἀνεῖται ('if ye shall indeed slay me, law is annulled', E. *Or.* 940-1). If Orestes is put to death, the hearer witnesses the complete and lasting annihilation of the law. Again, as in the case of the *praesens pro futuro*, the message is brought home forcefully: in view of the consequences Orestes should not be put to death. Cp. also § 24.2, Note 3.

10.2   Of stative verbs

In the case of verbs whose present stem forms already to some degree express a state, the perfect expresses the highest degree of that state (so-called *intensive* perfect). Examples are ἥγημαι 'be firmly convinced' (ἡγοῦμαι 'believe, think'), τεθαύμακα 'be surprised' (θαυμάζω 'wonder, marvel'), πεφόβημαι 'be terrified' (φοβοῦμαι 'be afraid'), σεσιώπηκα 'maintain complete silence' (σιωπῶ 'be silent').

§ 11 Pluperfect

Just as the perfect expresses a state existing in the present, the pluperfect locates the state resulting from the completion of the preceding state of affairs *in the past*. As to the notion 'state', what was said with regard to the perfect (§ 10.1) equally holds for the pluperfect, as appears from the following examples:

(77)   ταῦτα μὲν νῦν ὁ Σικυώνιος Κλεισθένης ἐπεποιήκεε, ὁ δὲ δὴ
        Ἀθηναῖος Κλεισθένης ... ('This, then, Cleisthenes from Sikyon
        had done, but Cleisthenes from Athens, on the other hand, ...', Hdt.
        5.69.1)

(78)   ταῦτα μὲν ἐς Ἄδρηστόν οἱ ἐπεποίητο ... ('These actions had been
        undertaken by him against Adrastus', Hdt. 5.68.1)

Notice that in (77), as in (75) above, the emphasis is clearly on the person having carried out the state of affairs: the deeds of one Cleisthenes are contrasted with those of the other.

   In many cases the pluperfect serves to express a 'past-in-the-past', i.e.: the state expressed by the pluperfect is located before a state of affairs mentioned in the preceding context, as in:

(79)   ἔπεμπε Ξέρξης κατάσκοπον ἱππέα ἰδέσθαι ὁκόσοι εἰσὶ ...
        ἀκηκόεε δὲ ... ὡς ἁλισμένη εἴη ταύτῃ στρατιὴ ὀλίγη ('Xerxes
        sent a scout on horseback to ascertain their strength ... For he had
        heard ... that a small force was concentrated there', Hdt. 7.208.1)

Cp. the comparable use of the aorist indicative (which does not explicitly express the resulting state), § 6.3.1.

§ 12 Future perfect

The future perfect, of which practically only middle (-passive) forms occur, expresses a state existing in the future, resulting from the completion of the preceding state of affairs.

An example:

(80) φίλος ἡμῖν οὐδεὶς λελείψεται ('No friend will be left to us', X. *An.* 2.4.5)

Note 1 The use of the active future perfect is virtually limited to ἑστήξω 'I will stand' and τεθνήξω 'I will be dead'. Besides these forms periphrastic constructions occur, consisting of an active perfect participle + ἔσομαι, e.g. ἐσόμεθ' ἐγνωκότες 'we will (once and for all) be aware'. Cp. also § 39.

§ 13 Subjunctive

The subjunctive is used in 1) iussive sentences ((ad)hortative and prohibitive subjunctive) and 2) interrogative sentences (deliberative subjunctive) (cp. also § 4).

13.1 In iussive sentences

(i) The adhortative subjunctive only occurs in the 1st person, more often plural than singular. It signifies that the speaker considers it necessary that a state of affairs be carried out, either by himself or by two or more people including himself; the negative is μή, see (ii).

Some examples:

(81) φέρε δή, ἦ δ' ὅς, πειραθῶ πιθανώτερον πρὸς ὑμᾶς ἀπολογή-σασθαι ('Well then, he said, let me try to conduct a more plausible defence before you', Pl. *Phd.* 63b)

(82) ἐπίσχες· ἐμβάλωμεν εἰς ἄλλον λόγον ('Stop; let us change the subject', E. *El.* 962)

(ii) The prohibitive subjunctive almost exclusively occurs in the 2nd person, occasionally in the 3rd, and is limited to the aorist stem. It expresses a prohibition:

(83) ἀλλὰ μή μ' ἀφῇς ἔρημον ('But don't leave me all by myself', S. *Ph.* 486)

(84) νομίσῃ τε μηδεὶς ... κίνδυνον ἕξειν ('No one should think that he will run risks ...', Th. 3.13.5)

Note 1 Prohibitions in the present stem are expressed by the imperative, cp. § 15. In general, this holds for prohibitions in the 3rd person of the aorist stem as well: μηδέ σε κινησάτω τις ('And no one shall move you', S. *Aj.* 1181).

Note 2 The use of the subjunctive in prohibitions in the 2nd person of the aorist stem is difficult to explain; a certain nuance of *fear* - present in cases like (with the 1st person of the aorist) μὴ πατέρ(α) ... ὄλωμαι ('for fear that I lose my father', *Od.* 15.90) - may underlie this use. Nevertheless, it is remarkable that this is limited to the aorist stem.

Note 3 On μή, μή οὐ and οὐ μή + subjunctive in declarative sentences cp. § 20, Note 3.

Note 4 Here too, of course, the question of the difference between present and aorist stem arises. This problem will be dealt with separately in § 16.

13.2 In interrogative sentences

The deliberative (or dubitative) subjunctive is confined to the 1st person, usually plural. It signifies that the speaker is not sure whether or not to carry out the state of affairs or that he is uncertain concerning a certain aspect of the state of affairs; the negative is μή.

Some examples:

(85) πότερον βίαν φῶμεν ἢ μὴ φῶμεν εἶναι; ('Should we call this violence or should we not call it that', X. *Mem.* 1.2.45)

(86) οἴμοι, τί δράσω; ποῖ φύγω μητρὸς χέρας; ('Oh, what shall I do? Where can I escape my mother's hands?' E. *Med.* 1271)

§ 14 Optative

14.1   In wishes (without ἄν; cupitive optative)

The optative without ἄν (cupitive optative) occurs in wishes. It presents the realization of the state of affairs as desirable and possible. It is often preceded by wish-particles like εἴθε and εἰ γάρ; the negative is μή.

Some examples:

(87)   εἴθ', ὁ λῷστε σύ, τοιοῦτος ὢν φίλος ἡμῖν <u>γένοιο</u> ('My good man, may you, a man of such value, become our friend', X. *HG* 4.1.38)

(88)   <u>μὴ</u> πλείω κακὰ <u>πάθοιεν</u> ('May they be grieved no more', S. *Ant.* 928)

> *Note 1* For imperfect and aorist indicative in unrealizable wishes cp. § 8.2.

14.2   In declarative sentences (with ἄν; potential optative)

The declarative sentences not only function as statements (§ 14.2.1) but may also have iussive force (§ 14.2.2).

14.2.1 In statements

The optative + ἄν presents the realization of the state of affairs as possible. The negative is οὐ. The potential optative often serves as a cautious variant of the indicative. In combination with οὐ, however, the aorist optative + ἄν expresses an emphatic negation: it is not even possible that the state of affairs should occur.

Some examples:

(89)   ἀρετὴ μὲν ἄρα, ὡς ἔοικεν, ὑγίειά τέ τις <u>ἂν εἴη</u> καὶ κάλλος καὶ εὐεξία ψυχῆς ('then virtue, as it seems, would be a kind of health and beauty and good condition', Pl. *R.* 444d)

(90)   ἐάν τις αὐτοῖς συμβουλεύσηται, οὐκ <u>ἂν εἴποιεν</u> ἃ νοοῦσιν, ἀλλὰ ... ἄλλα λέγουσι παρὰ τὴν αὐτῶν δόξαν ('When someone asks their advice they by no means say what they think but they say something else, contrary to their own opinion', Pl. *La.* 178b)

(91)   οὔτε γὰρ ἄν τοι δοίην ἔτι θυγατέρα τὴν ἐμὴν γῆμαι, οὔτε ἐκείνη πλεῦνα χρόνον συνοικήσεις ('I will no more give you my daughter to marry; yet you shall live no longer with that woman', Hdt. 9.111.5)

In (90) οὐκ ἂν εἴποιεν could in principle be replaced by (non-emphatic) οὐ λέγουσιν; note the coordination with λέγουσιν. The statement in (91) refers to the future; note the coordination with συνοικήσεις.

14.2.2 With iussive force

In dialogue the second person of the potential optative, especially in the present stem, is often used with iussive force, serving as a cautious variant of the imperative.

Some examples:

(92)   λέγοις ἄν, εἴ τι τῶνδ' ἔχεις ὑπέρτερον :: ... λέξω, κελεύεις γάρ, τὸν ἐκ φρενὸς λόγον ('If you have a better proposal, speak! :: ... I will voice my inmost thoughts, since you command me', A. *Ch.* 105-7)

(93)   κρίνοις ἄν ('You may tell us what you think', Ar. *Ra.* 1467)

Observe that, in (92), in spite of the cautious phrasing λέγοις ἄν is perceived as an order (κελεύεις γάρ).

Note 1 For the difference between present and aorist stem see § 16.

14.3   In interrogative sentences (with ἄν; potential optative)

The speaker wants to know whether the realization of the state of affairs is possible, as in

(94)   τρώγοις ἂν ἐρεβίνθους; ('Would you eat chickpeas?', Ar. *Ach.* 801)

or seeks further information about a possible state of affairs, e.g.

(94a) ποῦ δῆτ' ἂν εἴη; πότερον ἐκτὸς ἢ 'ν δόμοις; ('Where might he be? Outside? Or in the palace?', E. *Hel.* 467)

§ 15 Imperative

The imperative occurs in iussive sentences, in the 2nd or 3rd person. It signifies that the speaker thinks it necessary that the state of affairs be carried out, by someone other than himself. The negative is μή. The imperative is often preceded by an adhortative particle like ἄγε, φέρε, ἴθι (usually with δή): 'come on', 'go ahead'.

Some examples:

(95) <u>φέρε δή</u> μοι τόδε <u>εἰπέ</u> ('Come on, tell me this', Pl. *Cra.* 385b)

(96) <u>λεγέτω</u>, εἴ τι ἔχει τοιοῦτον ('Let him say so, if he possesses such a thing', Pl. *Ap.* 34a)

In 2nd person prohibitions the imperative is used in the present stem, the subjunctive in the aorist stem (cp. § 13). In the 3rd person both present and aorist imperatives occur (sometimes the aorist subjunctive as well, cp. (84)).

Some examples:

(97) καὶ <u>μὴ βράδυνε μηδ' ἐπιμνησθῇς</u> ἔτι Τροίας ('And tarry not, and speak no more of Troy', S. *Ph.* 1400-1)

(98) καὶ <u>μηδείς</u> γε ὑμῶν ἔχων ταῦτα <u>νομισάτω</u> ἀλλότρια ἔχειν ('And let not one of you think that in having these things he has what does not belong to him', X. *Cyr.* 7.5.73)

The imperative may not only express an order or a prohibition, but also a concession (examples (99) - (100)) or a supposition (example (101)). Cp. English: *let it be that way; go ahead, do it; ask me and I'll tell you* (= if you ask me ...):

(99) σὺ πάλιν αὖ λόγους ἐμοὺς <u>θαύμαζ'</u>· ἐμοὶ γὰρ θαύματ' ἐστὶ τὰ παρὰ σοῦ ('You be, in your turn, surprised at my words; for what you say is surprising to me', E. *IA* 843-4)

(100) <u>λεγέτω</u> μὲν οὖν περὶ αὐτοῦ ὡς ἕκαστος γιγνώσκει ('Now may everyone speak about this according to his personal opinion', Th. 2.48.3)

(101) <u>δειξάτω</u>, κἀγὼ στέρξω καὶ σιωπήσομαι ('Let him prove it, and I'll accept it and be silent', D. 18.112)

Note 1 The imperative also occurs in dependent clauses, especially δρᾶσον and ποίησον in questions after οἶσθα, e.g. οἶσθ' οὖν ὃ δρᾶσον; ('Do you know what you must do?', E. *Hel.* 1233). These idiomatic expressions, which are almost confined to drama, are usually not real questions but introduce an advice: 'Do you know what you must do?' = 'I'll tell you what you should do'. Thus, the above sentence is followed by τῶν πάρος λαθώμεθα 'let's forget the past'. The use of the imperative in a dependent clause is a rather remarkable phenomenon, of which as yet no satisfactory explanation has been given. Perhaps οἶσθ' ὅ originally had a function comparable to that of advisory 'You know what?' in English, or 'Weet je wat?' in Dutch, while δρᾶσον or ποίησον in a general way announced the following, more specific, imperatives.

Note 2 For the difference between present and aorist stem see § 16.

§ 16 The semantic difference between present and aorist stem in the constructions of §§ 13-15

16.1   Introduction

This section will deal with some applications of the semantic values given in § 1 of the present stem (: signifies that a state of affairs is being carried out and is, therefore, not-completed) and of the aorist stem (: signifies that a state of affairs is completed), in the constructions discussed in §§ 13-15. The treatment is by no means exhaustive, since many details are unclear and require further research. The emphasis will be on the imperative and the optative.

16.2   Imperative

In the case of the imperative (and adhortative subjunctive) the following applications of the values 'not-completed' and 'completed' may, among others, be distinguished:

(i) the present imperative is used in order to command someone to proceed with a state of affairs which he was carrying out already, or, with μή, not to proceed with it (*(dis)continuative* use):

(102)   ὅθεν οὖν ἀπέλιπες ἀποκρίνου ('So go on answering where you left off', Pl. *Grg.* 497c)

(103) νῦν δ' <u>ἀναγίγνωσκε</u> τὸν ἑξῆς νόμον ('And now go on and read the next law', D. 24.49)

(104) πότερον οὖν ἔτι πλείω ἐρωτῶ, ἢ ὁμολογεῖς ...; :: ὁμολογῶ, ἀλλὰ <u>μὴ ἐρώτα</u> ('Then am I to ask you further questions, or do you admit that ...? :: I admit it, do not question me further', Pl. *Grg.* 496d)

(104a) γυναικὶ δὴ ταύτῃ τῇ νῦν συνοικέεις <u>μὴ συνοίκεε</u> ('Stop living with that woman with whom you are living now', Hdt. 9.111.2)

In (102) the addressee had already been answering Socrates' questions, but rather reluctantly, and had eventually refused to answer at all anymore. He is now urged to continue answering the questions, cp. ὅθεν ... ἀπέλιπες. In (103) the clerk of the court is ordered to go on reading, i.e. to read the next law in a series, the reading of which had been announced already. In (104) the combination μή + present imperative is interpreted as 'do not continue asking questions'; note the preceding question 'should I ask any more?'. In (104a), finally, the content of the relative clause τῇ ... συνοικέεις clearly characterizes the use of the present imperative as discontinuative.

(ii) When someone is ordered to carry out a state of affairs which is not yet being carried out, the *present* imperative emphasizes the *process*, the *course* of the state of affairs, either relative to other states of affairs (cp. the use of the imperfect, § 6.1), or in 'absolute' use, i.e. without reference to a point of orientation. (See also § 1, Note 1). The *aorist* imperative, on the other hand, emphasizes the *completion* of the state of affairs. In cases where an aorist imperative occurs in a sequence of imperatives it is implied that the state of affairs expressed in the aorist must be completed before another state of affairs is carried out; an aorist imperative used 'absolutely' often refers to a single, well-defined state of affairs.

Some examples:

(105) <u>σκοπεῖτε</u> δὴ καὶ <u>λογίσασθ'</u> ἐν ὑμῖν αὐτοῖς, εἰ ... ('Consider the case and decide for yourselves, whether ...', D. 20.87)

(106) <u>ἔκστρεψον</u> ὡς τάχιστα τοὺς σαυτοῦ τρόπους, καὶ <u>μάνθαν'</u> ἐλθὼν ἂν ἐγὼ παραινέσω ('Change your way of life, and then come here and learn what I'll advise you', Ar. *Nu.* 88-9)

(107) καὶ νῦν δὴ τούτων ὁπότερον βούλει ποίει, ἐρώτα ἢ ἀποκρίνου ('So now, take whichever course you like: either put questions, or answer them', Pl. *Grg.* 462b)

(108) βούλομαι ... πυθέσθαι ἀπ' αὐτοῦ τίς ... (-). ἦ καλῶς λέγεις, ὦ Χαιρεφῶν. ἐροῦ αὐτόν ('I want to find out from the man what ... (-). What a good idea! Ask him, Chaerephon', Pl. *Grg.* 447c)

(109) βούλει οὖν, ἐπειδὴ τιμᾷς τὸ χαρίζεσθαι, σμικρόν τί μοι χαρίσασθαι; :: ἔγωγε. :: ἐροῦ νῦν με ... ('Then please, since you value "gratification", be so good as to gratify me in a small matter. :: I will. :: Then ask me ...', Pl. *Grg.* 462d)

(110) ἀναγνώσεται πρῶτον ὑμῖν τὸν τούτου νόμον, εἶτα τοὺς ἄλλους, ... ἀναγίγνωσκε ('First he will read to you his law, then the other laws, ... Please read.', D. 24.39)

(111) λαβὲ δ' αὐτοῖς τὴν γραφὴν αὐτὴν καὶ μέχρι τοῦ πρώτου μέρους ἀνάγνωθι τὸν νόμον ('Take, for their benefit, the actual bill and read the law as far as the end of the first section', D. 24.71)

(112) ἀνάγνωθι δὲ καὶ τούτους τοὺς νόμους ('And read those laws as well', D. 24.104)

In (105) the persons addressed are told to carefully think the case over (present imperative), while considering a specific point (aorist imperative). In (106) the aorist imperative signifies that the addressee should *first* change his way of life and *then* (present imperative) devote his attention to the speaker's advice. In (107) the present imperatives indicate that Socrates invites his interlocutor to a discussion, i.e. an as yet unspecified series of questions and answers. In (108), on the other hand, the issue is not an 'open' discussion, but a question about a single well-defined problem: hence the aorist imperative. The aorist imperative ἐροῦ in (109) may be explained in a similar way: one specific question is involved, prepared by σμικρόν τι and the aorist infinitive. In English the distinction between ἐρώτα and ἐροῦ may often be made explicit by means of translations like 'question me' and 'ask me a question', respectively.

In (110) it is announced that a series of laws will be read; the addressee is thus prepared for the command that follows. In such a case the present imperative may be interpreted as 'fire away', 'go ahead and speak' (*immediative* use of the present imperative, cp. the immediative use of the imperfect § 6.2.3). In (111) the addressee is to take the bill and read a well-delineated part of it (cp. also (108)). Finally, ἀνάγνωθι in (112) is used to order the reading of a number of laws, which are to be read as a single whole.

Note 1 The aspectual difference between imperatives like ἐρώτα (cp. (107)) and ἐροῦ (cp. (108), (109)), ἀποκρίνου and ἀπόκριναι, λέγε and εἰπέ, σκόπει and σκέψαι, plays an important role in the organisation of the Platonic dialogue. For details see the articles collected in Jacquinod (2000).

16.3   Cupitive optative and potential optative

In the other constructions discussed in §§ 13-15 we may observe similar applications of the values 'not-completed' and 'completed' of present and aorist stem, respectively.

Some examples of the cupitive optative:

(113) ληφθείς γ' ὑπὸ λῃστῶν <u>ἐσθίοι</u> κριθὰς μόνος ('May he be captured by bandits and eat only barley', Ar. *Pax* 449)

(114) καὶ <u>μήποτ'</u> αὐτῆς μᾶζαν ἡδίω <u>φάγοι</u> ('And may it never eat a tastier cake than that one', Ar. *Pax* 3)

In (113) the emphasis is on the 'not-completedness' of the act of eating: 'may the only food available to him be ...'; in (114), on the other hand, the speaker wishes that the state of affairs be restricted to the particular cake which he has just served.

Some examples of the potential optative:

(115) ὡς ἡδέως <u>ἄν</u> σου λίθῳ τοὺς γομφίους <u>κόπτοιμ' ἄν</u> ('How I'd like to kick out your teeth with a stone', Ar. *Ra.* 572-3)

(116) τίς ἀγορεύειν βούλεται; :: ἐγώ. :: περίθου δὴ τὸν στέφανον τύχἀγαθῇ. :: ἰδού. :: <u>λέγοις ἄν</u>. ('Who will speak? :: I will. :: Wear this chaplet then, and luck be with you! :: There. :: Speak away', Ar. *Ec.* 130-2)

(117) ἔγωγε πολὺ <u>ἄν</u> ἥδιον μετὰ σοῦ <u>σκοποίμην</u> εἴτ' ἀληθὲς εἴτε μὴ τὸ λεχθέν ('For my part I would greatly prefer to have you as partner in the inquiry as to whether what was said is true or not', Pl. *Chrm.* 162e)

(118) ἀλλ' ἔγωγε ἐκεῖνο <u>ἄν</u> ἥδιστα, ὅπερ ἠρόμην τὸ πρῶτον, καὶ <u>σκεψαίμην καὶ ἀκούσαιμι</u> ... ('But for my part I would like best of all to examine that question I asked at first, and hear your view', Pl. *Men.* 86c)

(119) οὐκ ἂν βαδίσαιμι τὴν ὁδὸν ταύτην ('No, I shall not follow that road', Ar. *Ra.* 135)

In (115) repeated 'kicking' is meant; κόψαιμι would have indicated that one single blow was concerned. λέγοις ἄν in (116) is a neat parallel to the immediative use of the present imperative (cp. (110) and also (92)). In (117) Socrates declares his willingness to look into a certain problem, without setting any limit as to scope or duration: it will be an 'open' discussion (cp. the present imperative in (107)). In (118), on the other hand, the issue is one single specific question which Meno would like to discuss. The aorist optative + ἄν with the negative οὐ in (119) expresses an emphatic refusal (cp. § 14.2.1), a frequent construction. The use of the aorist here is readily understandable, since the present optative would stress the course of the state of affairs concerned, a rather meaningless implication, since it is expressly stated that the state of affairs will *not* be carried out.

III THE USE OF MOODS AND TENSES IN DEPENDENT CLAUSES

§ 17 Introduction

This chapter will deal with the use of moods and tenses in *dependent* clauses (also called *embedded* or *subordinate* clauses). First (IIIA) those clauses will be discussed which function as *obligatory* constituents, i.e. constituents which must necessarily occur with a certain verb (are an *argument* of that verb). These clauses function as object or subject with verbs like 'say' ('They say that John is at home'; 'It is said that John is at home'), 'see', 'fear', etc. Then (IIIB) *non-obligatory*, or optional, clauses will be dealt with, i.e. clauses which may but need not necessarily occur with a certain verb (are a *satellite* of that verb). These are, for instance, temporal, conditional, and purpose clauses ('When John had found a hotel he went into town'; 'If John finds a hotel, he will go into town'; 'John went into town in order to find a hotel'). Finally (IIIC) clauses occurring at noun phrase level (*relative* clauses) will be discussed.

Note 1 For the terms 'argument' and 'satellite' cp. Dik (1997: 96-91). Cp. also below § 41.3.

Note 2 Since from a syntactic point of view dependent clauses with the function object/subject may be compared with nouns ('I tell you that ...', cp. 'I tell you the truth'), optional clauses with adverbs ('When John had found a hotel he went ...' cp. 'Finally, he went ...') and relative clauses with adjectives ('The man who is happy' cp. 'The happy man'), they are traditionally also called substantive clauses, adverb(ial) clauses, and adjective clauses, respectively.

Note 3 One type of relative clause functions, syntactically speaking, as an obligatory constituent with the verb, viz. so-called 'autonomous' clauses, cp. Engl. 'What he saw was amazing', where 'What he saw' is subject, and 'He didn't like what he saw', where 'what he saw' is object. I have preferred, however, to discuss these relative clauses together with the other ones, rather than with the subject/object clauses mentioned above.

IIIA CLAUSES WITH THE FUNCTION OBJECT OR SUBJECT (OBLIGATORY CLAUSES)

§ 18 With verbs of perception and emotion and with verbs of saying

These clauses are introduced by the conjunctions ὅτι 'that' and ὡς 'that; how'; the negative is οὐ. They occur with two types of verbs.

Note 1 For other constructions with these verbs see § 18.3, Note 1 (general remark); § 31.1 (b), § 32 and § 33.2 (infinitive after verbs of saying); § 37 (i) (participle).

18.1 With verbs of perception ('see', 'know', 'perceive', etc.) and emotion

This category consists of verbs like ὁρῶ, οἶδα, ἐπίσταμαι, μανθάνω, γιγνώσκω, (ἐν)νοῶ, θαυμάζω, ἥδομαι, χαίρω, ἀγανακτῶ, etc. An important semantic characteristic shared by these verbs is that, in this construction, the content of the dependent clause is *factive*: they express a sensory or intellectual perception of, or an emotional reaction to, something which already existed, independently of that perception or reaction. In the dependent clause the language user may, therefore, use the same moods and tenses that he would use if he were to express the content of that dependent clause in an independent sentence. This may be illustrated by some English examples, exhibiting the same factive features. Someone who utters the sentence 'John saw that the house was on fire' does not only tell us something about a certain perception on John's part, but also presents 'the house was on fire' as an *independent fact*, i.e. a fact that existed independently of John's perceiving it. This property of the verb 'see' is even more clearly illustrated when the main verb is negated: 'John did not see that the house was on fire'. Here 'the house was on fire' is still presented as an independent fact.

Some Greek examples:

(120)   εὖ δ' ἴστε, ..., <u>ὅτι</u> πλεῖστον <u>διαφέρει</u> φήμη καὶ συκοφαντία ('You know very well that there is the greatest difference between common report and slander', Aeschin. 2.145)

(121) ὁρῶντες ὅτι μόνος ἐφρόνει οἷα δεῖ τὸν ἄρχοντα ('... because they saw that he alone possessed the wisdom which a commander should have', X. *An.* 2.2.5)

(122) μετεμέλοντο ... (οἱ Ἀθηναῖοι) ὅτι ... οὐ ξυνέβησαν (τοῖς Λακεδαιμονίοις) ('(The Athenians) repented that they had not come to terms (with the Lacedaemonians)', Th. 5.14.2)

(123) ἐν πολλῇ ... ἀπορίᾳ ἦσαν οἱ Ἕλληνες, ἐννοούμενοι ὅτι ἐπὶ ταῖς βασιλέως θύραις ἦσαν ... ('The Greeks were in great perplexity, realizing that they were at the King's gates ...', X. *An.* 3.1.2)

Note 1 From 'factive' one must distinguish 'factual', as used in e.g. § 4 (i). 'Factual' is a modal notion, and is opposed to other modal notions, like 'potential' and 'counterfactual', cp. § 4 (i). It relates, then, to the attitude of the speaker vis-à-vis the reality of the information he is presenting. *John is ill* expresses a state of affairs that is, according to the speaker, a fact, as opposed to *John might be ill* and *John would have been ill*. It need not be a fact, of course, for instance because the speaker is mistaken or lying. 'Factive', on the other hand, is beyond modality, so to speak, and belongs to the domain of presuppositions. A factive state of affairs is a state of affairs whose reality is simply taken for granted. The speaker's attitude is irrelevant here. Cp. also § 18.2, Note 1 on presupposition.

18.2   With verbs of saying; indirect speech

Verbs of saying are, for instance, λέγω, ἀγγέλλω, ἀποκρίνομαι, δηλῶ (and also ἀκούω 'hear' = 'I am told that ...'). Dependent clauses occurring with these verbs - indirectly - represent a statement, reply, etc. of the subject of the main verb (*indirect speech*; also: *indirect discourse, reported speech*). Here, the content of the dependent clause is *not* presented as an independent fact; the statement, reply, etc. of the subject of the main verb is simply reported. In the dependent clause those moods and tenses are used which the subject of the main clause would have used in direct speech. In Greek this also holds for cases where the main verb is a past tense - a construction different from that in English, where a shift in the tense of the verb in the dependent clause occurs (cp., e.g. (126) and (129) below).

Some Greek examples:

(124) λέγει δ' (ὁ κατήγορος) ὡς ὑβριστής εἰμι ('The accuser says that I am insolent', Lys. 24.15; direct speech: (with shift of person)

ὑβριστὴς εἶ, or ὑβριστής ἐστι - simultaneous with the state of affairs of the main clause)

(125) καὶ οὔποτε ἐρεῖ οὐδεὶς ὡς ἐγὼ ... τὴν τῶν βαρβάρων φιλίαν εἰλόμην ('And no one will ever say that I chose the friendship of the barbarians', X. An. 1.3.5; direct speech: εἵλετο - anterior to the state of affairs of the main clause)

(126) ... τινες ... εἶπον ὅτι νῆες ἐκεῖναι ἐπιπλέουσι ('Some said that those ships were sailing against them', Th. 1.51.2; direct speech: ἐπιπλέουσι - simultaneous with the state of affairs of the main clause)

(127) ἀπεκρίνατο ... ὅτι πειθομένοις αὐτοῖς οὐ μεταμελήσει ('He answered that if they were obedient they would not be sorry for it', X. An. 7.1.34; direct speech: οὐχ ὑμῖν μεταμελήσει - posterior to the state of affairs of the main clause)

(128) ἀκούσας δὲ Ξενοφῶν ἔλεγεν ὅτι ὀρθῶς ἠτιῶντο ('After hearing this Xenophon said that they had been right in finding fault with him', X. An. 3.3.12; direct speech: ὀρθῶς ἠτιᾶσθε - anterior to the state of affairs of the main clause)

(129) ἠγγέλθη αὐτῷ ὅτι Μέγαρα ἀφέστηκε καὶ Πελοποννήσιοι μέλλουσι ἐσβαλεῖν ἐς τὴν Ἀττικὴν καὶ οἱ φρουροὶ Ἀθηναίων διεφθαρμένοι εἰσὶν ὑπὸ Μεγαρέων ('Word was brought to him (: Pericles) that Megara had revolted, and that the Peloponnesians were going to invade Attica and that the Athenian garrison had been destroyed by the Megarians', Th. 1.114.1; direct speech: ἀφέστηκε ... καὶ μέλλουσι ... καὶ ... διεφθαρμένοι εἰσίν - simultaneous with the state of affairs of the main clause)

In cases where the main clause has a past tense, the optative may be used where in direct speech an indicative would occur (so-called *oblique optative*). The optative has the temporal value which the corresponding indicative would have had. It should be noted that in principle a present optative may represent both a primary present indicative and an imperfect. Actually, however, the present optative usually represents a present indicative, while in cases where in direct speech an imperfect would be used an imperfect usually occurs in the dependent clause as well (cp. (128) above). Thereby, a possible source of confusion as to the temporal value of the optative is avoided.

Some examples:

(130) ἀπεκρινάμην αὐτῷ ὅτι σκεύη ... οὐ λάβοιμι ('I answered that I had taken no equipment', [D.] 50.36; direct speech: οὐκ ἔλαβον)

(131) ὑπειπὼν ... ὅτι αὐτὸς τἀκεῖ πράξοι ᾤχετο ('After adding that he would himself look after matters there, he departed', Th. 1.90.4; direct speech: τἀκεῖ πράξω)

(132) καί μιν πυθόμενοι ὡς εἴη Μιλτιάδεω παῖς ἀνήγαγον παρὰ βασιλέα ('And hearing that he was Miltiades' son they brought him up to the king', Hdt. 6.41.3; direct speech: ἔστι ... παῖς)

(133) ἐλέχθη ... ὡς οἱ Πελοποννήσιοι φάρμακα ἐσβεβλήκοιεν ἐς τὰ φρέατα ('It was said that the Peloponnesians had put poison in the cisterns', Th. 2.48.2; direct speech: ἐσβεβλήκασι (for the value of the perfect cp. (129) and § 10.1))

There is a pragmatic difference between the use of the oblique optative and that of the mood and tense of direct speech. In the construction with the oblique optative, the optative is the formal sign that the clause depends on a past tense main verb; the words reported belong, therefore, to the past as well. This means that they are presented from the perspective of the narrator. The construction which uses the tense and mood of direct speech, on the other hand, suggests that the words reported are quoted almost *verbatim* (almost, for it is not a direct quotation). Now, since their pastness is cancelled, so to speak, the words reported are presented from the perspective of the original speaker and/or addressee. This often suggests that these words are of immediate concern to speaker and/or addressee. Thus, in (129) the three events reported force the addressee, Pericles, to abandon immediately the expedition he was engaged in.

The two constructions may also be combined, as in:

(133a) οὗτοι ἔλεγον ὅτι Κῦρος μὲν τέθνηκεν, Ἀριαῖος δὲ πεφευγὼς ἐν τῷ σταθμῷ εἴη ('They told that Cyrus was dead, and that Ariaeus had fled and was now at the stopping-place', X. An. 2.1.3)

In such contrastive pairs it is suggested that, in the context at hand, the state of affairs in the direct speech tense (here Κῦρος ... τέθνηκεν) is of more direct concern to the speaker and the addressee than that in the oblique optative (here Ἀριαῖος ... εἴη).

Note 1 The semantic difference between verbs like 'see', 'know', etc. and verbs like 'say' is often said to be a difference in *presupposition*. The first group belongs to the class of so-called *presupposition-triggers*: they presuppose the reality of the state of affairs expressed in the dependent clause. The verbs of saying lack this feature. For the notion 'presupposition-trigger' see Levinson (1983: 181ff.).

18.3   *'Indirect speech' with verbs of perception and emotion*

Verbs of perception (but not ὁρῶ) and emotion (cp. § 18.1) are often construed in the same way as verbs of saying: if the main clause has a past tense, the ὅτι- or ὡς-clause may either have the mood and tense of direct speech, or the optative. In the latter case the 'words' or 'thoughts' are presented from the perspective of the narrator (cp. the remark at the end of the preceding section). The effect of the 'indirect speech' construction is that the dependent state of affairs is no longer factive.

Some examples:

(134) τοῦτο γὰρ καλῶς ἠπίσταντο, <u>ὅτι</u> ... <u>οὐχ οἷοί τ' ἔσονται</u> περιγενέσθαι ('For they knew very well that ... they would not be able to get the upper hand', Lys. 12.45; 'direct speech': οὐχ οἷοί τ' ἐσόμεθα)

(135) ἠπιστάμην <u>ὅτι οὐ</u> περὶ τῶν μειρακίων ὁ λόγος <u>ἔσοιτο</u> ('I knew that our discussion would not be about the boys', Pl. *La.* 188b; 'direct speech': οὐκ ... ἔσται)

(136) ἥσθη <u>ὅτι ἕξοι</u> τὸν συγκορυβαντιῶντα ('he was glad that he would have a companion to his manic frenzy', Pl. *Phdr.* 228b; 'direct speech': ἕξω)

Note 1 Besides ὅτι- and ὡς-clauses other dependent constructions occur with verbs like 'see', etc., and verbs like 'say': the former are construed with the accusative plus participle (cp. § 37), the latter with the infinitive or accusative plus infinitive (cp. § 31). The accusative plus infinitive construction is practically obligatory with φημί and common with verbs meaning 'promise', 'think', 'judge', 'hope', 'believe', 'swear', 'deny'. Some verbs (e.g. 'hear') may be construed both with the accusative plus participle and with the accusative plus infinitive (with a difference in meaning; § 37, Note 1).
Note 2 The optative of the future stem only occurs in indirect speech.

18.4   Temporal and other clauses in indirect speech

For temporal, conditional and other clauses in indirect speech the same rules apply as for ὅτι-and ὡς-clauses: mood and tense of direct speech are used, but in case of a past main verb the oblique optative may occur. Some examples:

(137) λέγουσιν <u>ὡς</u>, <u>ἐπειδάν</u> τις ἀγαθὸς ὢν <u>τελευτήσῃ</u>, μεγάλην μοῖραν καὶ τιμὴν <u>ἔχει</u> ('(... all those who) say that when a good man dies he has a great portion and honour among the dead', Pl. *Cra.* 398b)

(138) Περικλῆς ... προηγόρευε τοῖς 'Αθηναίοις ... <u>ὅτι</u> ... τοὺς ... ἀγροὺς τοὺς ἑαυτοῦ καὶ οἰκίας, ἢν ἄρα <u>μὴ δηώσωσιν</u> οἱ πολέμιοι ..., <u>ἀφίησιν</u> αὐτὰ δημόσια εἶναι ('Pericles announced to the Athenians that as for his fields and houses, unless the enemy devastated them, he gave them up to be public property', Th. 2.13.1; direct speech: ἢν ἄρα μὴ ... δηώσωσιν, ἀφίημι)

(139) ᾔδει γὰρ <u>ὅτι</u>, <u>εἰ</u> μάχης ποτὲ <u>δεήσοι</u>, ἐκ τούτων αὐτῷ ... παραστάτας ... <u>ληπτέον εἴη</u> ('For he knew that if ever there should be occasion for fighting, he would have to select his helpers from their number', X. *Cyr.* 8.1.10; 'direct speech': εἰ δεήσει, ληπτέον ἐστίν)

(140) εἶπεν ὁ Σάτυρος <u>ὅτι οἰμώξοιτο, εἰ μὴ σιωπήσειεν</u> ('Satyrus said that he would be sorry if he did not shut up', X. *HG* 2.3.56; direct speech: οἰμώξῃ ἐὰν μὴ σιωπήσῃς)

Note 6 The present optative (without ἄν) usually represents a present indicative or a present subjunctive + ἄν, the aorist optative represents an aorist subjunctive + ἄν. Imperfect and aorist indicative are usually retained. The future optative can, of course, only replace a future indicative.

§ 19   With verbs of asking, inquiring, etc.

19.1   Introduction: direct questions

Two types of interrogative sentences may be distinguished (cp. § 4): *specifying* questions, introduced by interrogative pronouns and adverbs like τίς, ποῖος, πῶς, etc., in which information is requested concerning an aspect of the state of affairs; and *yes-no* questions, i.e. questions which seek a positive or negative answer. The latter type is often introduced by an interrogative particle like ἦ, ἆρα, οὐ, μή, μῶν, etc., enabling the speaker to give an indication of the answer which he expects. A subtype of *yes-no*-questions are *alternative* questions, formed with πότερον ... ἤ ...; ((either) ... or ...?). In direct questions the same moods occur as in declarative sentences, i.e. indicative, optative + ἄν, secondary indicative + ἄν, and also the dubitative subjunctive (cp. § 13.2).

Some examples:

(141) τί ποθ᾽ ἄνδρες οὐχ ἥκουσιν; ('Why haven't the men come yet?', Ar. *Ec.* 877)

(142) ποῦ δῆτ᾽ ἂν εἶεν οἱ ξένοι; δίδασκέ με ('Where could the strangers possibly be? Tell me', S. *El.* 1450)

(143) ἡμεῖς δὲ προσμένωμεν; ἢ τί χρὴ ποεῖν; ('Should we stay? Or what are we to do?', S. *Tr.* 390)

19.2   Indirect questions

Indirect questions occur with verbs like ἐρωτῶ ('ask'), βουλεύομαι ('deliberate'), ἀπορῶ ('be at a loss'), θαυμάζω ('wonder'), but also with other verbs expressing uncertainty or lack of knowledge, e.g. ὁρῶ ('see', 'consider'), πυνθάνομαι ('inquire'), σκοπῶ ('see', 'inquire, examine'), and especially with negatived οἶδα, γιγνώσκω (οὐκ οἶδα, οὐ γιγνώσκω 'I do not know': pragmatically equivalent to 'I ask') and the imperative of λέγω (λέγε/εἰπέ: 'tell me' = 'I ask you'). *Specifying* questions are introduced by the interrogative words used in direct questions or by indefinite relative pronouns and adverbs like ὅστις, ὁποῖος, ὅπως, etc. *Yes-no*-questions are usually introduced by εἰ ('if', 'whether'), alternative questions by πότερον (-α) ... ἤ ..., or by εἰ ... ἤ ..., εἰ ... εἴτε ..., εἴτε ... εἴτε ... ('whether ... or ...').

As to the use of moods and tenses, the rules of indirect speech apply: the moods and tenses of the direct question are used in the indirect question, but when the main verb is a past tense an indicative or deliberative subjunctive occurring in the direct question may be represented by the oblique optative. For the pragmatic differences cp. end of § 18.2.

Some examples:

(144) συμβουλευόμεθά σοι <u>τί χρὴ</u> ποιεῖν ('We ask you to advise us what we ought to do', X. *An.* 2.1.16; direct question: τί χρὴ ποιεῖν;)

(145) <u>ὅπως</u> δὲ ταῦτα <u>γένοιτ' ἄν</u> οὐ δύναμαι γνῶναι ('But how that could come about I cannot see', X. *Mem.* 3.5.1; direct question: πῶς ταῦτα γένοιτ' ἄν; - potential optative)

(146) ἐρωτᾷ ... <u>πῶς</u> με <u>θάπτῃ</u> ('He asks how he should bury me', Pl. *Phd.* 115d; direct question: πῶς σε θάπτω; - deliberative subjunctive)

(147) ᾔδει δὲ οὐδεὶς <u>ὅποι στρατεύουσιν</u> ('No one knew whither they were marching', Th. 5.54.1; direct question: ποῖ στρατεύομεν;)

(148) ἐχρηστηριάζοντο ... οἱ Πελασγοὶ <u>εἰ ἀνέλωνται</u> τὰ οὐνόματα τὰ ἀπὸ τῶν βαρβάρων ἥκοντα ('The Pelasgians asked the oracle whether they should adopt the names that had come from foreign parts', Hdt. 2.52.3; direct question: ἀνελώμεθα; - deliberative subjunctive)

(149) ἡ μήτηρ διηρώτα τὸν Κῦρον <u>πότερον βούλοιτο</u> μένειν ἢ ἀπιέναι ('His mother asked Cyrus whether he wished to stay or go', X. *Cyr.* 1.3.15; direct question: πότερον βούλει ... ἢ ...;)

(150) ἐχρηστηριάζετο <u>εἰ ἐκβάλοι</u> τὸν Ἄδρηστον ('He asked the oracle whether he should cast Adrastus out', Hdt. 5.67.2; direct question: ἐκβάλω; - deliberative subjunctive)

Note 1 Indirect questions may, in the main clause, be prepared by pronominal elements like τοῦτο; this illustrates the fact that they have the syntactic function object or subject.

Note 2 With some of these verbs (but not those of 'asking') a *relative* clause introduced by ὅς may occur. In that case we are not dealing with a question but with a so-called autonomous relative clause functioning as syntactic object or subject; e.g., with οἶδα, ἔξοιδ' ἀκούων τῶνδ' <u>ὅς</u> ἐσθ' ὁ προστάτης ('I know, and have learnt from them, who is their leader' = 'I know (the man who is) their leader', S. *OC* 1171), where ὅς ἐσθ' ὁ προστάτης is syntactically comparable with a noun in the accusative (τὸν προστάτην). Similarly e.g. πέμπει πρὸς τὸν Κῦρον εἰπὼν <u>ὅς</u> ἦν ('he sent a messenger to Cyrus, after he had told who he was', X. *Cyr.* 6.1.46). Cp. also § 29.2. For details about the differences between ὅστις and ὅς see the collection of papers edited by B. Jacquinod (Jacquinod 1999).

Note 3 A present optative usually represents a present indicative or present (deliberative) subjunctive; an aorist optative usually represents an aorist (deliberative) subjunctive. Imperfect and aorist indicative are generally retained.

§ 20 With verbs of fearing

Dependent clauses occurring with these verbs are introduced by the conjunction μή 'that', negative μὴ οὐ. Verbs expressing 'fear' or 'anxiety' are, for instance: φοβοῦμαι, δέδοικα ('fear'), κίνδυνός ἐστιν, δεινόν ἐστιν ('there is danger that'), φυλάττομαι, σκοπῶ, ὁρῶ ('take care lest'), etc.

When a primary verb form occurs in the main clause the verb in the dependent clause is a subjunctive; when a past tense occurs in the main clause the verb in the dependent clause is, according to the rules of indirect speech, an oblique optative or a subjunctive.

Some examples:

(151) δέδοικα μὴ ... ἐπιλαθώμεθα τῆς οἴκαδε ὁδοῦ ('I fear that we may forget the way home', X. *An.* 3.2.25)

(152) αὐτὸ τοῦτο φοβοῦμαι, μὴ διὰ τὴν ἀπειρίαν οὐ δυνηθῶ δηλῶσαι περὶ τῶν πραγμάτων ὑμῖν ('This I fear, that because of my lack of experience I may be unable to explain my case before you', D. 41.2)

(153) ὅρα μὴ ἐξ ὑστέρης σεωυτὸν ἐν αἰτίῃ σχῇς ('Take care lest you have cause to blame yourself hereafter', Hdt. 5.106.2)

(154) ἐφοβεῖτο γὰρ μὴ οἱ Λακεδαιμόνιοι σφᾶς ... οὐκέτι ἀφῶσιν ('For he was afraid that the Lacedaemonians would refuse to let them go', Th. 1.91.3)

(155) ἐφοβεῖτο ... μὴ οὐ δύναιτο ... ἐξελθεῖν ('He was afraid that he would not be able to get away', X. *An.* 3.1.12)

Note 1 For an indication of the object-function of these clauses cp. (152): αὐτὸ τοῦτο.

Note 2 The verbs discussed in this section may also be followed by μή + present or perfect *indicative*, when it is implied that the content of the dependent clause, i.e. the object of fear, etc., is or has become a fact; the perfect indicative is particularly frequent in this type of clause, e.g. φοβοῦμαι ... μὴ ... λόγοις τισὶν τοιούτοις ἐντετυχήκαμεν ('I am afraid that we've ended up in that kind of arguments', Pl. *Ly.* 218d). A similar example of the present indicative with ὁρῶ: ὁρῶμεν μὴ Νικίας οἴεταί τι λέγειν ('Let us watch out: Nicias may think that he has a point', Pl. *La.* 196c).

Note 3 μή and μὴ οὐ + subjunctive may also be used independently, i.e. without a verb of fearing. These constructions express a, sometimes ironical, anxiety (with μή that something is, with μὴ οὐ that something is not the case) and often function as cautious statements; e.g. μὴ ἀγροικότερον ᾖ τὸ ἀληθὲς εἰπεῖν ('It is perhaps rather rude to tell the truth', Pl. *Grg.* 462e); with μὴ οὐ: ἀλλὰ μᾶλλον μὴ οὐ τοῦτο ᾖ τὸ χρηστήριον ('But that the oracle surely does not mean to say', Hdt. 5.79.2).

When a μή + subjunctive clause is *preceded* by οὐ it expresses a strong conviction on the part of the speaker that the state of affairs will not be realized: οὐ μὴ πίθηται ('He will certainly not be persuaded', S. *Ph.* 103), κοὐ μή ποτέ σου παρὰ τὰς κάννας οὐρήσω μηδ᾽ ἀποπάρδω ('I shall never ever piss or fart on your fence', Ar. *V.* 394).

Note 4 The οὐ μή + subjunctive construction of Note 3 must be distinguished from the use of οὐ μή + second person future indicative in questions, which expresses an emphatic prohibition, cp. § 9, example (74), with Note 1. For details about these constructions I refer to Rijksbaron (1991: pp. 167-74 'The constructions of οὐ μή').

Note 5 Occasionally, verbs of fearing are construed with ὅπως μή + subjunctive or future indicative, e.g. δέδοιχ᾽ ὅπως / μὴ ᾽κ τῆς σιωπῆς τῆσδ᾽ ἀναρρήξει κακά ('I misdoubt, a storm of sorrow will break forth from this silence', S. *OT* 1074-5). Since ὅπως μή is regularly found after verbs of contriving (see § 21), the construction with δέδοικα and the like may imply 'a desire to avert ... the thing feared', as Jebb puts it at *OT* 1074.

§ 21 With verbs of contriving, etc.

Dependent clauses occurring with these verbs are introduced by the conjunction ὅπως (occasionally ὡς) 'that', negated ὅπως μή. Verbs of contriving, i.e. verbs expressing a state of affairs meant to reach a certain goal or to create a certain effect, are, for instance: ἐπιμέλομαι (-οῦμαι), φροντίζω ('take care that'), παρασκευάζομαι ('make preparations in order that'), σκοπῶ (-οῦμαι) ('see that'), σπεύδω ('strive to'), μηχανῶμαι ('contrive that').

When a primary verb form occurs in the main clause the future indicative, sometimes the subjunctive, is used in the dependent clause. When the verb of the main clause is a past tense the rules of indirect speech apply: the future indicative (most often) or the subjunctive is used, but sometimes we find the oblique optative.

Some examples:

(156) τοῦτο δεῖ παρασκευάσασθαι ὅπως ὡς κράτιστα μαχούμεθα ('Our preparation should have this end in view, to make the strongest possible fight', X. *An.* 4.6.10)

(157) ἐπιμελητέον (ἐστὶν) ... ὅπως τρέφωνται οἱ ἵπποι ('Care should be taken that the horses are fed well', X. *Eq. Mag.* 1.3)

(158) ἐσκοπούμην ... ὅπως αὐτὸς ἀπολυθήσομαι τῆς ἐγγύης ('I set about considering how I might get myself free from my pledge', D. 33.10)

(159) ἐπεμελεῖτο ... ὅπως μήτε ἄσιτοι μήτε ἄποτοι ἔσοιντο ('He took care that they should not suffer any deprivation in food or drink', X. *Cyr.* 8.1.43)

Note 1 For an indication of the object-function of these clauses cp. (156) τοῦτο.

Note 2 Besides ὅπως (μή) + subjunctive the construction with ὅπως ἄν (μή) + subjunctive also occurs. ἄν indicates that, *in the circumstances concerned*, it is plausible that the verbal action expressed in the dependent clause will be realized. This use of the subjunctive + ἄν is called *prospective*.

Note 3 In the case of ὅπως + future indicative it is often difficult to determine whether we are dealing with an object-clause with a verb of contriving, or with one in which ὅπως functions as an indefinite relative adverb of manner, as in δεῖ σκοπεῖν ὅπως ἀπαλλαγησόμεθα ('We must consider how we shall liberate ourselves' or 'We must take care that ...', Isoc. 4.172); cp. also example (158). In general, the verbs discussed in this section may have an implicit semantic characteristic such as 'attempt to find a way in which a certain state of affairs may be realized'. Notice, furthermore, that the conjunction ἵνα, which is not an indefinite relative adverb of manner, cannŗot be used to introduce obligatory dependent clauses with these verbs.

Note 4 ὅπως and ὅπως μή + future indicative are also used - without a preceding main verb - to introduce an emphatic exhortation or warning, respectively; e.g. ὅπως οὖν ἔσεσθε ἄνδρες ἄξιοι τῆς ἐλευθερίας ('Be sure, therefore, to be men worthy of the freedom ...', X. *An.* 1.7.3) and ὅπως δὲ τοῦτο μὴ διδάξεις μηδένα ('But mind: don't whisper this to anyone', Ar. *Nu.* 824). Such a clause may be coordinated with an imperative, as in: ἀλλ᾽ ἔμβα χὥπως ἀρεῖς / τὴν Σώτειραν ... ('Well, go ahead and make sure you'll extol Soteira ...', Ar. *Ra.* 377).

IIIB CLAUSES WITH THE FUNCTION SATELLITE (OPTIONAL CLAUSES)

§ 22 Purpose clauses

Purpose clauses (or final clauses) are introduced by the conjunctions ἵνα, ὡς, ὅπως ('in order that'); negative ἵνα (ὡς, ὅπως) μή or simply μή ('in order that not', 'lest'). They express the purpose which the subject of the state of affairs of the main clause wants to achieve with this state of affairs.

When a primary tense form occurs in the main clause the verb in the dependent clause is a subjunctive; when a secondary tense form occurs in the main clause either the oblique optative is used in the dependent clause, according to the rules of indirect speech, or the subjunctive, the mood of the 'direct speech', is retained. In the first case the content of the dependent clause is presented from the perspective of the narrator, in the second case from that of the subject of the main verb. Compare also § 18.2.

Some examples:

(160) διανοεῖται αὐτὴν (sc. τὴν γέφυραν) λῦσαι ..., ὡς μὴ διαβῆτε ἀλλ' ἐν μέσῳ ἀποληφθῆτε ('He intends to destroy it (the bridge) ... in order that you may not cross but are cut off in the middle', X. An. 2.4.17)

(161) ἐγὼ δ' ἄπειμι, μὴ κατοπτευθῶ παρών ('But I will go away, lest I be seen here', S. Ph. 124)

(162) ἀπεκάλει ... (τὸν Κῦρον), ὅπως τὰ ἐν Πέρσαις ἐπιχώρια ἐπιτελόίη ('He called Cyrus back to complete the regular curriculum in Persia', X. Cyr. 1.4.25)

(163) ... πλοίοις, ἃ τότε 'Αβροκόμας ... κατέκαυσεν, ἵνα μὴ Κῦρος διαβῇ ('... the ships, which Abrocomas had burned, lest Cyrus cross (in order to prevent Cyrus from crossing)', X. An. 1.4.18)

When, after a secondary tense form, a purpose clause occurs which contains both a subjunctive and an oblique optative, the subjunctive clause, which purports to represent the original thoughts of the subject of the main verb, presents the purpose that is of immediate concern to the subject concerned, while the optative presents rather a more remote purpose. An example is:

(164) τῶνδε δὲ εἵνεκα ἀνῆγον τὰς νέας, <u>ἵνα</u> δὴ τοῖσι Ἕλλησι <u>μηδὲ</u> φυγεῖν <u>ἐξῇ</u>, ἀλλ᾿ ἀπολαμφθέντες ἐν τῇ Σαλαμῖνι <u>δοῖεν</u> τίσιν τῶν ἐπ᾿ Ἀρτεμισίῳ ἀγωνισμάτων ('The purpose of their putting out to sea was that the Greeks might have no liberty even to flee, but should be hemmed in at Salamis and punished for their fighting off Artemisium', Hdt. 8.76.2)

Note 1 When a purpose clause follows an imperative it is often the purpose of the speaker which is relevant rather than that of the subject of the main verb (the imperative). The speaker wants the addressee to do something, in order that he, the speaker, may achieve a certain goal. An example is: <u>ἀπόδος</u> δάμαρτος νέκυν, <u>ὅπως</u> χώσω τάφῳ ('Give back the body of my wife, in order that I may bury her', E. *Or.* 1585).

Note 2 Besides ὡς (μή) and ὅπως (μή) + subjunctive ὡς ἄν (μή) and ὅπως ἄν (μή) + subjunctive occur as well (ἵνα ἄν and μὴ ἄν are not found). ἄν indicates that, once the state of affairs of the main clause is realized, it is very well possible that the state of affairs of the dependent clause will be realized as well (prospective subjunctive, cp. § 21, Note 2).

Note 3 A constative aorist in direct speech (cp. § 8.3.1) is usually followed by a subjunctive in the dependent clause: though the state of affairs of the main clause has (just) been completed, the speakers' intention is still valid at the moment of utterance; e.g. ὑμέας νῦν ἐγὼ συνέλεξα, <u>ἵνα</u> τὸ νοέω πρήσσειν <u>ὑπερθέωμαι</u> ὑμῖν ('I have now summoned you together, in order that I may tell you what I intend to do', Hdt. 7.8α.2). Conversely, a primary tense is sometimes followed by an optative, e.g. τοῦτον δ᾿ ὀχῶ, / <u>ἵνα μὴ ταλαιπωροῖτο</u> μηδ᾿ ἄχθος <u>φέροι</u> ('... I let him ride, lest he would toil and carry the burden', Ar. *Ra.* 23-4). The optative indicates that the intention of the speaker, Dionysus, was formed in the past, viz. when he put his slave, Xanthias, on a donkey, and that it is no longer valid.

Note 4 In a purpose clause the optative may also occur following an optative + ἄν or an optative in a wish in the main clause, as a result of which the dependent clause is incorporated into the modal value of the main clause. This phenomenon is called *modal attraction (attractio modorum)*; e.g. βούλοιντ᾿ ἂν ἡμᾶς πάντας ἐξολωλέναι, <u>ἵνα</u> τὰς τελετὰς <u>λάβοιεν</u> αὐτοί ('They'd want us all annihilated, so they could take over the rites of the gods themselves', Ar. *Pax* 412-3). Similarly, in a purpose clause occurring after a counterfactual verb form (imperfect, aorist or pluperfect + ἄν) the dependent verb is a secondary tense form (without ἄν), as in: οὐκ ἂν δοκῶ ὑμῖν ... τοῖς φίλοις παραγγεῖλαι, <u>ἵν᾿</u> ὡς ἀσφαλέστατα ... <u>εἰσῄα</u> ...; ('Do you not think that I ... would have passed the word to my friends, in order that I might have gone in ... with all possible safety?', Lys. 1.42). The same phenomenon is found in purpose clauses after modal imperfects like χρῆν, ἔδει etc. (cp. § 8.1), e.g. οὐκοῦν ἐχρῆν σε Πηγάσου ζεῦξαι πτερόν, / <u>ὅπως</u> <u>ἐφαίνου</u> τοῖς θεοῖς τραγικώτερος ('Well, you should have harnessed the

wings of Pegasus, to make a more tragic impression on the gods', Ar. *Pax*
135-6), and after unrealizable wishes, e.g. εἶθ᾽ ἦν ἐμαυτὸν προσβλέπειν
ἐναντίον / στάνθ᾽, ὡς ἐδάκρυσ᾽ οἷα πάσχομεν κακά ('Ah, to stand face to
face and see myself, / That for the wrongs I suffer I might weep', E. *Hipp.*
1079).

§ 23 Consecutive clauses

Consecutive clauses (also: result clauses, clauses of consequence) are
introduced by ὥστε (seldom ὡς). The following uses may be distinguished:

(i) ὥστε is followed by the moods and tenses found in declarative
sentences. An indicative verb form locates the consequence at a particular
point in time; the consequence is presented as a fact. An optative + ἄν
expresses a possible consequence, and the secondary indicative + ἄν a
consequence that did not come about. The negative is οὐ.

Some examples:

(165) ἐπιπίπτει (historic present) χιὼν ἄπλετος, ὥστε ἀπέκρυψε καὶ τὰ
ὅπλα καὶ τοὺς ἀνθρώπους ('But there came such a tremendous fall
of snow that it completely covered both the arms and the men', X.
An. 4.4.11)

(166) πλοῖα δ᾽ ὑμῖν πάρεστιν, ὥστε ὅπῃ ἂν βούλησθε ἐξαίφνης ἂν
ἐπιπέσοιτε ('You have ships at your disposition, so that you may
make a sudden attack at whatever point you may wish', X. *An.*
5.6.20)

(167) κατεφαίνετο πάντα αὐτόθεν, ὥστε οὐκ ἂν ἔλαθεν αὐτὸν
ὁρμώμενος ὁ Κλέων τῷ στρατῷ ('This place commanded a view
in all directions, so that Cleon would not have remained unnoticed
while moving his army', Th. 5.6.3)

(ii) ὥστε may also be followed by an infinitive. The negative is μή. These
ὥστε-clauses have in common that the consequence is not located at a
particular point in time; this means that the dependent clause in principle
expresses a *possible* consequence: the state of affairs of the main clause
is of such a nature as to make it possible, or, when μή is present,
impossible, for the dependent state of affairs to be realized. Whether or not
the consequence actually came about is not explicitly indicated. In past
contexts, however, just as with Engl. *could* in sentences like *He spoke in*

a loud voice, so that everybody could hear him, or Dutch *kon* in *Hij sprak luid, zodat iedereen hem kon horen,* it is usually implied that the consequence is a fact. Unlike *John spoke in a loud voice, so that everybody heard him,* where the consequence is ascertained as a mere fact, the '*could*-clause' suggests that the 'hearing' was a natural consequence of John's speaking in a loud voice, and perhaps also that John wanted to be heard.

As for Greek ὥστε, depending on the context a number of nuances can be discerned.

Some examples:

(168) ἔχω γὰρ τριήρεις <u>ὥστε ἑλεῖν</u> τὸ ἐκείνων πλοῖον ('For I have men-of-war so that I can overtake their craft', X. *An.* 1.4.8)

(169) κραυγὴν πολλὴν ἐποίουν καλοῦντες ἀλλήλους, <u>ὥστε</u> καὶ τοὺς πολεμίους <u>ἀκούειν</u> ('They made a great uproar with calling one another, so that the enemy could also hear it', X. *An.* 2.2.17)

(170) εἰ δὲ Νικίας ἢ Λάχης ηὕρηκεν ἢ μεμάθηκεν, οὐκ ἂν θαυμά-σαιμι· καὶ γὰρ χρήμασιν ἐμοῦ δυνατώτεροι, <u>ὥστε μαθεῖν</u> παρ' ἄλλων, καὶ ἅμα πρεσβύτεροι, <u>ὥστε</u> ἤδη <u>ηὑρηκέναι</u>. ('But I should not be surprised if Nicias or Laches has discovered or learnt it (viz. the art of teaching); for they have more means at their command, so that they have been able to learn from others, and they are also older, so that they had the opportunity to discover it', Pl. *La.* 186c)

(171) ἐνταῦθα δ' ἔστησαν οἱ Ἕλληνες· ὑπὲρ γὰρ τῆς κώμης γήλοφος ἦν, ... τῶν δ' ἱππέων ὁ λόφος ἐνεπλήσθη, <u>ὥστε</u> τὸ ποιούμενον <u>μὴ γιγνώσκειν</u> ('There the Greeks halted; for above the village was a hill,... but the hill was covered with horsemen, so that they could not perceive what was going on', X. *An.* 1.10.12)

(172) σὺ δὲ σχολάζεις, <u>ὥστε θαυμάζειν ἐμέ</u> ('But you are delaying, so that I have cause for wonder', E. *Hec.* 730)

(173) ... παραυτίκα μὲν ἡ νεότης ἐπέζεσε, <u>ὥστε ἀεικέστερα ἀπορρῖψαι</u> ἔπεα ἐς ἄνδρα πρεσβύτερον ἢ χρεόν· ('... my youthful spirit did for the nonce take fire, whereby there brake from me a more unseemly answer to one older than myself than was fit', Hdt. 7.13.2)

In most of these examples ((168) - (171)) possibility amounts to ability. In (168), the possession of ships enables Cyrus to overtake the generals who have defected. Since a future state of affairs is involved, the consequence is obviously not a fact. In (169), the level of the noise enabled the enemy to hear it. As in the English examples discussed above, a suggestion may be present that the 'hearing' was a natural consequence of the uproar made by the soldiers, and that the soldiers wanted the enemy to hear them. As appears from the context they did, in fact, hear it, for Xenophon continues as follows: ὥστε οἱ μὲν ἐγγύτατα τῶν πολεμίων καὶ ἔφυγον ('The result was that the nearest of the enemy actually took to flight'). In (170), the qualifications given in the main clauses (δυνατώτεροι and πρεσβύτεροι, respectively) have enabled Nicias and Laches to learn and to discover the art of teaching. Note that the consequence is not presented as an indisputable fact (cp. also the conditional clause with neutral value, see next §). In (171), too, we are dealing with an ability; here, it is simply implied that the not-perceiving of the Greeks was a fact. In (172), however, there is no ability involved; the consecutive clause expresses rather a natural, inevitable, consequence, again implying that the speaker is, indeed, astonished. In (173), finally, the ὥστε-clause *does* unambiguously refer to a fact, since Xerxes *has* insulted the addressee, his uncle Artabanus. The notion 'ability' is not relevant here either. By the use of the infinitive, Herodotus makes Xerxes present his misbehaviour as a but too natural result of his youthful touchiness.

The difference between ὥστε + indicative and ὥστε + infinitive can be illustrated neatly by the following examples:

(174)   οὕτω σκαιὸς εἶ καὶ ἀναίσθητος, ὥστ' οὐ δύνασαι λογίσασθαι ὡς ... ('You are so clumsy and stupid that you cannot take into account that', D. 18.120)

(175)   δυσπρόσοδόν τε αὐτὸν παρεῖχε καὶ τῇ ὀργῇ οὕτω χαλεπῇ ἐχρῆτο ἐς πάντας ὁμοίως ὥστε μηδένα δύνασθαι προσιέναι ('And so he (Pausanias) made himself difficult, and indulged in such a violent temper towards everybody that no one could come near him', Th. 1.130.2)

In (174), we are dealing with a consequence which obtains there and then: the addressee is right now, as the speaker is speaking to him, not able to take account of the event expressed in the ὥστε-clause. In (175), on the other hand, the ὥστε-clause expresses a consequence that is not limited to a particular occasion: during some unspecified period it was not possible for anybody to approach Pausanias, the implication being, as usual, that people did, in fact, not approach Pausanias.

Note 1 For the use of ὥστε + (obligatory) infinitive after verbs like πείθω see § 33.1 (vi).

Note 2 ὥστε is a derivation of the relative adverb of manner ὡς 'such as'. This meaning of ὡς may sometimes be felt in ὥστε, as in (169), where ὥστε could be rendered as 'in such a way that'.

Note 3 ὥστε may be prepared by intensifying adverbs and adjectives like οὕτως ('so, thus'), τοιοῦτος ('such'), τοσοῦτος ('so large') etc., which explicitly indicate that it was in the nature of the state of affairs of the main clause to be followed by the consequence expressed in the ὥστε-clause. These words may also be followed by οἷος etc. + infinitive; e.g. ἐγὼ (sc. εἰμὶ) ... τοιοῦτος, <u>οἷος</u> ... μηδένι ἄλλῳ πείθεσθαι ἢ τῷ λόγῳ ('I am ... a man who follows nothing but reason', Pl. *Cri.* 46b). οἷος etc. + infinitive also occurs without τοιοῦτος etc. preceding it: ἐλείπετο τῆς νυκτὸς <u>ὅσον</u> (= τοσοῦτον ὥστε) σκοταίους διελθεῖν τὸ πεδίον ('So much of the night remained that they could cross the plain in the dark', X. *An.* 4.1.5). While οἷος + infinitive expresses a natural disposition, the combination οἷος τε + infinitive primarily expresses an ability or capability: 'be able to', 'be capable of'; e.g. ὡς ... τινὸς ἤκουον, ἀνδρὸς οὐδαμῶς <u>οἵου τε</u> ψεύδεσθαι ('As I learnt from someone, a man incapable of falsehood', D. 2.17). Cp. also § 29.3, Note 4.

Note 4 ὥστε may also be interpreted as 'on the condition that', 'provided that', especially following a verb of promising; e.g. ταῦτα δὲ ἔλεγεν εἰδὼς ἃ Τιμασίωνι ... ὑπισχνοῦντο <u>ὥστε</u> ἐκπλεῖν ('All this he said with full knowledge of what they were promising Timasion provided that he sailed away', X. *An.* 5.6.26). More frequently we find ἐφ' ᾧ or ἐφ' ᾧτε.

Note 5 ὥστε sometimes occurs at the beginning of an independent sentence, particularly when followed by an imperative or a direct question; in these cases ὥστε functions as a (consecutive) adverb: 'therefore'. E.g.: <u>ὥστε</u> πῶς οὐ βοηθήσουσιν ἡμῖν ...; ('Why, therefore, won't they help us ...?', D. 16.13).

§ 24 Conditional clauses

24.1 Introduction

Conditional clauses are introduced by the conjunction εἰ. The negative is μή. The conditional clause (also called *protasis*) and the main clause (also called *apodosis*) are usually related in such a way that it is implied that the realization of the state of affairs expressed in the main clause is dependent upon the realization of the state of affairs expressed in the εἰ-clause.

Together the conditional clause and the main clause form a *conditional period*.

> *Note 1* The brief definition given here applies to most but not to all conditional clauses, as may be illustrated by the following English examples:
> > (a) If they can raise the money our company will be taken over;
> > (b) If I am to believe the news reports our company will be taken over;
> > (c) If you're interested: our company will be taken over.
>
> Only in (a) does the realization of the main state of affairs depend upon that of the conditional clause. In (b) the taking over of the company obviously does not depend upon my beliefs, nor, in (c), upon the interest displayed by my addressee. Rather, the conditional clause in (b) specifies a condition for the *truth* of the main clause, while that in (c) specifies a condition for the *appropriateness* of (putting forward) that clause. (Conditional clauses of type (c) are often called 'illocutionary' clauses). An important semantic difference between type (a), on the one hand, and types (b) and (c), on the other, is that while (a) necessarily involves a temporal relationship (here, a relationship of anteriority: the raising of the money must precede the taking over of the company), there is, strictly speaking, no temporal relationship at all in (b) and (c). This appears e.g. from the fact that one could change the main clause of (b) and (c) to: *our company has been taken over*, without affecting the relationship between conditional clause and main clause. This is impossible in (a).
>
> The distinctions mentioned above are also relevant for Greek. Of the examples given below (176) and (180) belong to type (b), (181) belongs to type (c). All others belong to type (a). - Greek conditional clauses are discussed in detail in Wakker (1994).
>
> *Note 2* Conditional clauses are also called hypothetical clauses, since the condition is usually based on a hypothesis.

A common semantic feature of all conditional clauses (except the counter-factual ones), is that they express a 'disjunctive situation': the state of affairs may or may not be (have been) realized. There are several possible constructions in Greek indicating to what degree the condition is, in the speaker's opinion, (likely to be) fulfilled. These constructions will be dealt with in the following sections.

> *Note 3* In counterfactual clauses fulfilment of the condition is impossible, cp. § 24.5.

24.2 εἰ + *indicative*

The conditional clause refers to the present, past or future, depending on the nature of the indicative. No indication is given concerning the likelihood of fulfilment of the condition (*neutral* condition): 'if it is the case that ...', 'if it is true that ...'. The verb in the main clause may be expressed in any mood or tense.

Some examples:

(176) εἰ δέ εἰσι ὑπερβόρεοί τινες ἄνθρωποι, εἰσὶ καὶ ὑπερνότιοι ἄλλοι ('But if there are men beyond the north wind, then there are others beyond the south', Hdt. 4.36.1)

(177) εἰ ψεύδομαι, ἐξέλεγχε ('If I am lying, refute me', Pl. *Smp.* 217b)

(178) εἰ αὕτη ἡ πόλις ληφθήσεται, ἔχεται καὶ ἡ πᾶσα Σικελία ('If this city is taken, all of Sicily is lost as well', Th. 6.91.3)

(179) εἰ δέ τινα ὑμῶν λήψομαι ἐν τῇ θαλάττῃ, καταδύσω ('If I catch anyone of you on the sea, I will sink him', X. *An.* 7.2.13)

(180) Ἀλκμεωνίδαι δὲ ἐμφανέως ἠλευθέρωσαν, εἰ δὴ οὗτοί γε ἀληθέως ἦσαν οἱ τὴν Πυθίην ἀναπείσαντες προσημαίνειν Λακεδαιμονίοισι ἐλευθεροῦν τὰς Ἀθήνας ('It is clear that the Alcmeonids set (the city) free, if indeed it is true that they were the people who persuaded the Pythia to signify to the Lacedaemonians that they should free Athens', Hdt. 6.123.2)

(181) μέλλω κτενεῖν σου θυγατέρ', εἰ βούλῃ μαθεῖν ('I intend to kill your daughter, if you're interested', E. *Or.* 1578)

Note 1 The neutral value of indicative conditional clauses was recognized by ancient grammarians, cp. the following scholion on Dionysius Thrax (p. 284-285 Hilgard): ἐὰν εἴπω «εἴπερ ὁ ἥλιος ὑπὲρ γῆς» ἄδηλον εἰ ὑπὲρ γῆς ἐστιν. With ἐπείπερ, on the other hand, reality is involved (it ὑφίστησι τὸ πρᾶγμα 'treats the reality as subsisting', or, in modern terminology, 'presupposes reality'). Cp. § 26.3 on ἐπεί.

Note 2 The use of the indicative often suggests a certain scepticism on the part of the speaker concerning the fulfilment of the condition. This nuance may be explicitly expressed by means of so-called attitudinal modifiers (i.e. modifiers indicating a speaker's attitude concerning the content of his words), such as ἀληθέως in (180): 'if ... in truth ...', 'if ... really ...'.

Note 3 In the case of εἰ + future indicative the speaker's scepticism (cp. Note 2 above) may imply that he considers fulfilment of the condition undesirable, particularly in cases where the apodosis refers to something undesirable or unpleasant, as in (178) (cp. also § 7.3, Note 5) and (179). It is clear from the unpleasant consequences that the addressee had better take care lest the condition be fulfilled.

Note 4 For εἰ + secondary indicative in counterfactual clauses see below § 24.5.

24.3   ἐάν (ἤν, ἄν) + subjunctive

24.3.1 With a future indicative or some other form with future reference in the apodosis

The condition refers to the future; on account of the situation or general circumstances the speaker considers fulfilment of the condition very well possible (*prospective* condition; cp. also § 21, Note 2). The present subjunctive indicates that the state of affairs of the protasis is simultaneous with that of the apodosis; the aorist subjunctive indicates that the state of affairs of the protasis is anterior to that of the apodosis.

Some examples:

(182) ἢν κρατήσωμεν, οὐ μή τις ἡμῖν ἄλλος στρατὸς ἀντιστῇ ('If we are victorious, it is certain that no other army will resist us', Hdt. 7.53.2; for οὐ μὴ cp. § 20, Note 3)

(183) τοὺς ξυμμάχους, ἢν σωφρονῶμεν, οὐ περιοψόμεθα ἀδικουμένους ('If we are in our right minds, we shall not permit our allies to be wronged', Th. 1.86.2)

Sometimes two conditions with ἐάν + subjunctive are coordinated (ἐάν μέν ... ἐάν δέ): fulfilment of both conditions is equally possible. εἰ + future indicative may be contrasted with ἐάν + subjunctive, in which case the speaker considers fulfilment of only one of the conditions really possible; e.g.:

(184) τοῦτο μὲν δή, εἰ νικήσεις, τί σφεας ἀπαιρήσεαι ...; τοῦτο δέ, ἢν νικηθῇς, μάθε ὅσα ἀγαθὰ ἀποβαλέεις ('On the one hand, if you conquer them, of what will you deprive them ...? But if, on the other hand, you are conquered, then see how many good things you will lose', Hdt. 1.71.3)

The use of the moods makes clear that the speaker, who tries to convince his addressee of the dangers of an expedition planned by the latter, considers the chances of being conquered (ἢν + subjunctive) higher than those of conquering the enemy (εἰ + future indicative).

Note 1 Sceptical modifiers like ἀληθῶς (cp. § 24.2, Note 2) naturally do not occur with ἐάν + subjunctive. We do find modifiers which emphasize that fulfilment of the condition is, indeed, possible, as in ἢν ... <u>τὰ ἐγὼ ἐλπίζω</u> γένηται καὶ νικήσωμεν τῇσι νηυσί ('If things go the way I expect them to and we conquer them with the ships ...', Hdt. 8.60.γ).

24.3.2 With a generic present indicative in the apodosis

The condition refers to a habitual state of affairs and does not have a specific temporal reference (cp. § 3, Note 1 and § 5.3). The condition is repeatedly fulfilled, in that every repetition of the state of affairs of the protasis involves a repetition of the state of affairs of the apodosis. The present subjunctive indicates simultaneity, the aorist subjunctive anteriority.

Some examples:

(185) ταύτῃ ὦν δεῖ τὸ πλοῖον διαδήσαντας ἀμφοτέρωθεν κατά περ βοῦν πορεύεσθαι· <u>ἢν δὲ ἀπορραγῇ</u>, τὸ πλοῖον οἴχεται φερόμενον ὑπὸ ἰσχύος τοῦ ῥόου ('Here one must pass with the boat roped on both sides as men harness an ox; and if the rope breaks, the boat is carried away by the strength of the current', Hdt. 2.29.2)

(186) <u>ἐὰν</u> οὖν τις <u>αἰσχύνηται</u> καὶ <u>μὴ τολμᾷ</u> λέγειν ἅπερ νοεῖ, ἀναγκάζεται ἐναντία λέγειν ('If a man is ashamed and dares not say what he thinks, he is forced to contradict himself', Pl. *Grg.* 482e)

Note 1 This use of the subjunctive is called *(distributive-)iterative.*
Note 2 Here we are no longer dealing with a strict hypothesis: real events are referred to, though events which *sometimes* occur in the situation at hand; in the situation described in (185) the rope may, of course, also *not* break. In such contexts, then, conditional clauses may be called 'partially' factive, as opposed to the related temporal clauses, which are fully factive, cp. § 26.6. Thus, replacement of ἢν by ἐπεάν in (185) would express that the rope always broke: 'After the rope has broken ...' (which in the context is of course quite absurd).

24.4   εἰ + optative

24.4.1   With an optative + ἄν in the apodosis

The speaker considers fulfilment of the condition possible, but no more than that (*potential* condition). By expressing a mere possibility an optative conditional clause often suggests that, in the situation at hand, the condition is only remotely relevant: the speaker is simply exploring all conceivable possibilities, even those which he considers unattractive (cp. ex. (187)). There may, in fact, be such a wide gap between the actual situation and that described in the conditional clause that an optative conditional clause comes close to a counterfactual, as in example (188).

The present optative indicates simultaneity, the aorist optative anteriority.

(187)   <u>εἰ</u> δ᾽ ὡς μάλιστ᾽ <u>ἀπεχοίμεθ᾽</u> οὗ σὺ δὴ λέγεις,
        ὃ μὴ γένοιτο, μᾶλλον ἂν διὰ τουτογὶ
        γένοιτ᾽ ἂν εἰρήνη;
        ('But if we would abstain as much as possible from what you say, which I wish may not happen, would there be peace because of that?', Ar. *Lys.* 146-48)

(188)   τὸ μὲν αὐτῶν (sc. ὀίων) ἕτερον (γένος) ἔχει τὰς οὐράς μακράς, ..., τὰς <u>εἴ</u> τις <u>ἐπείη</u> σφι ἐπέλκειν, ἕλκεα ἂν ἔχοιεν ...· νῦν δ᾽ ...
        ('One of these (kinds of sheep) has long tails; if they were permitted to trail these after them, they would have wounds ...; but as it is ...', Hdt. 3.113.1)

Notice, in (188), the presence of νῦν δέ in the main clause, a combination which often introduces the main clause after a counterfactual protasis (cp. ex. (192) below). By choosing an optative, though, Herodotus indicates that the possibility of letting trail the tails of the sheep cannot be excluded.

In contexts where εἰ + optative is contrasted with ἐάν + subjunctive their respective semantic values are apparent. An example is:

(189)   <u>εἰ</u> οὖν <u>ἴδοιεν</u> καὶ νὼ ... ἐν μεσημβρίᾳ μὴ διαλεγομένους ἀλλὰ νυστάζοντας, δικαίως ἂν καταγελῷεν, ...· <u>ἐὰν δὲ ὁρῶσι</u> διαλεγομένους ..., ὃ γέρας παρὰ θεῶν ἔχουσιν ἀνθρώποις διδόναι, τάχ᾽ ἂν δοῖεν ἀγασθέντες ('If they should see us not conversing at mid-day ... but dozing, they would quite justly laugh at us; but if they see us conversing perhaps they may respect us

and give us that gift which they have from the gods to give to men', Pl. *Phdr.* 259a)

Here, Socrates is playfully imagining a situation where cicadas are looking down on Phaedrus and himself, and are going to comment upon their activities. The use of the optative indicates that he considers the first alternative a mere possibility; he is reckoning rather with realization of the second alternative, as suggested by the prospective subjunctive. In the situation at hand this means that he hopes for realization of that alternative. Notice, incidentally, the opposition of the aorist form ἴδοιεν and the present stem form ὁρῶσι. While the former denotes a momentaneous state of affairs, ὁρῶσι has rather a durative value: one look suffices for the cicadas to start laughing, if Socrates and Phaedrus are not conversing, but they will continue looking at them if they have a real conversation, just like the cicadas themselves.

> *Note 1* Occasionally the main clause contains a (generic) present indicative, or a future indicative, e.g. (pres. ind.) (Ag.) τίς οὕτω δυστυχὴς ἔφυ γυνή; / (Hek.) οὐκ ἔστιν, εἰ μὴ τὴν Τύχην αὐτὴν λέγοις ('What woman ever suffered such misfortune? / None, unless you named Lady Misfortune herself', E. *Hec.* 786-7); there is, however, a variant λέγεις); (fut. ind.) μιᾷ τε νίκῃ ναυμαχίας κατὰ τὸ εἰκὸς ἁλίσκονται· εἰ δ᾽ ἀντίσχοιεν, μελετήσομεν καὶ ἡμεῖς ἐν πλέονι χρόνῳ τὰ ναυτικά ('If we win a single victory at sea, in all probability they are defeated. If, however, they should still hold out, we on our part shall have more time for practice in seamanship', Th. 1.121.4). Notice, in the latter example, the clearly 'remote' relevance of the optative condition: it is contrasted with a situation that is presented as likely (κατὰ τὸ εἰκός).

24.4.2 With an imperfect in the apodosis

This construction refers to habitual states of affairs in the past; it is, therefore, the 'past' counterpart of the construction discussed in § 24.3.2. The condition is repeatedly fulfilled in the past, in that every repetition of the state of affairs of the protasis involves a repetition of the state of affairs of the apodosis.

Some examples:

(190) τάδε δὲ ἄλλα ἐκεκοσμέατό οἱ· εἴ τινα πυνθάνοιτο ὑβρίζοντα, τοῦτον ... κατ᾽ ἀξίην ἑκάστου ἀδικήματος ἐδικαίευ ('But this too had been arranged by him: if he heard that someone was doing

violence he would punish him as befitted each offence', Hdt. 1.100.2)

(191) εἰ μὲν ἐπίοιεν οἱ ᾽Αθηναῖοι, ὑπεχώρουν, εἰ δ᾽ ἀναχωροῖεν, ἐπέκειντο ('If the Athenians attacked they retreated, but if they retreated they charged', Th. 7.79.5)

Note 1 This *distributive-iterative* use of the optative is also simply called *iterative*.
Note 2 Here too (cp. § 24.3.2, Note 2), we are dealing with real events which *sometimes* occurred, rather than with hypotheses. Cp. also § 26 for temporal clauses.

24.5 εἰ + *secondary indicative*

In the apodosis a *secondary indicative* + ἄν is used. The speaker considers fulfilment of the condition impossible, or no longer possible (*counterfactual* or *contrary-to-fact* condition). In conditions referring to the present the imperfect is most common; in conditions referring to the past the aorist indicative is usually found. This construction presupposes the existence of another state of affairs (cp. also §§ 8.1 and 8.2), which often is mentioned *expressis verbis*.

Some examples:

(192) εἰ μὲν ἠπιστάμεθα σαφῶς ὅτι ἥξει πλοῖα Χειρίσοφος ἄγων ἱκανά, οὐδὲν ἂν ἔδει ὧν μέλλω λέγειν· νῦν δ᾽ ἐπεὶ τοῦτο ἄδηλον ... ('If we knew beyond doubt that Cheirisophos would bring back with him an adequate number of ships, there would be no need of what I am about to say; but since that is uncertain ...'. X. *An.* 5.1.10)

(193) εἰ δ᾽ ἐκεῖνά γε προσέθηκεν, οὐδεὶς ἀντεχειροτόνησεν ἄν ('And if he had added this, no one would have voted against him', Ar. *Ec.* 422-3)

Note 1 The use of the imperfect in conditions referring to the present raises the same problems as the 'present' use of the imperfect of modal verbs. Cp. the remarks in § 8.1, Note 1.

24.6   Appendix: ἐάν- and εἰ-clauses with purpose value

There is a type of conditional clauses which, rather than expressing a condition, have purpose value. They nearly always follow after the main clause, as opposed to the types of conditional clauses discussed above, which most often precede the main clause. With reference to a future state of affairs ἐάν + subjunctive, with reference to a past state of affairs εἰ + optative is used. This construction is especially frequent in Homer.

Some examples from Classical Greek:

(194)   καί σε στρατηγὸν αἱ γυναῖκες αὐτόθεν / αἱρούμεθ', ᾗν ταῦθ' ἀπινοεῖς κατεργάσῃ ('We, the women, elect you here and now as our leader, in the hope that you will accomplish what you have in mind', Ar. *Ec.* 246-7)

(195)   καὶ ἔπεμψαν μὲν ἐς Καρχηδόνα τριήρη περὶ φιλίας, εἰ δύναιντό τι ὠφελεῖσθαι ('And they sent a trireme to Carthage on a mission of friendship, in the hope that they might be able to get some aid', Th. 6.88.6)

The ἐάν- (εἰ-) clause may be translated by means of 'in the hope that'.

Note 1 These clauses differ from regular purpose clauses (cp. § 22) in that they, like conditional clauses, have an inherent nuance of uncertainty concerning the realization of the state of affairs, a nuance which purpose clauses (introduced by ἵνα, ὅπως etc.) lack.

§ 25 Concessive clauses

Concessive clauses are a variant of conditional clauses. They are introduced by εἰ καί and καὶ εἰ 'even if' and express an exceptional or unlikely condition, i.e. a condition that may be considered unfavourable for the realization of the state of affairs of the apodosis: *even in that case* the state of affairs of the apodosis has been, will be, could be (potential) or would have been (contrary-to-fact) realized. A certain nuance of surprise is often present. Sometimes the contrast is emphasized by means of expressions like ὅμως 'nevertheless' in the apodosis. Moods and tenses are used as in conditional clauses, as well as the negative (μή).

Some examples:

(196) τὰ δὲ Μηδικὰ ..., εἰ καὶ δι' ὄχλου μᾶλλον ἔσται αἰεὶ προβαλλο-
μένοις, ἀνάγκη λέγειν ('But concerning the Persian wars ... we
needs must speak, even if it will be rather irksome to mention
them, since they are always being paraded', Th. 1.73.2; εἰ καί +
indicative: neutral (cp. § 24.2))

(197) τῶνδ' εἰ καὶ κρατήσαιμεν, διὰ πολλοῦ γε καὶ πολλῶν ὄντων
χαλεπῶς ἂν ἄρχειν δυναίμεθα ('But even if we could defeat
them, we should find it hard to govern them, far off as they are and
formidable in numbers', Th. 6.11.1; εἰ καί + optative: potential (cp.
§ 24.4.1))

(198) οὐδ' ἢν ὁ Λάκων ἐπιῇ τοι ἄρχειν αὐτῆς, ἡμεῖς ἐπήσομεν ('Even
if the Laconian should allow you to command it, not so shall we',
Hdt. 7.161.2; οὐδ' ἢν (negative of καὶ ἤν) + subjunctive:
prospective (cp. § 24.3.1))

(199) εἰ καὶ τὸν ἄλλον χρόνον εἴθιστο συκοφαντεῖν, τότ' ἂν ἐπαύσατο
('Even if he had been accustomed in former times to bring
malicious accusations, then he would have given up the practice',
Isoc. 21.11; εἰ καί + secondary indicative: contrary-to-fact (cp. §
24.5))

(200) καὶ γὰρ εἰ μυθώδης ὁ λόγος γέγονεν, ὅμως αὐτῷ καὶ νῦν
ῥηθῆναι προσήκει ('For even if the story has taken the form of a
myth, yet it deserves to be told again', Isoc. 4.28; καὶ εἰ +
indicative: neutral (cp. § 24.2))

Note 1 Sometimes an indicative in the protasis refers to a factive state of
affairs, i.e. the reality of the state of affairs is presupposed (cp. § 18.2, Note
1), in which case εἰ καί and καὶ εἰ come to mean 'although'; e.g. καὶ γὰρ
εἰ πένης ἔφυν, οὔτοι τό γ' ἦθος δυσγενὲς παρέξομαι ('For even if I am
poor by nature (although I am ...), yet I will show that I have no mean
character', E. *El.* 362-3). Usually, however, a factive concessive relationship
is expressed by means of καίπερ + participle (cp. § 38 (iv)).
Note 2 καὶ εἰ may have a stronger effect than εἰ καί in that it explicitly
presents the condition as an exceptional one, but usually there is no marked
difference.

§ 26 Temporal clauses

Temporal clauses establish a temporal relationship between two states of affairs. Relative to the state of affairs of the main clause that of the dependent clause may be anterior, simultaneous or posterior; the dependent clause may express both single and repeated states of affairs, in past, present, or future, as well as habitual states of affairs.

26.1 Single past states of affairs

The verb of the dependent clause is expressed in the indicative; the state of affairs is factive (cp. Note 2 below). The negative is οὐ. The following types of clauses may be distinguished:

(a) ἐπεί, ἐπειδή, ὅτε, ὡς + aorist indicative: the state of affairs of the dependent clause is anterior to that of the main clause: 'when', 'after'.
(b) ἐπεί, ἐπειδή, ὅτε, ὡς, as well as ἕως, ἐν ᾧ + imperfect: the state of affairs of the dependent clause is simultaneous with that of the main clause: 'when'; ἕως 'so long as', ἐν ᾧ 'while'.
(c) ἕως, πρίν + aorist indicative: the state of affairs of the dependent clause is posterior to that of the main clause: ἕως 'until', πρίν 'before'.
Some examples ((a): (201); (b): (202) - (204); (c): (205) - (206)):

(201) <u>ἐπεὶ</u> ὦν ὁ βουκόλος σπουδῇ πολλῇ καλεόμενος <u>ἀπίκετο</u>, ἔλεγε ὁ Ἅρπαγος τάδε ('So when the cowherd had come with all speed at the summons, Harpagus said the following', Hdt. 1.110.3)
(202) καὶ <u>ὅτε</u> δὴ <u>ἦν</u> δεκαέτης ὁ παῖς, πρῆγμα ἐς αὐτὸν τοιόνδε γενόμενον ἐξέφηνέ μιν ('And when the boy was ten years old, the following occurrence revealed his identity', Hdt. 1.114.1)
(203) καὶ <u>ἕως</u> μὲν <u>ἐτιμᾶτο</u>, πιστὸν ἑαυτὸν παρεῖχεν· <u>ἐπειδὴ</u> δὲ Πείσανδρον μὲν καὶ Κάλλαισχρον καὶ ἑτέρους <u>ἑώρα</u> προτέρους αὑτοῦ γιγνομένους ..., τότ' ἤδη ... μετέσχε τῶν Ἀριστοκράτους ἔργων ('So long as he found favour, he showed himself loyal; but when he saw Peisandros, Kallaischros, and other getting in advance of him ..., then he began to co-operate with Aristokrates', Lys. 12.66-7)
(204) ... ἐθωρακίζετο καὶ οἱ σὺν αὐτῷ. <u>ἐν ᾧ</u> δὲ <u>ὡπλίζοντο</u> ἧκον ... οἱ ... σκοποί ('... he put on his breastplate and so did those who were

with him. While they were arming themselves, however, the scouts returned ...', X. *An.* 2.2.14-5)

(205) αὕτη δὲ ἐφύλαττεν (sc. αὐτόν), <u>ἕως ἐξηῦρεν</u> ὅτι εἴη τὸ αἴτιον ('And she kept a close watch on him, until she discovered what was the cause', Lys. 1.15)

(206) παραπλήσια δὲ καὶ οἱ ἐπὶ τῶν νεῶν αὐτοῖς ἔπασχον, <u>πρίν</u> γε δὴ οἱ Συρακόσιοι ... <u>ἔτρεψαν</u> τοὺς 'Αθηναίους ('The men aboard the ships were affected in a similar way, at least before the Syracusans routed the Athenians', Th. 7.71.5)

Note 1 Besides the aorist indicative and the imperfect, the pluperfect may sometimes follow ἐπεί, ἐπειδή, ὅτε and ὡς: the state expressed in the dependent clause is simultaneous with the state of affairs of the main clause; e.g.: <u>ἐπεὶ δὲ ὑπελέλειπτο</u> ὁ βουκόλος μοῦνος ..., τάδε αὐτὸν εἴρετο ὁ 'Αστυάγης ('And when the cowherd was left alone, Astyages asked him the following', Hdt. 1.116.3)

Note 2 Temporal conjunctions function as *presupposition-triggers* (cp. § 18.2, Note 1): they presuppose the reality of the state of affairs expressed in the dependent clause. See Levinson (1983: 182). One of Levinson's examples runs: '*Since* Churchill died, we've lacked/we haven't lacked a leader'. This presupposes: Churchill died.

26.2   Particulars

(i) Dependent clauses of types (a) en (b) usually precede the main clause; those of type (c) usually follow the main clause (but see (vi) below).

(ii) In the case of (a) and (b) any secondary indicative may occur in the main clause, while in the case of (c) the imperfect is usually found (but see (vi) below).

(iii) Both ἕως and ἐν ᾧ + imperfect express 'during the time in which' but differ in that ἕως (particularly ἕως μέν) is often used with a conditional nuance: the state of affairs of the main clause is carried out *as long as* the state of affairs of the dependent clause is carried out, and is, therefore, dependent on it. ἐν ᾧ never has this nuance; it simply connects two simultaneous states of affairs: 'while'.

(iv) In some cases a temporal clause may have a causal nuance, especially in cases where the main clause describes a *reaction* to the state of affairs of the dependent clause (so-called *circumstantial* use of a temporal clause), cp. ἐπειδὴ ... ἑώρα in (203).

(v) There sometimes does not seem to be a clear difference in meaning between ἕως 'until' and πρίν 'before' (in (206) ἕως could have been used as well). In both cases the state of affairs of the dependent clause marks the end of the state of affairs of the main clause: 'x lasted until y occurred'. Πρίν is used in particular after a negative main clause : οὐ ... πρίν 'not ... before'.

Some examples:

(207) πρότερον δ' οὐκ ἦν γένος ἀθανάτων, πρὶν "Ερως ξυνέμειξεν ἅπαντα ('Earlier there was no race of immortals, before Love had blended everything', Ar. Av. 700)

(208) οὐ πρόσθεν ἐπαύσαντο πολεμοῦντες, πρὶν ἐποίησαν πᾶσαν τὴν πόλιν ὁμολογεῖν Λακεδαιμονίους καὶ αὐτῶν ἡγεμόνας εἶναι ('They did not cease waging war before they had made the entire city acknowledge that the Lacedaemonians were their leaders also', X. An. 6.1.27)

The construction οὐκ A πρὶν B ('not A before B') often implies ἐπεὶ B, A ('(only) after B, A'), as in (207) and (208).

(vi) πρίν is also frequently followed by the *infinitive*, particularly in cases where the main clause is affirmative (not-negative). Unlike the construction discussed in (v) above πρίν + infinitive often precedes the main clause, while the verb of the main clause need not be an imperfect.

Some examples:

(209) λέγεται γὰρ 'Αλκιβιάδην, πρὶν εἴκοσιν ἐτῶν εἶναι, Περικλεῖ ... τοιάδε διαλεχθῆναι περὶ νόμων ('For it is said that Alcibiades, before he was twenty years old, had the following conversation about laws with Pericles', X. Mem. 1.2.40)

(210) ὀλίγον δὲ πρὶν ἡμᾶς ἀπιέναι, μάχη ἐγεγόνει ἐν τῇ Ποτειδαίᾳ ('And shortly before we left there had been a battle at Potidaea', Pl. Chrm. 153b)

(211) ἦσαν δὲ καὶ ἀνάριστοι· πρὶν γὰρ δὴ καταλῦσαι τὸ στράτευμα πρὸς ἄριστον βασιλεὺς ἐφάνη ('And they had had no breakfast, either, for the king had appeared before the time when the army could halt for breakfast', X. An. 1.10.19)

In this construction the state of affairs of the main clause either simply occurs at a moment before the occurrence of the state of affairs of the dependent clause (as in (209) and (210)) or before the state of affairs of the dependent clause could occur (as in (211)): in the latter case the state of affairs of the main clause precludes the occurrence of the state of affairs of the dependent clause.

The interpretation depends on the context: in (210) it is clear that the 'we' did indeed leave; in another context πρὶν ἡμᾶς ἀπιέναι could also be interpreted as 'before we were able to leave'. In (211) the interpretation is determined by the preceding statement 'they did not have breakfast'. In the use with the infinitive πρίν *cannot* be replaced by ἕως.

Note 1 Unlike πρίν + indicative, πρίν + infinitive clauses are not inherently factive.

Note 2 Other, less frequently used, temporal conjunctions are μέχρι (οὗ), ἄχρι (οὗ), ἔστε 'until', 'so long as'; ἡνίκα 'at the moment when', 'when'; ὁπότε, ὅπως 'when(ever)'; ἀφ' οὗ, ἐξ οὗ 'from the moment when', 'since'. ἐπεί (ἐπειδή) and ὡς may be combined with (τὸ) πρῶτον or τάχιστα: ἐπεὶ τάχιστα 'as soon as'. In Ionic ἐπείτε is used besides ἐπεί (ἐπειδή).

26.3   ἐπεί-*clauses with causal value*

In direct speech ἐπεί + primary present indicative, + constative aorist indicative (cp. § 8.3.1), or + primary perfect indicative has causal value; on the basis of the state of affairs expressed in the ἐπεί-clause the speaker draws a certain conclusion, often in the form of a request or command: 'now that/since/seeing that x has occurred, you must do y'. Thus also ἐπειδή, and ὅτε and ὡς (seldom) are used. The negative is οὐ.

Some examples:

(212)   ἐπεὶ ... οὐ <u>δύναμαί</u> σε πείθειν ..., σὺ δὲ ὧδε ποίησον ('Now that I cannot convince you ..., you must act as follows: ...', Hdt. 1.112.2)

(213)   <u>ἐπειδὴ</u> δ' ὑμῖν τὰ Ἐρασιφῶντος δημεύειν <u>ἔδοξεν</u>, ... τὰ Ἐρασιστράτου ἀξιῶ μοι ψηφισθῆναι ('Now that you have seen fit to confiscate the property of Erasiphon, ... I claim that the property of Erasistratos be adjudged to me', Lys. 17.6)

Note 1 Unlike εἰ + present indicative (cp. § 24.2), ἐπεί is, again, a presupposition-trigger: it presupposes that the state of affairs concerned is a fact. Cp. also § 24.2, Note 1.

Note 2 For causal ἐπεί following the main clause with the value of γάρ see § 27, Note 4.

26.4   Single future states of affairs

The conjunctions of types (a) - (c) (see above), except ὡς, are construed with ἄν and the subjunctive in cases where the state of affairs of the dependent clause is located in the future. A future indicative or some other form with future reference usually occurs in the main clause. The negative in the dependent clause is μή.

Note 1 ὅτε + ἄν = ὅταν; ἐπεί + ἄν = ἐπάν or ἐπήν, Ionic also ἐπεάν; ἐπειδή + ἄν = ἐπειδάν.
Note 2 ὡς ἄν does occur, but only as a (relative) conjunction of manner: 'in the way ...', and in purpose clauses (§ 22, Note 2).

(a) ἐπήν, ὅταν etc. + aorist subjunctive: the state of affairs of the dependent clause is anterior to that of the main clause: 'after', 'when';
(b) ἐπήν, ὅταν etc. + present subjunctive: the state of affairs of the dependent clause is simultaneous with that of the main clause: 'when'; ἕως ἄν 'so long as';
(c) ἕως ἄν + aorist subjunctive: the state of affairs of the dependent clause is posterior to that of the main clause: 'until'. For πρίν see below.
Some examples ((a): (214) - (215); (b): (216); (c): (217) - (218)):

(214)   νῦν ὦν μοι δοκέει, ἐπεὰν τάχιστα νὺξ ἐπέλθῃ ... ἀπαλλάσσεσθαι ('Now therefore my counsel is to depart as soon as night has fallen', Hdt. 4.134.3)
(215)   τάφος δὲ ποῖος δέξεταί μ', ὅταν θάνω; ('And what kind of tomb shall receive me ̣after I have died?', E. *IT* 625)
(216)   ἕωσπερ ἂν ἐμπνέω καὶ οἷός τε ὦ, οὐ μὴ παύσωμαι φιλοσοφῶν ('So long as I live and am able to continue, I shall never give up philosophy', Pl. *Ap.* 29d; for οὐ μή cp. § 20, Note 3)
(217)   δεῖ μὴ περιμένειν ἕως ἂν ἐπιστῶσιν ('You must not wait until they are upon you', Isoc. 4.165)
(218)   ἔδοξεν αὐτοῖς ... προϊέναι εἰς τὸ πρόσθεν, ἕως Κύρῳ συμμείξειαν ('They resolved to push forward until they should join forces with Cyrus', X. *An.* 2.1.2; indirect speech: συμμείξειαν is an oblique optative, ἂν συμμείξωσιν would have been possible as well)

26.5   Particulars

πρίν (ἄν) + subjunctive (usually aorist subjunctive) only occurs in cases where the main clause is negative (cp. also (207) and (208) above). Some examples:

(219) μὴ προκαταγίγνωσκ', ὦ πάτερ, <u>πρὶν ἄν γ' ἀκούσῃς</u> ἀμφοτέρων ('Don't decide against us, father, before you have heard both sides', Ar. V. 919-20)

(220) μὴ ἀπέλθητε <u>πρὶν ἂν ἀκούσητε</u> ... ('Do not go away before you have heard ...', X. An. 5.7.12)

In indirect speech (cp. also § 18.4) πρίν-clauses either retain the subjunctive of direct speech (ex. (221)), or they have an oblique optative (ex. (222)):

(221) οὐ προεθυμήθησαν ξυμπλεῖν, <u>πρὶν</u> τὰ Ἴσθμια ... <u>διεορτάσωσιν</u> ('They were not disposed to sail with them before they should have fully celebrated the Isthmian games', Th. 8.9.1)

(222) ... ὑποσχόμενος αὐτοῖς ... μὴ πρόσθεν παύσεσθαι <u>πρὶν</u> αὐτοὺς <u>καταγάγοι</u> οἴκαδε ('... having promised them that ... he would not stop before he had restored them to their homes', X. An. 1.2.2; direct speech: οὐ παύσομαι πρὶν (ἂν) ὑμᾶς καταγάγω)

In the case of an affirmative main clause πρίν is construed with the infinitive (cp. also § 26.2 (vi)):

(223) νῦν ὦν μοι δοκέει ... ἀπαλλάσσεσθαι, <u>πρὶν</u> ... ἐπὶ τὸν Ἴστρον <u>ἰθῦσαι</u> Σκύθας ('Now therefore my counsel is to depart ... before the Scythians can march straight to the Ister', Hdt. 4.134.3)

Note 1 In temporal clauses the future indicative does *not* occur, since it is not suited for the expression of temporal relationships like anteriority and simultaneity.

Note 2 Though states of affairs located in the future cannot, strictly speaking, be called factive, the states of affairs in these dependent clauses are presented as such; in particular this holds for clauses introduced by the presupposition-triggers ὅταν, ἐπειδάν etc. as opposed to the corresponding conditional clauses (cp. § 24). In the literature it is often held that there is little or no difference between ἐάν + subjunctive and ὅταν + subjunctive, but this is, in general, untrue: the conditional clauses express a condition which is based on a hypothesis, while in the case of ὅταν-clauses we are neither dealing with a condition nor with a hypothesis, but with events whose reality is presupposed (cp. § 26.1, Note 2). From this it follows that the term 'prospective subjunctive' (cp. § 21, Note 2 and § 24.3.1) is not applicable here: notions like 'it is (very well) possible that the state of affairs will be carried out' play no part here, even less so since here the alternative construction with a future indicative in the dependent clause does not exist. Where a speaker may choose between alternatives, as in the case of ἐάν + subjunctive and εἰ + future indicative, it is useful to make a clear distinction; in the case of ὅταν, however, the construction with the subjunctive is the only possible one.

26.6 Habitual non-past states of affairs

Conjunctions and present and aorist subjunctives are used as discussed in the preceding section. A generic present indicative occurs in the main clause: '(each time) when/after ...', etc. The state of affairs in the dependent clause is factive. The negative is μή.

(224) (The Assyrians build strangely shaped boats to sail down the Euphrates) ἐπεὰν ὧν ἀπίκωνται πλέοντες ἐς τὴν Βαβυλῶνα ... τὰς ... διφθέρας ἐπισάξαντες ἐπὶ τοὺς ὄνους ἀπελαύνουσι ἐς τοὺς Ἀρμενίους. (...) ἐπεὰν δὲ ... ἀπίκωνται ὀπίσω ἐς τοὺς Ἀρμενίους, ἄλλα τρόπῳ τῷ αὐτῷ ποιεῦνται πλοῖα ('So when they have sailed down to Babylon ... they load the hides on the backs of donkeys and return to the Armenians. (...) And when they have arrived in Armenia, they make other boats in the same way', Hdt. 1.194.4-5)

(225) τότε γὰρ πλεῖστα κερδαίνουσιν, ὅταν κακοῦ τινος ἀπαγγελ-θέντος τῇ πόλει τίμιον τὸν σῖτον πωλῶσιν ('For they make most profit when at the announcement to the city of some disaster they sell their corn at a high price', Lys. 22.14)

(226) ἕως ἂν σῴζηται τὸ σκάφος, ... τότε χρὴ ... προθύμους εἶναι ...· ἐπειδὰν δ' ἡ θάλαττα ὑπέρσχῃ, μάταιος ἡ σπουδή ('So long as the vessel is safe, you must be willing; but when the sea has overhelmed it, zeal is useless', D. 9.69)

(227) ποιοῦμεν ταῦθ' ἑκάστοθ' ... ἕως ἂν αὐτὸν ἐμβάλωμεν ἐς κακόν ('We do this every time ... until we have driven him into misery', Ar. Nu. 1458-60)

πρίν (ἄν) + subjunctive following a negative main clause:

(228) οὐ πρότερον παύονται, <u>πρὶν ἂν πείσωσιν</u> οὓς ἠδίκησαν ('They do not stop until they have persuaded those whom they have wronged', Pl. *Phd.* 114b)

Note 1 This use of the subjunctive is called distributive-iterative; cp. § 24.3.2, Note 1. These temporal clauses introduced by ὅταν, ἐπειδάν, etc. and the corresponding conditional clauses introduced by ἐάν (cp. § 24.3.2) differ in that the latter clauses present the state of affairs of the dependent clause as *sometimes* occurring in a given situation, whereas in the case of the clauses introduced by ὅταν, etc. it is implied - due to the factive value of the conjunction - that the state of affairs of the dependent clause *always* occurs in the situation at hand. Thus in (224) a series of subsequent states of affairs is described: 'after x, y; after y, z'. The use of ἤν here would have implied that the Assyrians sometimes did not arrive in Babylon. On the other hand, as was observed above (§ 24.3.2, Note 2), the use of ἐπεάν instead of ἤν in (185) would imply that the rope always broke.

26.7   Habitual past states of affairs

Here we are dealing with the past counterpart of the construction discussed in the preceding section. ἐπεί and the other conjunctions are followed by the (distributive-iterative) optative; an imperfect occurs in the main clause: '(each time) when/after ...'.

Some examples:

(229) <u>ὡς</u> δὲ ἐς τὴν Μιλησίην <u>ἀπίκοιτο</u>, οἰκήματα μὲν ... οὔτε κατέβαλλε οὔτε ἐνεπίμπρη ..., ἔα δὲ ... ἐστάναι ('And whenever he came to the Milesian territory, he neither demolished the houses nor burnt them ..., but let them stand unharmed', Hdt. 1.17.2)

(230) ἐθήρευεν ἀπὸ ἵππου, <u>ὁπότε</u> γυμνάσαι <u>βούλοιτο</u> ἑαυτόν τε καὶ τοὺς ἵππους ('He used to hunt on horseback whenever he wished to give himself and his horses exercise', X. *An.* 1.2.7)

(231) αἰεὶ γὰρ δὴ καὶ τὰς πρόσθεν ἡμέρας εἰώθεμεν φοιτᾶν ... παρὰ τὸν Σωκράτη, ... περιεμένομεν οὖν ἑκάστοτε, <u>ἕως ἀνοιχθείη</u> τὸ δεσμωτήριον· ... <u>ἐπειδὴ</u> δὲ <u>ἀνοιχθείη</u>, εἰσῇμεν παρὰ τὸν Σωκράτη ('On the previous days we had always been in the habit of visiting Socrates ... Every day we used to wait about, until the prison was opened; and when it was opened, we went in to Socrates', Pl. *Phd.* 59d)

Note 1 πρίν is never construed with the distributive-iterative optative; instead πρίν + infinitive is used.

Note 2 The distributive-iterative optative is used with ὁπότε in particular; in Herodotus with ὅκως (= ὅπως) 'when' as well.

§ 27 Causal clauses

Causal clauses are introduced by ὅτι and διότι 'because'; they express the reason or cause underlying the state of affairs of the main clause. The moods are used as in independent declarative clauses (usually the indicative). These conjunctions function, again, as presupposition-triggers: they presuppose that the dependent state of affairs is a fact. The negative is οὐ.

Some examples:

(232) ἔγραψα δὲ αὐτὰ ... διὰ τόδε, <u>ὅτι</u> τοῖς πρὸ ἐμοῦ ἅπασιν ἐκλιπὲς τοῦτο <u>ἦν</u> τὸ χωρίον ('I have written this ... for this reason, because this period has been omitted by all my predecessors', Th. 1.97.2)

(233) Ἀθηναῖοι ἐνόμιζον ἡσσᾶσθαι, <u>ὅτι</u> οὐ πολὺ <u>ἐνίκων</u> ('The Athenians thought they were defeated, because they were not signally victorious', Th. 7.34.7)

In third person narrative, as in (233), it is the narrator who assigns the reason or cause involved (therefore a comma should be put after ἡσσᾶσθαι, as in the Budé-text). This is borne out by the fact that causal ὅτι-clauses may be modified by attitudinal modifiers like *in my* (i.e. the narrator's) *opinion, presumably*, as in

(234) μετὰ δὲ Σόλωνα οἰχόμενον ἔλαβε ἐκ θεοῦ νέμεσις μεγάλη Κροῖσον, <u>ὡς εἰκάσαι, ὅτι</u> ἐνόμισε ἑωυτὸν εἶναι ἀνθρώπων ἁπάντων ὀλβιώτατον ('But after Solon's departure, the divine anger fell heavily on Croesus, presumably because he supposed himself to be blest beyond all other men', Hdt. 1.34.1)

After a past tense in the main clause a future indicative or an oblique optative may occur in the dependent clause, indicating that we are dealing with 'indirect speech' (cp. p. 52): the reason is presented as a consideration of the subject of the main clause. Such clauses are no longer factive.

Two examples:

(235) τὸν Περικλέα ... ἐκάκιζον <u>ὅτι</u> στρατηγὸς ὢν οὐκ <u>ἐπεξάγοι</u> ('They abused Pericles on the ground that, though their general, he did not lead them out', Th. 2.21.3; 'direct speech': οὐκ ἐπεξάγει).

(236) ἀρρώδεον δέ, <u>ὅτι</u> αὐτοὶ ... ναυμαχέειν <u>μέλλοιεν</u>, νικηθέντες τε ... <u>πολιορκήσονται</u> ('They were frightened, because, in their opinion, they were about to fight a sea-battle, and after a defeat would be under siege', Hdt. 8.70.2; 'direct speech': μέλλομεν, πολιορκησόμεθα; for the pragmatic differences between the optative and the indicative see § 18.2, p. 53)

Note 1 Observe that, in (236), the ὅτι-clause is not an object clause, for with verbs of fearing these are introduced by μή (§ 20). - It should be noted that causal clauses with a future indicative or an optative after a past tense (cp. (236)) are rare. In this respect, then, causal ὅτι-clauses differ from object clauses with ὅτι (and ὡς) in real indirect discourse, cp. § 18.2. Perhaps the rareness of such causal ὅτι-clauses after a past tense is due to the fact that Greek has at its disposal an altogether different construction to present a so-called 'subjective' reason or cause, viz. ὡς + participle. The difference between the two causal types is well illustrated by: οἱ Κορίνθιοι εὐθὺς τροπαῖον ἔστησαν <u>ὡς</u> νικῶντες, <u>ὅτι</u> πλείους τῶν ἐναντίων ναῦς ἄπλους ἐποίησαν ('... the Corinthians at once set up a trophy, considering themselves the victors, because they had disabled a larger number of the enemy's ships', Th. 7.34.7). Here, the ὡς-phrase expresses the considerations of the Corinthians, while the ὅτι-clause explains why, according to Thucydides, the Corinthians believed they had won. For ὡς + participle, and for its 'objective' counterpart ἅτε + participle, see § 38 (ii).

Note 2 It is sometimes impossible to determine whether a ὅτι-clause is an (optional) causal clause or on (obligatory) object clause, especially after verbs of emotion. An example is (136) above: ἥσθη <u>ὅτι</u> ἕξοι τὸν συγκορυβαντιῶντα ('he was glad that he would have a companion to his manic frenzy', Pl. Phdr. 228b; 'because', however, is also possible). Be that as it may, the states of affairs referred to are, of course, highly similar, if not identical.

Note 3 Besides the strictly causal dependent clauses discussed here there are several other constructions which may have a causal nuance:

– ἐπεί + present indicative in direct speech (cp. § 26.3 and (212) - (213)): on the basis of the state of affairs of the dependent clause the speaker draws a conclusion.

–   Sometimes temporal clauses with ἐπεί, ὡς, etc. + imperfect or aorist indicative, cp. § 26.1 with example (203), and § 26.2 (iv).

Note 4 ἐπεί and ὡς frequently function as causal coordinator-like conjunctions ('for', 'namely'), comparable to γάρ. The content of such ἐπεί- and ὡς-clauses usually consists of a *motivation* for the preceding statement: οὐ σύ γε ἡμέας ἀπολείψεις, ἐπεί τοι ἐγὼ μέζω δῶρα δώσω ('You will not leave us behind, for I shall give you larger gifts', Hdt. 8.5.2); πέμπειν δὲ χρὴ καὶ ὑμέας στρατιὴν πολλήν, ὡς, εἰ μὴ πέμψετε, ἐπίστασθε ἡμέας ὁμολογήσειν τῷ Πέρσῃ ('But you too must send a great force; for if you will not send it, be assured that we shall make terms with the Persians', Hdt. 7.172.2). In this use the ἐπεί- and ὡς-clauses always *follow* the clauses or sentences they modify.

IIIC RELATIVE CLAUSES

§ 28 Introduction

Relative clauses are introduced by the relative pronouns ὅς and ὅστις, by relative adjectives such as οἷος and ὅσος, and by relative adverbs such as οὗ 'where', οἷ 'whither', ὡς 'as'.

Syntactically, two groups may be distinguished:

(i) *Anaphoric* relative clauses: the clause modifies an antecedent (also called the head noun) which is a constituent of the main clause. Within this group two subtypes may be distinguished:

(a) *determinative* (or: *restrictive*) clauses: the clause contains the information which allows the antecedent to be identified, i.e. the information from which it becomes clear to which entity the antecedent refers. English: the man *whom you see* is my brother; Greek: ὁ ἀνὴρ <u>ὃν ὁρᾷς</u> ἀδελφός μου ἐστίν.

(b) *digressive* clauses: the antecedent is identifiable without the information offered by the relative clause; the clause may, therefore, be characterized as a digression. English: The Rhine, *which flows through several countries*, is a major European river; Greek: ὁ Νεῖλος, <u>ὃς δι' Αἰγύπτου ῥεῖ</u>, ποταμὸς μέγας ἐστίν. Digressive clauses especially occur with proper names, which normally refer to a single identifiable entity.

(ii) *autonomous* relative clauses: the clause has no antecedent, but itself functions as a constituent (subject, object, etc.) of the main clause. These clauses are always determinative, for they allow the subject, object, etc. to be identified. English: What he has done is quite remarkable: *what he has done* is the subject of *is*; Greek: ἃ ἐποίησε πάνυ θαυμαστά ἐστιν· ἃ ἐποίησε is the subject of ἐστιν. As to their function such constituents resemble substantives (*what he has done* ~ *his deeds;* ἃ ἐποίησε ~ τὰ ἔργα) and also, in Greek, substantivally used participles: ἃ ἐποίησε ~ τὰ ποιηθέντα.

§ 29 The moods in relative clauses

In both groups of relative clauses the moods of the main clauses are used, in particular indicative, secondary indicative + ἄν, optative + ἄν and cupitive optative. In digressive clauses *only*, furthermore, imperative and adhortative subjunctive occur, and in determinative clauses *only*, the moods which are typically used in dependent clauses: prospective subjunctive + ἄν, distributive-iterative subjunctive + ἄν, optative of potential condition (cp. § 24.4.1), and distributive-iterative optative. As for the negative see below.

Some examples:

29.1 Anaphoric clauses

(i) Anaphoric determinative clauses:

(237) τοὺς θησαυρούς τ' αὐτοῖς δείξουσ' <u>οὓς</u> οἱ πρότεροι <u>κατέθεντο</u> ('They will show to them the treasures which their forefathers have hidden', Ar. *Av.* 599; indicative)

(238) τῷ ἀνδρὶ <u>ὃν ἂν ἕλησθε</u> πείσομαι ('I shall obey the man whom you choose', X. *An.* 1.3.15; prospective subjunctive)

(239) ... ἀποτίνει ζημίην <u>τὴν ἂν</u> οἱ ἱρέες <u>τάξωνται</u> ('... he pays whatever penalty the priests appoint', Hdt. 2.65.5; distributive-iterative subjunctive)

(240) οὐκ ἂν ἀποδοίην οὐδ' ἂν ὀβολὸν οὐδενὶ <u>ὅστις καλέσειε</u> κάρδοπον τὴν καρδόπην ('No, I wouldn't repay a single penny to anyone who called the kardope kardopos', Ar. *Nu.* 1250-1; optative of potential condition)

(241) πάντας γὰρ δὴ ... Λακεδαιμόνιοι <u>ὅσους λάβοιεν</u> ἐν τῇ θαλάσσῃ ... διέφθειρον ('For the Lacedaemonians killed all persons whom they captured at sea', Th. 2.67.4; distributive-iterative optative)

(ii) Anaphoric digressive clauses:

(242) Ἀρταΰκτης ..., <u>ὃς</u> Σηστὸν ... <u>ἐπετρόπευε</u> ('Artayctes, who was governor of Sestus', Hdt. 7.78; indicative)

(243) ἥξετε ἐπὶ ... ῎Αλυν, ..., <u>ὃν οὐκ ἂν δύναισθε</u> ἄνευ πλοίων
διαβῆναι ('You will come to ... the Halys, which you could not
cross without boats', X. *An.* 5.6.9; optative + ἄν)

(244) εἰς καλὸν ἡμῖν ῎Ανυτος ὅδε παρεκαθέζετο, <u>ᾧ μεταδῶμεν</u> τῆς
ζητήσεως ('At the right moment Anytus here came to sit beside us,
whom we should make a partner to our quest (or: let us make
him...)', Pl. *Men.* 89e; adhortative subjunctive)

29.2 *Autonomous clauses*

(245) ἦ που σοφὸς ἦν <u>ὅστις ἔφασκεν</u> ... ('Whoever said ... was pretty
wise ...', Ar. *V.* 725; indicative, the clause functions as subject)

(246) ὁρᾷς <u>ἃ ποιεῖς</u>; ('Do you see what you are doing?', Ar. *Pl.* 932;
indicative, the clause functions as object)

(247) ἆρ᾽ οἶσθα θάνατον ὅτι προεῖφ᾽ ὁ Ζεὺς <u>ὃς ἂν</u> ταύτην ἀνορύττων
<u>εὑρεθῇ;</u>('Do you realize that Zeus has ordained death for anyone
caught digging her up?', Ar. *Pax* 371-2; prospective subjunctive,
the clause functions as indirect object in the dative case)

(248) <u>ὃ δὲ μὴ ἀγαπῴη</u>, οὐδ᾽ ἂν φιλοῖ ('And that which he does not
cherish he will not love', Pl. *Ly.* 215b; optative of potential
condition, the clause functions as object)

(249) καὶ <u>οὓς</u> μὲν <u>ἴδοι</u> εὐτάκτως καὶ σιωπῇ ἰόντας, ... τίνες ... εἶεν
ἠρώτα ('And those whom he saw marching in good order and
silence he asked who they were', X. *Cyr.* 5.3.55; distributive-
iterative optative, the clause functions as object)

Note 1 The syntactic function of the clause may be clarified by preparative
(cataphoric) and resumptive (anaphoric) constituents in the main clause: ...
εἴρηται <u>τούτου</u> μὴ καταγιγνώσκειν φόνον, <u>ὃς ἂν</u> ... <u>ταύτην</u> τὴν τιμωρίαν
ποιήσηται ('It has been stated that whoever takes this vengeance shall not
be convicted of murder', Lys. 1.30); <u>ἃ</u> δ᾽ ἐγὼ πέπονθα, <u>ταῦτα</u> λέξαι
βούλομαι ('But what I have experienced, that I am willing to tell you', Ar.
Th. 445).
Note 2 Constructions where a noun would be followed by two relative
clauses, with the relative pronoun appearing in different cases, are avoided.
Instead, the second clause either has no relative pronoun of its own, or it
contains an anaphoric pronoun. Cp.: (no rel. pronoun in second clause:)
Οὐκοῦν ὡμολόγηται <u>οὗ</u> ἐνδεής ἐστι καὶ μὴ <u>ἔχει</u>, τούτου ἐρᾶν; ('Well then,
haven't we agreed that he loves what he lacks and has not?', Pl. *Smp.* 201b;

for ὃ μὴ ἔχει); (anaphoric pronoun:) ἀπόκριναι τί ἐστιν τοῦτο ὃ φὴς σὺ μέγιστον ἀγαθὸν εἶναι ... καὶ σὲ δημιουργὸν εἶναι αὐτοῦ ('tell us what is this thing that you say is the greatest good ..., and that you claim to produce', Pl. *Grg.* 452d; for οὗ σέ).

Note 3 For the exceptional use of the imperatives δρᾶσον and ποίησον in autonomous clauses (οἶσθ᾽ οὖν ὃ δρᾶσον; and the like) see § 15, Note 1.

29.3   *Particulars*

(i) Autonomous clauses in which subjunctive + ἄν, optative of potential condition, and distributive-iterative optative are used greatly resemble conditional clauses (cp. § 24, 3-4). Thus ὃς ἄν ... εὑρεθῇ in (247) may, practically speaking, be paraphrased by ἐάν τις ... εὑρεθῇ, and ὃ μὴ ἀγαπῴη in (248) by εἴ τι μὴ ἀγαπῴη, and οὓς ... ἴδοι in (249) by εἴ τινας ... ἴδοι. As in conditional clauses, the negative is always μή.

(ii) Autonomous clauses with the indicative may also have a conditional nuance, particularly due to the presence of μή:

(250)   ὃς δὲ τούτους μὴ ὄπωπε, ἐγὼ ... σημανέω ('For him who has not seen them I shall describe them', Hdt. 3.37.2; the clause functions as indirect object)

ὃς ... μὴ ὄπωπε may be paraphrased by εἴ τις ... μὴ ὄπωπε. This construction, just as εἰ + indicative, does not specify whether or not the content of the dependent clause is a fact. Relative clauses with μή and indicative, therefore, are often of a generalizing nature rather than referring to a concrete, particular entity. The use of the negative οὐ, on the other hand, indicates that a particular entity is involved, in which case the relative clause cannot be paraphrased by εἴ τις ...:

(251)   ἀλλ᾽ ἠπίσταντο ἃ ἐγὼ οὐκ ἠπιστάμην ('But they knew what I did not', Pl. *Ap.* 22d; the clause functions as object)

(iii) Digressive anaphoric clauses are more loosely connected with the antecedent than determinative anaphoric clauses. Among other things, this appears from the fact that digressive clauses may be replaced by a sentence with a demonstrative pronoun instead of the relative pronoun; for determinative clauses this does not hold. Thus ᾧ μεταδῶμεν in (244) may be replaced by τούτῳ (or αὐτῷ) μεταδῶμεν. The use of the negative in digressive clauses is consonant with their main clause-status: οὐ with indicative and optative + ἄν, μή with subjunctive and cupitive optative. In some cases there is such a loose connection between antecedent and relative clause that the clause acquires the function of an independent sentence. This happens, for instance, in cases where ὅς is separated from its antecedent by a large number of constituents, as in:

(252) ἐς Λεωνίδην ἀνέβαινε ἡ βασιληίη, καὶ διότι πρότερος ἐγεγόνεε Κλεομβρότου ... καὶ δὴ καὶ εἶχε Κλεομένεος θυγατέρα. <u>ὃς τότε ἤιε ἐς</u> ... ('The succession fell to Leonidas, because he was older than Cleombrotus, and moreover had Cleomenes' daughter to wife. He then went to ...', Hdt. 7.205.1-2)

(iv) In determinative (never in digressive) anaphoric clauses *attraction* of the relative pronoun may occur, i.e. the relative pronoun is attracted from its proper case into the case of its antecedent. In particular, this occurs in cases where the antecedent has the genitive or dative case form, while the relative pronoun functions as object in the relative clause and would, therefore, have been expressed in the accusative.

Two examples:

(253) ... ἄγων ἀπὸ τῶν πόλεων <u>ὧν</u> (for ἃς) <u>ἔπεισε</u> στρατιάν ('... bringing from the cities which he had prevailed upon a body of troops', Th. 7.21.1)
(254) ... σὺν τοῖς θησαυροῖς <u>οἷς</u> (for οὓς) <u>ὁ πατὴρ κατέλιπεν</u> ('... with the treasures that my father left me', X. *Cyr.* 3.1.33)

The adaptation of the relative pronoun to the antecedent reinforces the formal connection between these two elements. This construction may have been developed on the analogy of the attributive passive participle: τῶν πόλεων ὧν ἔπεισε corresponds with τῶν πόλεων τῶν πεισθεισῶν. In fact, the 'attracted' relative clause may be considered the active counterpart to the construction with a passive participle; a construction involving an *active* participle was, of course, not possible.

Note 1 Conversely, the antecedent may also be attracted into the case of the relative pronoun (*attractio inversa*). This especially occurs in cases like the following, where the antecedent plus relative clause stand at the beginning of a sentence (as a so-called Topic or Theme constituent): <u>τάσδε δ' ἅσπερ εἰσορᾷς</u> /... εὑροῦσαι βίον / <u>χωροῦσι</u> πρὸς σέ ('The women who you see, having found a life ... are coming up to you', S. *Tr.* 283).

Note 2 In constructions such as ἐγὼ δέ σοι ὑπισχνοῦμαι ... ἀνθ' ὧν ἂν ἐμοὶ δανείσῃς, ... ἄλλα ... εὐεργετήσειν ('I promise you that in return for what you lend to me I shall do you other favours', X. *Cyr.* 3.1.34) we are not dealing with attraction but with an autonomous clause which, as a whole, has a function comparable to that of an article + noun-construction. As such, therefore, this combination may be construed with a preposition (as in English): ἀνθ' ὧν ἂν ... δανείσῃς = 'in return *for what* you lend to me'. ὧν ... δανείσῃς is, therefore, in a way the 'genitive case form' of ἅ ... δανείσῃς. Compare also the next subsection, examples (258) and (259).

(v) The formal connection between antecedent and relative clause is still stronger in a remarkable construction in which the antecedent has been *incorporated* into the relative clause, to use the traditional terminology. (Strictly speaking the terms 'antecedent' and 'relative clause' are no longer valid in such cases). Such clauses are like autonomous clauses in that they provide the subject, object etc. of the main clause. 'Relative pronoun' and noun usually appear in the case form required by the verb of the dependent clause, but their form may also be determined by some constituent of the main clause, e.g. a preposition. Some examples are, of the former:

(255) ὃν δ' ἐπιστείβεις τόπον / χθονὸς καλεῖται τῆσδε χαλκόπους ὁδός ('The place on which you tread is called the brazen treshold of this land', S. *OC* 56; the 'relative' clause functions as subject of καλεῖται)

(256) εἰ δέ τινα ὁρῴη ... κατασκευάζοντα ... ἧς ἄρχοι χώρας ('Whenever he saw that a man was organizing well the country over which he ruled ...', X. *An.* 1.9.19; the 'relative' clause functions as object of κατασκευάζοντα)

(257) ἔστησαν δὲ καὶ οἱ Πελοποννήσιοι τροπαῖον ... τῆς τροπῆς ἃς πρὸς τῇ γῇ διέφθειραν ναῦς ('But the Peloponnesians also set up ... a trophy for the defeat of the ships which they had disabled near the shore', Th. 2.92.5; the 'relative' clause functions as 'object' of τῆς τροπῆς; an 'objective genitive' (ὧν ... νεῶν) would have been possible)

and of the latter

(258) Ξέρξῃ συνεβούλευε λέγειν πρὸς τοῖσι ἔλεγε ἔπεσι, ὡς ('... this man counselled Xerxes to add to what he said another plea, to wit ...', Hdt. 7.3.2; the 'relative' clause depends on πρός)

(259) τούτους ... ἄρχοντας ἐποίει <u>ἧς κατεστρέφετο χώρας</u> ('He appointed them as rulers of the territory which he was subduing', X. *An.* 1.9.14; the 'relative' clause depends on ἄρχοντας)

Again, as in the case of type (iv) above, this construction can best be analysed as the active counterpart to the construction with an attributive passive participle. Thus, πρὸς τοῖσι ἔλεγε ἔπεσι in (258) is comparable to πρὸς τοῖσι λεχθεῖσι ἔπεσι. Note especially the attributive position of the finite verb in between the 'relative pronoun' and the noun. We are dealing, then, with a noun phrase consisting of 'relative pronoun' + finite verb + noun, which, as a whole, functions in exactly the same way as a regular noun phrase, consisting of article + adjective/participle + noun (cp. also Note 2 above on ἀνθ' ὧν ... δανείσῃς). In this case, too, the active construction has a finite verb because a parallel construction with an active participle was not possible.

(vi) ὅς and indefinite ὅστις differ in that τις indicates that the language user is unable or unwilling to further identify the constituent concerned; cp. (245) σοφὸς ἦν <u>ὅστις ἔφασκεν</u> 'wise was he, whoever he may be, who said ...' and (240) οὐδενὶ <u>ὅστις καλέσειε</u> 'no one, whoever he may be, who ...'. ὅς does not specify whether or not the entity referred to by the relative clause may be further identified.

(vii) In view of the value discussed in (vi) ὅστις was, in principle, not suitable for digressive clauses, for in such clauses the antecedent is pre-eminently identifiable. In Homer ὅστις does, in fact, not occur in this type of clause; in later Greek it does, in which case the relative clause often has a causal nuance.
  An example:

(260) οἴκτιρον ... με ..., <u>ὅστις</u> ὥστε παρθένος <u>βέβρυχα κλαίων</u> ('Have pity on me, who am crying loudly like a girl' (= 'because I ...'), S. *Tr.* 1070-2)

Digressive clauses with ὅς may be interpreted in this way as well:

(261) οὐ μόνον εἰς τῶν γενομένων Περσέων ἄριστος, ἀλλὰ καὶ τῶν ἐσομένων, <u>ὅς</u> τά τε ἄλλα λέγων <u>ἐπίκεο</u> ἄριστα ... ('You surpass not only all Persians that have been but also all that shall be, you

who have been most successful in speaking about all other matters ...' (= 'because you have been ...'), Hdt. 7.9.1)

Note 2 The negative in causal relative clauses is οὐ.

(viii) The use of the future indicative in (any type of) relative clauses often leads to a purpose interpretation, as in:

(262) ... ἡγεμόνα αἰτεῖν Κῦρον, <u>ὅστις ... ἀπάξει</u> ('... to ask Cyrus for a guide, who will lead them away' (= 'to lead ...'), X. *An.* 1.3.14; digressive, ὅστις)

(263) ἡ βουλὴ μέλλει αἱρεῖσθαι <u>ὅστις ἐρεῖ</u> ἐπὶ τοῖς ἀποθανοῦσι ('The Council is about to select someone who will make an oration over the dead' (= 'to make an oration ...'), Pl. *Mx.* 234b; autonomous, ὅστις)

(264) οὔτε πλοῖα ἔστιν <u>οἷς ἀποπλευσόμεθα</u> ... ('We neither have ships in which we shall sail away' (= 'in which to sail away'), X. *An.* 6.3.16; determinative, ὅς)

Note 3 The negative in these clauses is μή.
Note 4 After τοιοῦτος, οὕτως etc. ὅς and ὅστις often introduce *consecutive* clauses; e.g.: οὐδεὶς γὰρ <u>οὕτω</u> ἀνόητός ἐστι <u>ὅστις</u> πόλεμον πρὸ εἰρήνης <u>αἱρέεται</u> ('For no man is so foolish that he prefers war to peace', Hdt. 1.87.4). The negative in these consecutive clauses is οὐ. Cp. also § 23, Note 3.

IV NON-FINITE VERB FORMS: INFINITIVE AND PARTICIPLE

§ 30 Introduction

Since the non-finite verb forms have no endings indicating person, tense and mood, they in principle cannot express an independent state of affairs but are used as constituents of a finite verb form (but cp. Notes 2 and 3).

Note 1 Infinitive and participle are also called *nominal* verb forms, because, syntactically speaking, they resemble nouns and adjectives, respectively. Thus, cp. for the infinitive ταῦτα βούλομαι and ἀπιέναι βούλομαι and, for the participle, οἱ γελῶντες ἄνδρες and οἱ ἀγαθοὶ ἄνδρες. Furthermore, the infinitive may be combined with the article τό (see § 36 below) and the participle, like adjectives, expresses gender, number, and case.

Note 2 The infinitive is used independently in two constructions:
(i) with the value of a command or wish: ἐπὶ Σκύθας ... ἰέναι ἔασον ...· σὺ δέ ... ἐπὶ τὴν Ἑλλάδα <u>στρατεύεσθαι</u> ('Forbear to attack the Scythians ...; rather, march against Hellas', Hdt. 3.134.5).
(ii) in emotional exclamations (often substantival): τῆς μωρίας· τὸν Δία <u>νομίζειν</u> ὄντα τηλικουτονί ('What stupidity, believing in Zeus at your age', Ar. *Nu.* 818-9).

Note 3 The infinitive also occurs in a number of idiomatic expressions such as (ὡς) συνελόντι εἰπεῖν 'to put it briefly', ὡς (ἔπος) εἰπεῖν 'so to speak', ὀλίγου δεῖν 'practically, almost', ἑκὼν εἶναι 'voluntarily'. These infinitives have no syntactic relation with the finite verb.

IVA INFINITIVE

§ 31 Infinitive as an obligatory constituent; dynamic and declarative infinitive

31.1 Infinitive as an obligatory constituent

The infinitive is mainly used as an obligatory constituent (i.e., as an argument, cp. § 17) with a great number of verbs. (On the negative see below, p. 104 and 106). Two groups may be distinguished:

(a) Verbs denoting a desire or will, such as βούλομαι 'want, be willing', ἐθέλω 'be willing, wish', αἰσχύνομαι 'be ashamed' (= 'not be willing'), ἀναγκάζω 'force, compel', δέομαι 'ask', συμβουλεύω 'advise', κελεύω 'command, exhort'; verbs denoting an ability, such as δύναμαι 'be able'; μανθάνω 'learn (to)', διδάσκω 'teach'; ἄρχομαι 'begin'; furthermore, adjectives denoting a capability or quality, such as ἀγαθός 'good, capable', ἱκανός 'competent, adequate', ἐπιτήδειος 'suitable', etc.; finally, nouns like ἵμερος 'desire', ὥρα 'it is time', etc.

(b) Verbs of saying and thinking, such as λέγω, φημί, ἀγγέλλω, νομίζω, ἡγοῦμαι, οἴομαι, also ἀκούω, πυνθάνομαι.

Some examples of (a):

(265) ταῦτα ... <u>βουλόμενος εἰδέναι</u> ἱστόρεον ... ('Because I wanted to know those things I inquired ...', Hdt. 2.19.3)

(266) <u>αἰσχύνομαι</u> οὖν ὑμῖν <u>εἰπεῖν</u> ... τἀληθῆ ('Now I'm ashamed to tell you the truth', Pl. Ap. 22b)

(267) ἐγὼ ... σοὶ <u>οὐκ ἂν δυναίμην ἀντιλέγειν</u> ('I would not be able to contradict you', Pl. Smp. 201c)

(268) καὶ τέσσερας ἵππους <u>συζευγνύναι</u> παρὰ Λιβύων οἱ Ἕλληνες <u>μεμαθήκασι</u> ('And to yoke four horses the Greeks have learnt from the Libyans', Hdt. 4.189.3)

(269) <u>ἐδέοντο αὐτοῦ</u> παντὶ τρόπῳ <u>ἀπελθεῖν</u> ᾿Αθήνηθεν ('They asked him at all costs to leave Athens', Lys. 13.25)

(269a) βασιλεὺς ὁ Αἰθιόπων <u>συμβουλεύει τῷ</u> Περσέων <u>βασιλέϊ</u> ... ἐπεὰν ..., τότε ἐπ᾿ Αἰθίοπας ... <u>στρατεύεσθαι</u> ('The King of the Ethiopians counsels the King of the Persians, when ..., then ... to attack the Ethiopians', Hdt. 3.21.3)

(270)   ... τοὺς ἐπιτηδείους ... τούτων ἐπιμεληθῆναι ('... the proper persons to take care of these things', X. *An.* 5.2.12)

(271)   ὁ δὲ Κῦρος ἐκέλευε τὸν ἄγγελον ἀπαγγέλλειν ὅτι ... ('And Cyrus ordered the messenger to report that ...', Hdt. 1.127.2)

(272)   τοὺς Μήδους ἠνάγκασε ἓν πόλισμα ποιήσασθαι ('He constrained the Medes to make him one stronghold', Hdt. 1.98.3)

Some examples of (b):

(273)   ἔφη ὑπ' ἀνέμων ἀπενειχθεὶς ἀπικέσθαι ἐς Λιβύην ('He said that, having been driven out of his course by the winds, he had come to Libya', Hdt. 4.151.2)

(274)   ὑπώπτευον γὰρ ἤδη ἐπὶ βασιλέα ἰέναι ('For they suspected by this time that they were going against the king', X. *An.* 1.3.1)

(275)   ἔφη ... ἢ ἄξειν Λακεδαιμονίους ζῶντας ἢ αὐτοῦ ἀποκτενεῖν ('He said that he would either bring the Lacedaemonians alive or kill them on the spot', Th. 4.28.4)

(276)   οὕτω ... Ἰοῦν ἐς Αἴγυπτον ἀπικέσθαι λέγουσι Πέρσαι ('The Persians say that Io came to Egypt in this way', Hdt. 1.2.1)

(277)   ἥξειν νομίζεις παῖδα σὸν γαίας ὕπο; ('Do you think your son will return from beneath the earth?', E. *HF* 296)

31.2   Dynamic and declarative infinitive

There is an important semantic difference between these two groups. With verbs of saying and thinking the infinitive represents a statement or thought of the subject of the main verb concerning some state of affairs in the 'real' world. This means, in turn, that the infinitive has the temporal value of the corresponding verb forms of direct speech: an aorist infinitive is anterior to, a present infinitive simultaneous with (but cp. § 33.2 (i), p. 105), and a future infinitive posterior to, the main verb. Thus, ἀπικέσθαι in (273) represents ἀπικόμην 'I came/have come', ἰέναι in (274) ἴμεν 'we are going', and ἄξειν and ἀποκτενεῖν in (275) represent ἄξω and ἀποκτενῶ 'I will bring', 'I will kill'. With the verbs of group (a), on the other hand, the infinitive constitutes the content of the will, desire, ability, etc. of the subject of the main verb; the infinitive expresses, therefore, a potential state of affairs and is, thus, *always posterior* to the main verb. The infinitives of group (a) are called *dynamic* (the state of affairs exists δυνάμει 'potentially'); the infinitives of group (b) are called *declarative*, since they are dependent on verbs of saying or thinking. The difference can perhaps be illustrated most clearly by the aorist infinitive: in (269) 'dynamic' ἀπελθεῖν is posterior to ἐδέοντο, in (273) 'declarative' ἀπικέσθαι is anterior to ἔφη. Now since all dynamic infinitives are posterior, the question arises, of course, as to what differences there are between present and aorist dynamic infinitive. On this point, see below § 33.1 (ii).

Note 1 For verbs allowing both infinitive constructions (e.g. λέγω) see below § 33.3 (ii) and (iii).

Note 2 The *perfect* infinitive occurs with both groups, but rarely. It will not be dealt with here.

Note 3 With some verbs of group (a) e.g. ἄρχομαι and τολμῶ, the infinitive does not express a strictly potential state of affairs, since the realization of the main verb entails that the dependent state of affairs is realized as well: 'potentiality' passes into 'performance'. Cp. (272) and also e.g. ἄνδρες ῞Ελληνες, ... ἐτολμήσατε ἐμὲ σύμμαχον ... παρακαλέοντες ἐλθεῖν ('Men of Hellas, ... you have made bold to come hither and invite me to be your ally ...', Hdt. 1.158.1).

Note 4 The future infinitive is only used as a declarative infinitive, representing a statement or thought in the indicative.

Note 5 I use the terms 'dynamic' and 'declarative', which were introduced by Kurzová (1968), because they are now widely used in Greek linguistics. (The distinction as such was already made by the Danish scholar J.N. Madvig in his *Syntax der griechischen Sprache, besonders der attischen Sprachform, für Schulen*. Braunschweig 1847, pp. 187ff.). They have, to be sure, some disadvantages, since (1) 'dynamic' is also used for quite different linguistic phenomena, and (2) they do not express a clear-cut opposition. 'Referring' (: the infinitive after verbs of saying and thinking) and 'non-referring' (: the infinitive after volitional etc. verbs) would perhaps be better terms. As was noted above, the infinitive after verbs of saying and thinking refers to a state of affairs in the 'real' world, while the infinitive after volitional verbs does not refer to such a state of affairs.

Note 6 For indirect speech expressed by ὅτι- and ὡς-clauses see § 18.2. Unlike the verbs of saying those of volition do not allow ὅτι- and ὡς-clauses as an alternative to the infinitive.

§ 32 Supplementary infinitive and accusative plus infinitive

32.1 General observations

With both groups of verbs discussed in § 31 a single infinitive is found in cases where the subject of the infinitive is the same as that of the main verb. In technical terms: the subjects are *co-referential*, cp. (265) - (268) (group (a)), and (273) and (275) (group (b)). If, on the other hand, the subjects of main verb and infinitive are not co-referential, the subject of the infinitive must be expressed explicitly. In such cases the subject of a dynamic infinitive is expressed in the genitive, dative, or accusative, depending on the main verb; in syntactic terms, this subject-constituent is governed by the main verb, while the infinitive is appended (*supplementary infinitive*). The subject of a declarative infinitive, however, when not co-referential with that of the main verb, is *always* expressed in the accusative; in syntactic terms, this constituent is not governed by the main verb but is a constituent of the infinitive only. In this case an *accusative plus infinitive* construction is involved. Cp. for the dynamic infinitive ἐδέοντο <u>αὐτοῦ ἀπελθεῖν</u> (269), συμβουλεύει <u>τῷ βασιλέϊ στρατεύεσθαι</u> (269a), and <u>τοὺς Μήδους</u> ἠνάγκασε ... <u>ποιήσασθαι</u> (272), and for the declarative infinitive: <u>Ἰοῦν ἀπικέσθαι</u> λέγουσι (276) and (277) <u>ἥξειν νομίζεις παῖδα σὸν γαίας ὕπο</u>;. I should add, however, that some verbs that semantically belong in group (a) are construed with an accusative plus infinitive. This notably holds for βούλομαι. An example is:

(278)   οὐ γάρ <u>σε βουλόμεθα</u> οὐδὲν ἄχαρι πρὸς Ἀθηναίων <u>παθεῖν</u> ('For we would not that you would suffer any harm at Athenian hands', Hdt. 8.143.3)

Note 1 Notice the presence of οὐδέν (rather than μηδέν) with παθεῖν, another feature belonging to verbs of saying rather than to volitional verbs. Cp. § 33.1 (iii).
Note 2 In technical terms one might say that the object (or rather: second argument) of e.g. ἔφη in (276) is a state of affairs (viz. 'Ἰὼ ἀπίκετο'). Recall that ὅτι/ὡς-clauses after verbs of saying are also an argument of those verbs, cp. § 17. In the case of e.g. ἐκέλευε τὸν ἄγγελον ἀπαγγέλλειν in (271), there is an object (second argument, τὸν ἄγγελον) and a *third* argument (the infinitive).

32.2   Particulars

(i) Above, it was noted that the accusative, in an accusative with supplementary infinitive construction, is governed by the main verb, while this is not the case in an accusative plus infinitive construction. The difference can be clearly seen with verbs that allow both constructions, e.g. πείθω. Compare the following examples:

(279)   οὐδέ <u>σφεας</u> χρηστήρια φοβερὰ ... <u>ἔπεισε ἐκλιπεῖν</u> τὴν Ἑλλάδα ('Nor did the threatening oracles ... move them to desert Hellas', Hdt. 7.139.6)

(280)   τέλος ... <u>πείθει</u> τὸν ἄνδρα <u>ταῦτα ἔχειν οὕτω</u> ('finally, she convinced her husband that this was true', Hdt. 4.154.2)

In the first example the accusative σφεας is *both* the direct object of the main verb *and* the subject of the infinitive ἐκλιπεῖν, in the second the accusative ταῦτα is not the direct object of the main verb (this is rather τὸν ἄνδρα) but the subject of ἔχειν *only*. Semantically, this means that only σφεας is directly concerned by the main verb (as its Patient). With these syntactic-semantic differences corresponds a difference in meaning: when followed by an accusative with supplementary infinitive πείθω has the meaning 'persuade someone to do something' (a dynamic infinitive, cp. (279)), when followed by an accusative plus infinitive its meaning is 'convince (that)' (declarative infinitive, cp. (280)).

Note 1 The syntactic status of the accusative in the accusative plus infinitive construction is difficult to account for. It may perhaps be compared to that of the accusative in so-called proleptic constructions, e.g. with verbs of saying, as in: λέγουσι δ' ἡμᾶς ὡς ἀκίνδυνον βίον / ζῶμεν κατ' οἴκους ('They (the men) say (of us) that we lead a riskless life at home', E. *Med.* 248). Here the accusative ἡμᾶς, being the subject of the dependent ὡς-clause, is used proleptically and is not the direct object of λέγουσι. On the other hand, the fact that a 'pseudo-object' like ἡμᾶς turns up as the subject if the main verb is passivized (λέγουσιν ἡμᾶς ζῆν ≈ λεγόμεθα ζῆν; see also next §) indicates that such pseudo-objects shared the syntactic possibilities of regular objects.

Note 2 There has been much speculation about the origin of the accustaive plus infinitive. It is often held that this construction, with its rather remarkable 'non-object'-accusative, is a derivative phenomenon and has developed out of the acc. with supplementary infinitive after verbs like κελεύω. If so, the acc. plus infinitive might be the result of a re-analysis of constructions like κελεύω αὐτοὺς ἀπελθεῖν as *I issue orders that they should go away*, as against *I order them to go away* in the accusative with supplementary infinitive analysis. Another factor facilitating its development may have been the existence of the proleptic constructions discussed above. *Note 3* It is difficult to determine what, if any, differences there are between the (declarative) infinitive and the corresponding ὅτι-/ὡς-clauses. Perhaps there are pragmatic factors involved, as is suggested by the following passages from Herodotus: καί τις ... οἱ τῶν οἰκετέων <u>ἐξαγγέλλει ὡς</u> οἱ παῖς <u>γέγονε</u> ('one of his household came to tell him that a son was born to him', Hdt. 6.63.2); ... τὸ εἶπε Ἀρίστων τότε ὅτε οἱ <u>ἐξήγγειλε</u> ὁ οἰκέτης παῖδα <u>γεγονέναι</u> ('... what Ariston had said when the servant brought news of the birth of a son', Hdt. 6.65.3). In the first passage we find a historic present followed by a ὡς-clause with a 'direct speech' verb form. Both features create an 'eyewitness'-effect, and indicate that we are dealing with events that are important for the addressee, Ariston. In the second passage the same event is referred to, but now by means of a dependent infinitive. The infinitive occurs, moreover, in a temporal clause, where an aorist has been substituted for the historic present. As a result, both the reporting and the reported event are presented in a neutral way. Interestingly, the childbirth is yet another time referred to, this time by <u>ἠγγέλθης γεγενημένος</u> (Hdt. 6.69.4). Here the addressee is the child concerned, Demaratos, and his birth can naturally be presented as factive (cp. § 37). See also Crespo (1984).

(ii) When passivized, both the verbs that are construed with an accusative with supplementary infinitive and those construed with a (declarative) accusative plus infinitive are followed by a single infinitive, since subject of main verb and infinitive are co-referential. (Cp. also § 32.1). With both groups this construction is traditionally called *nominative plus infinitive*. E.g.:

(281) <u>ἠναγκάσθησαν</u> ... <u>ναυμαχῆσαι</u> πρὸς Φορμίωνα ('They were forced to fight with Phormio', Th. 2.83.1; semantically: dynamic infinitive)

(282) οἱ <u>θύειν</u> ἀπὸ βασιλέος <u>κελευόμενοι</u> ('the men who were bidden by the king to sacrifice', Hdt. 8.55; semantically: dynamic infinitive)

(283) ὁ Ἀσσύριος εἰς τὴν χώραν ... <u>ἐμβαλεῖν ἀγγέλλεται</u> ('The report comes that the Assyrian is going to invade the country (The Assyrian is reported to be going to invade the country)', X. *Cyr.* 5.3.30; semantically: declarative infinitive)

But of verbs of saying impersonal passive forms followed by an *accusative plus infinitive* occur as well:

(284) ἐς ... τοῦτον τὸν χῶρον <u>λέγεται ἀπικέσθαι</u> τὸν στρατόν ('Thus far, it is said, the army came', Hdt. 3.26.2).

§ 33 Dynamic and declarative infinitive, continued

33.1 The dynamic infinitive

(i) The dynamic (accusative plus) infinitive also occurs as 'subject-constituent' with impersonal verbs such as δεῖ, χρή, ἀναγκαῖόν ἐστι 'it is necessary, inevitable'; ἔστι, ἔξεστι 'it is possible'; πρέπει, δίκαιόν ἐστι 'it is fitting, right'; δοκεῖ 'it seems right, it is decided' (on δοκεῖ see also below); συμβαίνει 'it happens', and the like. Some examples:

(285) ἤτοι <u>κεῖνόν</u> γε ... <u>δεῖ ἀπόλλυσθαι</u> ἢ <u>σὲ</u> ('Either he must die or you ...', Hdt. 1.11.3)

(286) <u>κότερα</u> τούτων <u>αἱρετώτερά ἐστι</u>, ταῦτα τὰ νῦν ... πρήσσεις, ἢ τὴν τυραννίδα ... <u>παραλαμβάνειν</u>; ('Which of these things is preferable, your present way of life or to take over the sovereignty?', Hdt. 3.52.3)

(287) τοῖσι δὲ λοιποῖσι ῎Ιωσι <u>ἔδοξε</u> ... <u>πέμπειν</u> ἀγγέλους ('To the other Ionians it seemed right (the other Ionians decided) to send envoys', Hdt. 1.141.4)

Note 1 Besides the impersonal constructions with ἐστί sometimes a personal counterpart exists, like, for instance, besides δίκαιόν ἐστι + accusative plus infinitive the construction δίκαιός εἰμι + infinitive: ἡμεῖς ... <u>δίκαιοί ἐσμεν</u> ... <u>κινδυνεύειν</u> τοῦτον τὸν κίνδυνον ('It is right for us to run this risk', Pl. *Cri.* 45a).

(ii) As for the semantic difference between the present and aorist dynamic infinitive, this can perhaps best be illustrated from the use of the infinitive with a verb having iussive meaning like κελεύω. With this verb, the difference between the two infinitives is the same as that between the present and aorist *imperatives*, as discussed in § 16.2.

Two examples:

(288) κεῖνον ... <u>ἐκέλευον</u> ἀναβάντα ἐπὶ πύργον <u>ἀγορεῦσαι</u> ὡς ('They ordered him to go up on to a tower and declare that ...', Hdt. 3.74.3)

(289) ... ἀνεβίβασαν αὐτὸν ἐπὶ πύργον καὶ ἀγορεύειν ἐκέλευον ('They brought him up on to a tower and ordered him to speak', Hdt. 3.75.1)

Here the same person is twice commanded to do something. In (288) the persons commanding are exclusively concerned with the content of the order as such, as a well-defined state of affairs (ἀγορεῦσαι, aorist infinitive). It is a preliminary instruction: the addressee does not begin to speak immediately following the command. In (289), where the moment of speaking has arrived, the present infinitive ἀγορεύειν is used to express the command: now the concrete process of the execution of the instruction is concerned. As is often the case with the present imperative (cp. (110)), an immediative nuance may be discerned here: 'fire away'. The same immediative nuance may also be present with other expressions of obligation e.g.:

(290) ... ἠναγκάσθησαν ... ναυμαχῆσαι πρὸς Φορμίωνα ... (-) οὕτω δὴ ἀναγκάζονται ναυμαχεῖν κατὰ μέσον τὸν πορθμόν ('They were forced to fight with Phormio; ... under these circumstances they were forced to fight in the middle of the channel', Th. 2.83.1 and 3)

(291) σπεύδω ποι, καί μοι ὥρα ἀπιέναι ('I am in a hurry, and it is time for me to go', Pl. *Euthyphro* 15e)

In (290), just as in (288), the aorist infinitive 'paves the way' for the actual battle, which is expressed by the present infinitive. (291) is an example of the frequent use of ὥρα + present infinitive to express immediate action.

> *Note 2* Immediate action is also expressed by μέλλω + present infinitive (but not with stative verbs like εἶναι, see Note 3 below): 'be about to, be on the point of', e.g. Ἡνίκ᾽ ἔμελλον ... τὸν ποταμὸν διαβαίνειν, τὸ δαιμόνιον ... σημεῖον ἐγένετο - ἀεὶ δέ με ἐπίσχει ὃ ἂν μέλλω πράττειν - ('When I was about to cross the river, the supernatural sign occurred - it always holds me back from whatever I am about to do - ', Pl. *Phdr.* 242c; observe that the state of affairs can be interrupted, cp. § 1, Note 2). In the, much rarer, construction with the aorist infinitive, μέλλω rather anticipates the full realization of the state of affairs, with no indication of the time of the realization. Since the aorist stem, unlike the present stem, expresses that the state of affairs cannot be interrupted (cp. again § 1 Note 2), there is often a nuance of inevitability: 'be destined to, be doomed to'. E.g. ... σκεπτέον τίν᾽ ἂν τρόπον τοῦτον ὃν μέλλοι χρόνον βιῶναι ὡς ἄριστα βιοίη ('... he

should consider in what way he will best live out his allotted span of life',
Pl. *Grg.* 512e). - For μέλλω + *future* infinitive see § 9, Note 3.

Note 3 The other applications discussed in § 16 occur as well, also with
verbs denoting a desire or will or an ability; e.g. ἠξίουν ὑπὲρ τῶν
ἀσθενεστέρων ... διαμάχεσθαι μᾶλλον ἢ ... τοὺς ... ἀδικουμένους
ἐκδοῦναι ('They preferred to do battle for the weaker rather than give up
the men who had been wronged', Lys. 2.12): διαμάχεσθαι: continuing state
of affairs, ἐκδοῦναι: single, well-delineated state of affairs. Here, as often,
the present infinitive serves to express a general course of action. In a clause
like τὸ ἄροτρον, εἰ μέλλει καλὸν εἶναι ... ('the plough, if it is to be good',
Pl. *R.* 370c), the present infinitive εἶναι does not have an immediative, but
rather a durative value.

(iii) With the dynamic infinitive the negative is μή (cp. μή with the
imperative and prohibitive subjunctive, § 15 and § 13.1 (ii)). An example:

(292)   ἐγὼ νῦν παρακελεύομαί σοι μὴ ἀφίεσθαι Λάχητος ('I now call
        upon you not to release Laches', Pl. *La.* 186d)

(iv) μή + infinitive with verbs of forbidding etc.

Verbs with what may be called 'prophylactic' meaning, i.e. verbs
expressing that the dependent state of affairs should not or does not come
about (e.g. ἀπαγορεύω, ἀπεῖπον 'forbid'; εἴργω, ἀπέχω 'prevent';
φυλάττομαι 'beware of'; ἀπέχομαι 'abstain') are usually followed by μή
+ infinitive (cp. the use of μή in prohibitions, above (iii)). Otherwise than
in e.g. English, where the 'prophylactic' meaning resides solely in the
main verb, but just as in e.g. French *empêcher que ne*, in Greek this
meaning is a feature both of the main verb and of the dependent
construction. When the main verb itself is negated and, consequently, has
positive value (e.g. οὐκ ἀναβάλλομαι 'I do not delay' = 'I hasten'), it is
followed by μὴ οὐ + infinitive; thus the negative value of the infinitive is
cancelled and made positive as well. In English μή and μὴ οὐ are not
translated explicitly. Some examples:

(293)   τοῖς ... νέοις ἀπαγορευόντων αὐτῶν μὴ διαλέγεσθαι ('When they
        forbade him to talk with the young people', X. *Mem.* 4.4.3)
(294)   καὶ ἐπὶ ἓξ ἔτη ... καὶ δέκα μῆνας ἀπέσχοντο μὴ ἐπὶ τὴν
        ἑκατέρων γῆν στρατεῦσαι ('And during six years and ten months
        they abstained from marching against each other's territory', Th.
        5.25.3)

(295) Ἀθηναῖοι οὐκέτι ἀνεβάλλοντο μὴ οὐ τὸ πᾶν μηχανήσασθαι ἐπ' Αἰγινήτῃσι ('The Athenians delayed no longer to devise all mischief against the Aeginetans', Hdt. 6.88).

In cases where a main verb which in itself does not have prophylactic value is followed by μή + infinitive, the construction as a whole is negated by expressing οὐ both with the main verb and with the infinitive. This occurs particularly with verbs expressing notions like *ability* and *appropriateness*. Thus, e.g. δίκαιόν ἐστι μὴ ποιεῖν τοῦτο 'it is right not to do that' → οὐ δίκαιόν ἐστι μὴ οὐ ποιεῖν τοῦτο 'it is not right not to do that' = 'it is by all means right to do that'. In this case, then, the negative meaning of the infinitive is not cancelled. Some examples:

(296) δήμου ... ἄρχοντος ἀδύνατα μὴ οὐ κακότητα ἐγγίνεσθαι ('When the people are in charge evil-mindedness must of necessity arise' (lit. '... it is impossible that evil-mindedness does not arise'), Hdt. 3.82.4)

(297) οὐ τὰ ὑμέτερα ... αἰτιασόμεθα μὴ οὐχ ἕτοιμα εἶναι ... ('You will give us no ground for complaint on the score of your not being ready to ...', Pl. *La.* 189c)

Note 4 Verbs like ἀπαγορεύω etc. may also be construed with a single infinitive; e.g. (they sent people to Olynthus) ὅπως εἴργωσι τοὺς ἐκεῖθεν ἐπιβοηθεῖν ('... in order to prevent the people there to come to aid', Th. 1.62.4).

(v) When the subject of a dynamic infinitive appears in the genitive or dative and is modified by predicative nouns, adjectives or participles, these predicative modifiers either show concord with the subject-constituent of the infinitive or appear in the accusative; e.g. νῦν σοι ἔξεστιν ... ἀνδρὶ γενέσθαι ('Now is your opportunity to prove yourself a man', X. *An.* 7.1.21); συμβουλεύει τῷ Ξενοφῶντι ἐλθόντα εἰς Δελφοὺς ἀνακοινῶσαι τῷ θεῷ ('He advised Xenophon to go to Delphi and consult the god', X. *An.* 3.1.5). In the latter case the construction changes half-way to an accusative plus infinitive.

(vi) With most verbs of group (a) the infinitive has a final-consecutive value: it expresses a (potential) effect of the main verb. Several of these verbs may be followed by ὥστε + infinitive, whereby the final-consecutive value of the infinitive, somewhat redundantly, is made explicit. Dutch shows a similar phenomenon with these verbs: *Ik vroeg hem weg te gaan* alongside *Ik vroeg hem om weg te gaan*. This is especially frequent with πείθω. Two examples:

(298) χρόνῳ δὲ ... ἀνέπεισε Ξέρξεα ὥστε ποιέειν ταῦτα ('and finally he persuaded Xerxes to do as he said', Hdt. 7.6.1)

(299) ἀδύνατον ὑμῖν ὥστε Πρωταγόρου τοῦδε σοφώτερόν τινα ἑλέσθαι ('you cannot possibly choose someone who is wiser than our friend Protagoras', Pl. *Prt.* 338c)

> *Note 5* For the use of ὥστε + infinitive in satellites (optional clauses) see § 23.

(vii) The particle ἄν does not occur with the dynamic, but only with the declarative infinitive (see § 33.2 (iv)). This means that in a case like: ἀρχὴν κλύειν ἂν οὐδ' ἅπαξ ἐβουλόμην ('I should have wished not to hear them at all', S. *Ph.* 1239), ἄν must be construed with ἐβουλόμην, not with the dynamic infinitive κλύειν.

33.2 The declarative infinitive

(i) While the present (declarative) infinitive usually represents a present indicative, it may also represent an *imperfect*, as in:

(300) (οἱ Κρῆτες) ἀλίσκεσθαι γὰρ ἔφασαν τῷ δρόμῳ ('for they said they were about to be overtaken in the running', X. *An.* 5.2.31; direct: ἡλισκόμεθα; imperfect of likelihood, cp. § 6.2.2)

(301) Ἀλλ' οὕτω χρὴ ποιεῖν, εἴ σοι δοκεῖ, ἔφη φάναι τὸν Ἀγάθωνα ('"Very well then, as you judge best", Agathon replied, as he (Aristodemus) said', Pl. *Smp.* 175c; direct speech: ἔφη ('he said that Agathon said'))

(ii) with the declarative infinitive the negative is οὐ (cp. οὐ in declarative sentences, § 4 (i)).

(302) πρὸς ταῦτα ὁ Αἰθίοψ ἔφη οὐδὲν θωμάζειν ... ('Then the Ethiopian said that he was not at all surprised ...', Hdt. 3.22.4; declarative infinitive: οὐδὲν θωμάζω)

However, following verbs denoting a conviction μή may occur with the infinitive, expressing an emphatic denial, e.g.:

(303) ὄμνυσιν τὸν Διόνυσον μὴ πώποτ᾽ ἀμείνον᾽ ἔπη τούτων κωμῳδικὰ μηδέν᾽ ἀκοῦσαι ('He swears (= states under oath) by Dionysus that no one ever heard any comic poetry better than that', Ar. V. 1046-7)

Here, μηδέν᾽ ἀκοῦσαι represents μή + aorist indicative, again expressing an emphatic denial, as in:

(304) μὰ γῆν ... / μὴ 'γὼ νόημα κομψότερον ἤκουσά που ('Holy Earth, I've never heard a cleverer idea' Ar. Av. 194-5)

In such cases the very thought of the state of affairs involved being a reality is rejected. On ὄμνυμι see further below, § 33.3 (iii).

(iii) As is the case with the dynamic infinitive, and contrary to what might be expected on the basis of (ii) above, verbs of saying with negative meaning such as ἀρνοῦμαι 'deny'; ἀντιλέγω 'contradict'; ἀμφισβητῶ 'dispute' are usually followed by μή + infinitive. Again, then (cp. above (§ 33.1 (iv)), the negative meaning is a feature both of the main verb and of the dependent construction. The use of μή rather than of οὐ probably expresses an emphatic denial; compare the use of μή after ὄμνυμι (example (303) above). When the main verb itself is negated and, consequently, has positive value (οὐκ ἀρνοῦμαι 'I do not deny' = 'I admit'), it is followed by μὴ οὐ + infinitive; thus the negative value of the state of affairs expressed by the infinitive is cancelled and made positive as well. In English μή and μὴ οὐ are not translated explicitly. Some examples:

(305) ὁ Πρηξάσπης ἔξαρνος ἦν (= ἐξηρνέετο) μὴ ... ἀποκτεῖναι Σμέρδιν ('Prexaspes denied that he had killed Smerdis', Hdt. 3.67.1)
(306) ... οὔτ᾽ αὐτὸς ἐξαρνοῦμαι μὴ οὐ γεγονέναι ἐρωτικός ... ('Nor do I deny that I myself have been a lover ...', Aeschin. 1.136)
(307) οὐκ ἀμφισβητῶ μὴ οὐχὶ σὲ εἶναι σοφώτερον ἢ ἐμέ ('I do not dispute that you are wiser than I', Pl. Hp.Mi. 369d)

(iv) In contrast to the dynamic infinitive (cp. § 33.1 (vii) above), ἄν may occur with a declarative infinitive, in cases where the infinitive corresponds to an optative + ἄν or a secondary indicative + ἄν in direct speech. Two examples:

(308) ὑμᾶς ... ἡμεῖς <u>ἡγησάμενοι</u> ... ἁπλῶς <u>ἂν εἰπεῖν</u> ἃ δοκεῖ ὑμῖν ('Since we thought that you would simply say what was in your minds', Pl. *La.* 178b; direct speech: ἂν εἴποιτε)

(309) ἆρ' οὖν <u>ἄν</u> με οἴεσθε τοσάδε ἔτη <u>διαγενέσθαι</u>, εἰ ἔπραττον τὰ δημόσια ('Do you think that I could have lived so many years if I had been in public life?', Pl. *Ap.* 32e; direct speech: διεγενόμην ἄν, εἰ ...)

(v) Verbs denoting 'think', 'promise', etc. are practically always construed with the (accusative plus) infinitive rather than with a ὅτι/ὡς-clause, whereas with verbs of saying and reporting (accusative plus) infinitive and ὅτι/ὡς-clauses are equally frequent (cp. § 18.2). The rareness of ὅτι/ὡς-clauses with verbs of thinking (such as ἡγοῦμαι, νομίζω, οἴομαι and also φημί) may be explained by the fact that these clauses present the indirect speech as a quotation, whereas the infinitive is neutral in this respect and is, thus, more suited to verbs expressing an opinion.

> *Note 1* In dependent clauses which correspond to dependent clauses in direct speech the moods and tenses of direct speech are used, while in the case of a past main verb the oblique optative occurs as well (cp. § 18.4); e.g.: οὐκ <u>ἔφασαν ἰέναι</u>, <u>ἐὰν μή</u> τις αὐτοῖς χρήματα <u>διδῷ</u> ('They said that they would not continue unless someone gave them money', X. *An.* 1.4.2). With oblique optative: <u>ἡγεῖτο</u> γὰρ ἅπαν ποιήσειν αὐτόν, <u>εἴ</u> τις ἀργύριον <u>διδοίη</u> ('For he believed that he would do anything if someone gave him money', Lys. 12.14; direct speech: ἅπαν ποιήσει, ἐάν τις ... διδῷ). Furthermore, in such clauses the finite verb is often replaced by an (accusative +) infinitive, cp. λέγεται δὲ καὶ τάδε ...· ἐπειδὴ ἐκ τῆς Ὀάσιος ταύτης <u>ἰέναι</u> ..., ... ἐπιπνεῦσαι νότον μέγαν ('And this, too, is said: when they were leaving that Oasis ..., a great south wind arose', Hdt. 3.26.3).

33.3   *Verbs allowing both infinitive constructions*

Apart from πείθω, that was discussed in a different context (above, § 32.2 (i)), several other (types of) verbs may be construed both with a dynamic and with a declarative (accusative plus) infinitive.

Some examples:

(i) γιγνώσκω + dynamic infinitive = 'resolve, decide', + declarative infinitive = 'judge', e.g.:

(310) οἱ δὲ Κυμαῖοι <u>ἔγνωσαν</u> συμβουλῆς πέρι ἐς θεὸν <u>ἀνοῖσαι</u> τὸν ἐν Βραγχίδῃσι ('The Cymaeans resolved to make the god at Branchidae their judge as to what counsel they should take', Hdt. 1.157.3; dynamic aorist infinitive)

(311) <u>ἔγνωσαν</u> οἱ παραγενόμενοι Σπαρτιητέων ... ’Ἀριστόδημον ... ἔργα <u>ἀποδέξασθαι</u> μεγάλα ('Those Spartans that were there judged that Aristodemus had achieved great feats', Hdt. 9.71.3; declarative infin., ἀποδέξασθαι represents ἀπεδέξατο).

(ii) The verbs of saying belonging to group (b) may also be construed as verbs of commanding, and thus be followed by a dynamic infinitive, in which case both a dative + supplementary infinitive and an accusative plus infinitive may be used. The negative is μή. E.g.:

(312) <u>τούτοις</u> ἔλεγον <u>πλεῖν</u> ('I told them to sail away', D. 19.150)

(313) εἶπον <u>μηδένα τῶν ὄπισθεν κινεῖσθαι</u> ('I gave instructions that no one of those behind should stir', X. *Cyr.* 2.2.8).

Observe that the presence of οὐδένα in (313) instead of μηδένα would turn the infinitive into a declarative one: 'I said that nobody stirred'.

(iii) ἐλπίζω 'hope, expect', ὑπισχνοῦμαι 'promise', and ὄμνυμι 'swear' usually behave as verbs of saying/thinking, i.e. they are followed by a declarative infinitive. Sometimes, however, they function as verbs denoting a will, desire, etc. and are followed by a dynamic infinitive; in this case, present and aorist infinitive refer to *potential* states of affairs, as with βούλομαι, etc. These uses must be distinguished on the basis of the context. E.g.:

(314) = (303) <u>ὄμνυσιν</u> τὸν Διόνυσον μὴ πώποτ' ἀμείνον' ἔπη τούτων κωμῳδικὰ μηδέν' <u>ἀκοῦσαι</u> ('He swears (= states under oath) by Dionysus that no one ever heard any comic poetry better than that', Ar. *V.* 1046-7; for μή see above, at ex. (303))

and

(315) οἱ δὲ ’Ἀργεῖοι <u>ὀμόσαντες</u> ... εἰρήνην <u>ποιήσασθαι</u> ('The Argives, who had sworn (= bound themselves) to make peace', X. *HG* 7.4.11)

In a different context, the latter example could be interpreted as 'who had sworn (= stated under oath) that they had made peace'. Notice that the 'bind oneself to' interpretation is possible only if the subject of the infinitive is co-referential with that of the main verb. If, as in the former example, the subjects of infinitive and main verb differ, ὄμνυμι can, of course, never mean 'bind oneself'.

> *Note 1* Conversely, verbs expressing a will, desire etc., that are normally construed with a dynamic infinitive, are occasionally followed by a declarative infinitive, e.g.: ἐφιέμενοι ... τῆς πάσης ἄρξειν ('desiring to rule the whole (of Sicily)', Th. 6.6.1); πῦρ ἐνήσειν διενοοῦντο ἐς τὰ ξύλινα παραφράγματα ('they intended to throw fire into the wooden breastworks', Th. 4.115.2). Recall that the future infinitive is only used as a declarative infinitive (§ 31, Note 4). In this use, the will, desire etc. is presented - not unnaturally - as a thought of the subject. These future infinitives are often considered textually unsound, needlessly.

(iv) The verb δοκῶ is construed in a number of ways. The main constructions involving the infinitive are the following.

(a1) Personal forms + *dative* + *declarative infinitive*, i.e. δοκῶ functions as a verb of thinking 'seem', ('I seem to you' >) 'you think that I', e.g.:

(316)   εἰ μὲν ὅσιά σοι δοκῶ παθεῖν ('If you think the treatment I have received is such as the gods approve', E. *Hec.* 788)

Also with δοκῶ μοι ('I seem to me' >) 'I think that I', e.g.:

(317)   κόθεν δὲ οἰκὸς αὐτοὺς γίνεσθαι, ἐγώ μοι δοκῶ κατανοέειν τοῦτο ('Whence it is like that these come into being I believe that I can guess', Hdt. 2.93.6)

Without a dative constituent, i.e. when no specific observer is present, δοκῶ simply = 'seem, give the impression that', e.g.:

(318)   μαθοῦσα δὲ τὸ ποιηθὲν ἐκ τοῦ ἀνδρὸς οὔτε ἀνέβωσε ... οὔτε ἔδοξε μαθεῖν ('Having perceived what her husband had done ... she never cried out nor let it be seen that she had perceived aught', Hdt. 1.10.2)

In the above uses the basic meaning of δοκῶ is 'give the impression that'.

(a2) Personal forms + *declarative accusative plus infinitive*, or, if the subjects of main verb and infinitive are co-referential, plus *single declarative infinitive*. Again, δοκῶ functions as a verb of thinking, but here it is construed like νομίζω, ἡγοῦμαι and the like. Some examples:

(319) Γύγη, οὐ γάρ <u>σε δοκέω πείθεσθαί</u> μοι λέγοντι ... ('Gyges, since I think that you do not believe what I tell you ...', Hdt. 1.8.2)

(320) ... <u>ἔδοξα</u> προσπόλων τινὸς / ὑποστενούσης ἔνδον <u>αἰσθέσθαι</u> (' ... from the doors, methought, came the sound of some handmaid moaning within', S. *El.* 78)

(321) ... <u>τὴν</u> ἐγὼ τάλας / οὐκ <u>ἄν</u> ποτ' ἐς τοσοῦτον αἰκίας <u>πεσεῖν</u> / <u>ἔδοξ(α)</u> ('Alas, I had not thought that she could have fallen to such a depth of misery', S. *OC* 747-9; note the presence of ἄν)

In this use the basic meaning of δοκῶ is 'to be under the impression that'.

(b) Impersonal forms + dative + *dynamic infinitive* (or accusative plus infinitive). In this use δοκεῖ etc. has volitional meaning: 'it seems good, it pleases', often in the specialized sense 'someone decides, resolves', especially with ἔδοξε and δέδοκται. E.g.:

(322) νῦν ὦν <u>μοι δοκέει διαβάντας προελθεῖν</u> ὅσον ἄν ἐκεῖνοι ὑπεξίωσι ('Now therefore it is in my mind that we should cross and go forward as far as they go back ...', Hdt. 1.207.5; διαβάντας, scil. ἡμᾶς)

(323) ... <u>ἔδοξ</u>' Ἀχαιοῖς παῖδα σὴν Πολυξένην / <u>σφάξαι</u> ('The Greeks have resolved to slay your daughter Polyxena', E. *Hec.* 220-1)

(324) βούλομαι δέ σου κλύειν / πότερα <u>δέδοκταί σοι</u> μένοντι <u>καρτερεῖν</u>, / ἢ <u>πλεῖν</u> μεθ' ἡμῶν ('and I fain would learn whether thy resolve is to abide here and endure, or to sail with us', S. *Ph.* 1273-5)

Note 2 Semantically, this use of δοκεῖ may be compared to that of Dutch *het lijkt mij wel wat om dat te doen*, where we find impersonal *het lijkt* + infinitive = 'it seems attractive to me'. As in Greek, the personal forms of this verb have the meaning 'seem'. Cp. also (obsolete) Engl. *it likes me*.

§ 34 Infinitive as an optional constituent with verbs of giving, taking, etc.

With verbs like δίδωμι 'give', λαμβάνω 'take', παρέχω 'supply', and the like an optional - dynamic - infinitive may occur expressing the purpose which the subject of the main verb wants to achieve (cp. the final-consecutive value mentioned above, § 33.1 (vi)).

Some examples:

(325)   τοῖς Αἰγινήταις οἱ Λακεδαιμόνιοι <u>ἔδοσαν Θυρέαν οἰκεῖν</u> ('The Lacedaemonians gave the Aeginetans the town of Thurea to occupy', Th. 2.27.2)

(326)   <u>ταύτην τὴν χώραν ἐπέτρεψε διαρπάσαι</u> τοῖς Ἕλλησιν ('That country he gave over to the Greeks to plunder', X. An. 1.2.19)

§ 35 Articular infinitive

Above (§ 30, Note 1) it was remarked that, syntactically speaking, the infinitive resembles nouns; this substantival function is made explicit if the article τό is added to the infinitive; the accusative plus infinitive construction, too, may be used substantivally in this way. When it is combined with the article the infinitive may be used in practically all case forms and prepositional phrases, and in all syntactic functions, in which so-called 'action nouns' occur; e.g. τὸ μάχεσθαι - ἡ μάχη/τὴν μάχην, τοῦ μάχεσθαι - τῆς μάχης; μετὰ τὸ μάχεσθαι - μετὰ τὴν μάχην, etc. The articular infinitive and the regular action noun differ in that the infinitive has distinct forms expressing tense and voice, whereas the noun does not. Moreover, the infinitive fully retains its verbal nature: the object is expressed in the usual case form, adverbs and dependent clauses may occur, and the subject of the infinitive, if necessary, is expressed in the accusative; action nouns, on the other hand are construed with an objective and/or subjective genitive. Cp. τὸ ἀποδιδόναι τὰς ἐπιστόλας 'the delivering of the letters' - ἡ τῶν ἐπιστολῶν ἀπόδοσις (objective genitive) and τὸ εὐνοεῖν τοὺς πολίτας 'the citizens' being benevolent' - ἡ τῶν πολιτῶν εὕνοια (subjective genitive). The negative used with the articular infinitive is μή. As for the article, this often has an anaphoric function. Some examples of the use of the articular infinitive are:

(327) (nominative, as subject:) οὐκ ἄρα τὸ χαίρειν ἐστὶν εὖ πράττειν ('So to enjoy oneself is not to fare well', Pl. *Grg.* 497a3; anaphoric τό; τὸ χαίρειν refers back to χαίρειν in 496e10)

(328) (nominative, as apposition to a subject:) ἡ εὐεργασία ... ἡ ἐς Σαμίους, τὸ δι' ἡμᾶς Πελοποννησίους αὐτοῖς μὴ βοηθῆσαι, παρέσχεν ὑμῖν ... Σαμίων κόλασιν ('And this service and that we rendered in connection with the Samians - our preventing the Peloponnesians from aiding them - enabled you to chastise the Samians', Th. 1.41.2; τὸ μὴ βοηθῆσαι refers back to 1.40.5)

(329) (nominative, as subject:) τὸ λαβεῖν πολλάκις τῷ τόλμαν μόνον παρασχομένῳ ἐγένετο, τὸ δὲ λαβόντα κατέχειν οὐκέτι τοῦτο ἄνευ σωφροσύνης ... γίγνεται ('For to win falls often to the lot of one who has shown nothing but daring; but to win and hold - that is no longer a possibility without the exercise of self-control', X. *Cyr.* 7.5.76)

(330) (genitive, with a verb governing the genitive:) ἄρξαντες τοῦ διαβαίνειν ('Having begun the crossing over', X. *An.* 1.4.15; anaphoric τοῦ; τοῦ διαβαίνειν refers back to διαβῆναι in § 14)

(331) (genitive, with a phrase governing the genitive:) πρὸς τὴν πόλιν προσβαλόντες ἐς ἐλπίδα μὲν ἦλθον τοῦ ἑλεῖν ('... having attacked the city they at first had hopes of taking it', Th. 2.56.4)

(332) (genitive of comparison:) τί οὖν ἐστιν ... τοῦ τοῖς φίλοις ἀρήγειν κάλλιον ('What, then, is more noble than to assist one's friends', X. *Cyr.* 1.5.13)

(333) (genitive, with (pre- and) postpositions:) προεῖπον ... ταῦτα τοῦ μὴ λύειν ἕνεκα τὰς σπονδάς ('They gave them these orders in order not to break the treaty', Th. 1.45.3)

(334) (dative, with a verb governing the dative; articular accusative plus infinitive:) ... ἵνα ... ἀπιστῶσι τῷ ἐμὲ τετιμῆσθαι ὑπὸ δαιμόνων (' ... in order that they do not believe that I am honoured by the gods', X. *Ap.* 14)

(335) (dative of instrument/cause (very frequent); articular accusative plus infinitive:) ἦν ... ἡ βασιλέως ἀρχὴ ... τῷ διεσπάσθαι τὰς

δυνάμεις ἀσθενής ('The king's power was weakened because of the scattered condition of the forces', X. *An.* 1.5.9)

(336) (dative of instrument/cause; articular 'nominative' plus infinitive:) ὁ δὲ Νικίας ... ὁρῶν τοὺς στρατιώτας τῷ ... πολὺ ταῖς ναυσὶ κρατυνθῆναι ἀθυμοῦντας ('But Nicias, seeing that the soldiers were discouraged because ... they had been badly beaten at sea', Th. 7.60.5; τῷ κρατυνθῆναι refers back to chapters 52-53)

(337) (accusative, as object:) αὐτὸ ... τὸ ἀποθνῄσκειν οὐδεὶς φοβεῖται ('No one fears the mere act of dying', Pl. *Grg.* 522e; compare τὸν θάνατον in the preceding sentence)

(338) (accusative, with a preposition:) διὰ τὸ ... στέργειν πόσιν / καὶ ξυνθάνοιμ' ἄν ('For love of my husband I could even die together with him', E. *Hel.* 1401-2)

Notice that of these articular infinitives some have an *aorist* infinitive that is posterior to the main verb ((329) and (331)), while in other cases it refers to an anterior state of affairs ((328) and (336)). The infinitive ἑλεῖν in example (331) can be considered, in fact, a dynamic infinitive, since it depends on a verb phrase of 'hoping'. (On (329) see below). On the other hand, κρατυνθῆναι in (336) is anterior to ἀθυμοῦντας because of the factive properties of this verb of emotion: the dependent state of affairs is presented as an independent fact (cp. § 18.1 and § 37 (i)). Likewise, τὸ μὴ βοηθῆσαι in (328) is anterior because it is an apposition to a noun with factive properties: the 'service in connection with the Samians' presupposes that a service has been rendered.

Of the other ones the *present* infinitives of (327), (329), (332), (333) and (337) have a dynamic value. That of (333) is posterior to the main verb because of the postposition ἕνεκα, which is semantically comparable to a verb of volition. Those of (327), (329), (332) and (337) do not refer to any particular time-sphere at all, and are like the generic present indicatives discussed in § 5.3. Notice, in this connection, that these infinitives, unlike those to be discussed below, have no subject-constituent; they are, therefore, not about a definite person. The same applies to τὸ λαβεῖν in (329); note the parallellism with τὸ κατέχειν. On the other hand, the infinitive of (338) refers to a state of affairs that is simultaneous with the main verb. This is probably due to the causal meaning of the phrase: διά functions, then, as a presupposition-trigger (cp. § 27); observe also that in this case there *is* a definite subject ('I').

The *perfect* infinitives of examples (334) and (335) both refer to a simultaneous state, in (334) because τετιμῆσθαι depends on a - factive - verb of knowing, in (335) because of the causal meaning of the phrase (cp. above on (338)).

Finally, τοῦ διαβαίνειν in (330) belongs to the semi-dynamic type mentioned in § 31.1, Note 3, since it depends on ἄρξαντες.

Note 1 The construction with the article is obligatory (a) when the infinitive depends on a constituent requiring a particular case form, e.g. a comparative like καλλίον in (332); (b) when the infinitive functions as a satellite, e.g. (335), particularly in pre- and postpositional phrases (examples (333) and (338)).

Note 2 The construction τοῦ + infinitive, particularly τοῦ μή + infinitive, is sometimes used with a final nuance; e.g. περιεσταύρωσαν αὐτοὺς τοῖς δένδρεσιν ἃ ἔκοψαν, τοῦ μηδένα ἐπεξιέναι ('They surrounded them with a stockade made of the trees which they had felled, in order that no one might get out', Th. 2.75.1).

Note 3 The verbs of forbidding and denying, etc. discussed in § 33.1 (iv) and § 33.2 (iii), respectively, may not only be followed by μή and μὴ οὐ + infinitive, but also by τὸ μή and τὸ μὴ οὐ + infinitive: οὐκ ἀπεσχόμην τὸ μὴ οὐκ ἐπὶ τοῦτο ἐλθεῖν ('I could not refrain from turning to that topic', Pl. R. 354b). Constructions with τοῦ μή and τοῦ μὴ οὐ + infinitive occur as well.

IVB PARTICIPLE

§ 36 The participle as an obligatory or optional constituent with a main verb

The main use of the participle is to express a state of affairs accompanying the state of affairs expressed by a main verb. The negative is οὐ, except in some special cases (cp. below § 38 (iii)). Syntactically two main types may be distinguished, depending on whether or not the participle must necessarily occur with the finite verb; the second type has, in turn, two subtypes.

(i) The participle functions as an *obligatory constituent* of the main verb, i.e. as an *argument*. It is often called the *supplementary* participle.

If the subjects of main verb and participle are the same (are co-referential), the participle appears in the nominative: οἶδα θνητὸς ὤν 'I know that I am mortal', ἔχαιρε παροῦσα 'She was glad that she was present'. If the subjects are different the participle has its own subject constituent, in which case the whole of subject-constituent and participle appears in the case form required by the main verb: οἶδα τὸν ἄνδρα θνητὸν ὄντα 'I know that the man is mortal', ἔχαιρον τῇ γυναικὶ παρούσῃ 'I was glad that the woman was present'.

(ii) The participle functions as a *satellite*, i.e. as an *optional modifier* of the main verb. It is often called the *circumstantial* participle.

(a) The participle is syntactically connected with one of the constituents of the main verb, a constituent which expresses the subject of the state of affairs of the participle. The participle agrees with this constituent in gender, number, and case (so-called *participium coniunctum*, 'connected participle'): ὁ παῖς γελῶν ἀπῆλθεν 'the boy left laughing'.

(b) The participle has, syntactically speaking, no relation to a constituent of the main verb; in this case it has a subject-constituent of its own. The construction as a whole, consisting of subject-constituent and participle, is expressed in the genitive: *genitive absolute* ('released, free genitive'): τοῦ παιδὸς γελῶντος ἀπήλθομεν 'while the boy was laughing we left'.

Note 1 Besides the genitive absolute the *accusative absolute* occurs, though on a much smaller scale. See below, § 38, Note 2 and Note 3.

Note 2 In the above uses the participle never occurs between the article and the noun (if present), but either before or after the combination article + noun (so-called *predicative* position of the participle).

Note 3 For the use of the participle as modifier of a noun only see below § 40.

In general, the participles of the various tense stems express the following relationships with respect to the main verb. The *present* participle expresses that the state of affairs of the participle is *simultaneous* with that of the main verb, the *aorist* participle that it is *anterior*, the *future* participle that it is *posterior* with respect to the main verb. The *perfect* participle indicates that the state concerned is *simultaneous* with the main state of affairs. In the following sections the various participle-constructions will be dealt with in more detail.

§ 37 The participle as an obligatory constituent

Many Greek verbs are construed with a participle as an obligatory constituent. With these verbs the state of affairs expressed by the participle is presented as an independent fact. (For other constructions with a number of these verbs see § 18.1 (ὅτι/ὡς-clauses) and below p. 121 Note 6 (infinitive)). They may be grouped as follows:

(i) Verbs of perceiving and knowing, such as: ὁρῶ 'see'; ἀκούω 'hear'; πυνθάνομαι 'learn'; μανθάνω, αἰσθάνομαι 'perceive'; δείκνυμι 'show' (= cause to perceive); εὑρίσκω 'find out'; φαίνομαι, δῆλός εἰμι 'appear'; μέμνημαι 'remember'; οἶδα, ἐπίσταμαι 'know'; σύνοιδα 'be aware'; γιγνώσκω 'realize'; κατανοῶ 'perceive'; occasionally also verbs of saying, notably ἀγγέλλω 'report' (= make it known).

Some examples:

(339) εἶδον αὐτοὺς πελάζοντας ('They saw them approaching', X. *Cyr.* 1.4.20)

(340) τὸν ... Μῆδον ... ἴσμεν ... ἐπὶ τὴν Πελοπόννησον ἐλθόντα ('We know that the Medes have come to the Peloponnesos', Th. 1.69.5)

(341) πυνθάνομαι οὕτω τοῦτο γενόμενον ('I learn that this happened in this way', Hdt. 1.214.1)

(342) κατενόησαν οὐ πολλοὺς τοὺς Θηβαίους ὄντας ('They perceived that the Thebans were not numerous', Th. 2.3.2)

(343) Περικλῆς ... ἔγνω τὴν ἐσβολὴν ἐσομένην ('Pericles realized that the invasion would take place', Th. 2.13.1)

(344) ἤκουσε Κῦρον ἐν Κιλικίᾳ ὄντα ('He heard that Cyrus was in Cilicia', X. An. 1.4.5)

(345) ἤκουσα ... αὐτοῦ καὶ περὶ φίλων διαλεγομένου ('I heard him give a discourse on friendship', X. Mem. 2.4.1)

In (339) - (344) we are dealing with a so-called *accusative plus participle*-construction: there is a constituent in the accusative and a participle agreeing with that constituent; in (345) we find a so-called *genitive plus participle*-construction. In all cases the subject of the main state of affairs differs from the subject of the state of affairs of the participle.

Note 1 ἀκούω + genitive plus participle (cp. (345)) = 'hear someone make a sound' (direct perception); the state of affairs of the participle is presented as an independent fact.

ἀκούω + accusative plus participle (cp. (344)) = 'learn, be told' (indirect perception); the state of affairs of the participle is presented as an independent fact.

ἀκούω + accusative plus infinitive (cp. § 31.1) or + ὅτι/ὡς-clause (cp. § 18.2) = 'be told (as a rumour), learn'; the state of affairs of the infinitive (the ὅτι/ὡς-clause) is not presented as an independent fact. See also § 33.2, note 3, for possible differences between infinitive and ὅτι/ὡς-clause.

In English the value of ἀκούω + accusative plus participle may be made explicit by translating 'find (out)', in which case the state of affairs of the participle is presented as an independent fact as well.

Note 2 It might be argued that αὐτοῦ in (345) functions as the complement of ἤκουσα (cp. ἤκουσα φωνῆς), and that αὐτούς in (339) is the object of εἶδον, with διαλεγομένου and πελάζοντας as satellites ('I heard him while he gave a discourse', 'I saw them while they approached'). On the other hand, in the case of τὴν ἐσβολήν in (343) this is not possible: *ἔγνω τὴν ἐσβολήν ('*he realized the invasion'); τὴν ἐσβολήν is, therefore, a constituent of the participle *only*. The same syntactic phenomenon was discussed in § 32, in connection with ἀναγκάζω αὐτὸν ἀπελθεῖν (accusative followed by supplementary infinitive) as against ἡγοῦμαι αὐτὸν ἀπελθεῖν (*accusative plus infinitive*) (*ἡγοῦμαι αὐτόν). On the analogy of this pair we might distinguish between a 'real' accusative plus participle (as in (343)) and an accusative or genitive with a supplementary participle in (339) and (345), respectively. To this it may be objected, however, that in the so-called nominative plus participle use (see below), e.g. ὁρῶμεν ἀδύνατοι ὄντες περιγενέσθαι (cp. ex. (346)), it is hardly possible to assign an object function to an unexpressed 'we' in ἀδύνατοι ὄντες. For this reason I prefer, as already indicated in § 36 (i), analysing the accusative plus participle of ex. (339) as depending *as a whole* on εἶδον, in the case form required by that verb. In technical terms: the object (or rather: second argument) of εἶδον is the state of affairs 'πελάζουσι'. Likewise, the second argument of ὁρῶμεν in (346) is 'ἀδύνατοί ἐσμεν'. Cp. also § 32.1, Note 2. In (345), however, we might, in fact, be dealing with a genitive with a supplementary participle.

Note 3 Verbs like οἶδα, ἐπίσταμαι, γιγνώσκω may also be construed with a genitive absolute-construction preceded by ὡς; e.g. ὡς ὧδ' ἐχόντων τῶνδ' ἐπίστασθαί σε χρή ('You must know that these things stand thus', S. *Ai.* 281). ὡς + 'accusative plus participle' may be used in this way too: ὡς φανέν γε τοὔπος ὧδ' ἐπίστασο ('Be assured that thus the tale was first told', S. *OT* 848). As to the latter, it is difficult to determine whether this construction differs from the accusative plus participle-construction without ὡς (cp. (340)).

Note 4 These verbs may also be construed with a participle + ἄν, having potential or counterfactual value; e.g. ὁρῶν τὸ παρατείχισμα ..., εἰ ἐπικρατήσειέ τις ... τῆς ἀναβάσεως ..., ῥᾳδίως ἄν ... ληφθέν ('Seeing that the cross-wall could be easily captured, if someone could gain the command of the way up', Th. 7.42.4).

In cases where the subjects of main verb and participle do not differ (are *co-referential*) the participle is expressed in the nominative (so-called *nominative plus participle*). Some examples:

(346)   ἐπειδὴ ... ἀδύνατοι ὁρῶμεν ὄντες ... περιγενέσθαι ('Now that we see that we are unable to get the upper hand', Th. 1.32.5)

(347)   οἱ δ' ὡς ἔγνωσαν ἐξηπατημένοι ... ('When they found that they had been deceived ...'; Th. 2.4.1)

(348)   ὡς ... ἠγγέλλοντο αἱ ... νῆες ... τὴν περιοικίδα αὐτῶν πορθοῦσαι ('When the ships were reported to be laying waste to the country surrounding them', Th. 3.16.2)

(349)   δῆλον ... ἐποιήσατε ... μόνοι οὐ μηδίσαντες ('You have made it plain that you alone refused to join the Persian cause', Th. 3.64.1)

(350)   φαίνονται δὲ αἰεί ... τοῦτον ἀείδοντες ('They appear to always sing this song' ('It appears that they ...'), Hdt. 2.79.2)

(351)   πρὸς ἀνδρὸς ᾔσθετ' ἠδικημένη ('She learned that she had been wronged by her husband', E. *Med.* 26)

(ii) Verbs of emotion, such as χαίρω 'rejoice', ἥδομαι 'enjoy oneself', αἰσχύνομαι 'be ashamed', μεταμέλομαι 'regret', and the like.

Some examples:

(352) μετεμέλοντο τὰς σπονδὰς <u>οὐ δεξάμενοι</u> ('They regretted not having accepted the treaty', Th. 4.27.2; nominative plus participle)

(353) τοῦτο μὲν οὐκ <u>αἰσχύνομαι λέγων</u> ('My saying this does not make me feel ashamed', X. *Cyr.* 5.1.21; nominative plus participle)

(353a) <u>χαίρουσιν ἐξεταζομένοις τοῖς οἰομένοις</u> ... εἶναι <u>σοφοῖς</u> ('They like it when people who think they are wise are being examined', Pl. *Ap.* 33c; dative plus participle)

Note 5 With participles of this type one may sometimes hesitate beween an analysis as obligatory or as non-obligatory constituents: ἥδομαι ἀκούων 'I enjoy hearing ...', or 'I enjoy myself, now that I hear ...' See also note 2 above.

(iii) Verbs meaning 'endure', 'persist', 'put up with', such as περιορῶ 'allow, bear', ἀπαγορεύω 'give up', ἀνέχομαι 'bear, stand'.
    Some examples:

(354) ἐγὼ ... <u>ἀπείρηκα</u> ... <u>συσκευαζόμενος</u> καὶ <u>βαδίζων</u> καὶ ... ('I, for my part, am tired of packing up and walking and ...', X. *An.* 5.1.2; nominative plus participle)

(355) <u>τοὺς ξυμμάχους</u> ... οὐ <u>περιοψόμεθα ἀδικουμένους</u> ('We shall not allow our allies to be wronged', Th. 1.86.2; accusative plus participle)

(iv) So-called 'phasal verbs', i.e. verbs expressing beginning, continuation, and end of a state of affairs, such as ἄρχομαι 'begin', διατελῶ 'continue', παύω/παύομαι '(cause to) stop'. These verbs are *always* construed with the *present* participle. Cp. also § 1, Note 2.
    Some examples:

(356) <u>ἄρξομαι</u> ... ἀπὸ τῆς ἰατρικῆς <u>λέγων</u> ('I shall begin (by) speaking about medicine', Pl. *Smp.* 186b; nominative plus participle)

(357) οὐ γὰρ <u>ἀνίει ἐπιὼν</u> ὁ Δαρεῖος ('For Darius kept coming closer (... did not stop ...)', Hdt. 4.125.2; nominative plus participle)

(357a) σύ νυν τοῦτον <u>τὸν ἄνδρα παῦσον</u> ταῦτα <u>ποιεῦντα</u> ('do you then make this man stop doing these things', Hdt. 5.23.3; accusative plus participle)

(v) Finally, an obligatory participle occurs with verbs that express a way of being: λανθάνω 'be hidden, escape notice', οἴχομαι 'go away, be away', τυγχάνω 'happen to, chance to', φθάνω 'be beforehand with, be first to'. In translating we may often express λανθάνω by an adverbial element: ἔλαθον τοῦτο ποιήσας 'I did that unawares/without being noticed'. With λανθάνω and φθάνω an object may occur. The subjects of main verb and participle are necessarily co-referential. Some examples:

(358) βουλοίμην ἂν ... <u>λαθεῖν</u> αὐτὸν <u>ἀπελθών</u> ('I should like to leave without being noticed by him', X. An. 1.3.17)

(359) <u>ᾤχετο ἀπελαύνων</u> ('He went riding off', X. An. 2.4.24)

(360) <u>ἔτυχον</u> ... ἐν τῇ ἀγορᾷ ὁπλῖται <u>καθεύδοντες</u> ('Hoplites happened to be sleeping in the market-place', Th. 4.113.2)

(361) <u>ἔφθησαν</u> ... οἱ Σκύθαι τοὺς Πέρσας ἐπὶ τὴν γέφυραν <u>ἀπικόμενοι</u> ('The Scythians came to the bridge before the Persians', Hdt. 4.136.2)

Note 6 Several verbs discussed in this section may also be construed with a dynamic or declarative *infinitive* (as well as with ὅτι/ὡς-clauses, but these are ignored here, see § 18). There are clear semantic differences between the constructions with the participle and those with the infinitive. Cp.:

γιγνώσκω + participle: 'realize that'; + declarative infinitive: 'judge'; + dynamic infinitive: 'decide'; cp. also § 33.3 (i).

οἶδα, ἐπίσταμαι + participle: 'know that'; + (dynamic) infinitive: 'know how to, be able to'.

φαίνομαι + participle: 'appear'; + (declarative) infinitive: 'seem'.

αἰσχύνομαι + participle: 'be ashamed that'; + (dynamic) infinitive: 'shrink from'.

μέμνημαι + participle: 'remember that'; + (dynamic) infinitive: 'be mindful'.

ἀγγέλλω + participle: 'report (as an independent fact)'; + (declarative) infinitive: 'report (as a rumour)'.

ἀκούω + participle: 'hear (as an independent fact)'; + (declarative) infinitive: 'hear (as a rumour)'; cp. also Note 1 above, and § 32.2, Note 3.

ἀνέχομαι + participle: 'bear'; + (dynamic) infinitive: 'dare'.

ἄρχομαι + participle: 'begin -ing' (of states of affairs that are continued) (cp. (356); + (dynamic) infinitive: 'begin to' (of states of affairs that are not necessarily continued).

Note 7 The participle may also be used in such a way that the state of affairs expressed by the participle is indispensable for a correct interpretation of the sentence as a whole. Such participles are called '*dominant* participles'; they are, of course, *obligatory* constituents. The combination noun + participle as a whole functions in much the same way as an action noun +

subjective or objective genitive. Some examples: ἡ Ἀστυάγεος ... ἡγεμονίη <u>καταιρεθεῖσα</u> ... καὶ τὰ τῶν Περσέων πρήγματα <u>αὐξανόμενα</u> πένθεος ... Κροῖσον ἀπέπαυσε ('The destruction of the sovereignty of Astyages and the growth of the power of the Persians caused Croesus to cease from his mourning', Hdt. 1.46.1). After a preposition: μετὰ ... Σόλωνα <u>οἰχόμενον</u> ('After Solon's departure ...', Hdt. 1.34.1). Cp. the so-called *ab urbe condita*-construction in Latin.

§ 38 The participle as a satellite

Non-obligatory participles as well as genitive absolute-constructions (functioning as satellites, i.e. optional constituents, cp. § 17) may have a number of semantic relations with the main state of affairs, comparable to the functions fulfilled by dependent clauses as satellites (see Ch. III B). The interpretation of such participle constructions is determined by the context and by the semantic characteristics of the states of affairs involved. Some of these various semantic functions may be made explicit by means of adverbs occurring either with the participle or with the main verb. The following functions may be fulfilled by optional participles (and genitive absolute-constructions):

(i)   *Temporal* modifier (the participle often precedes the main verb):

(362) <u>ἀκούσας</u> δὲ ταῦτα ὁ Ἀστυάγης Μήδους ... ὥπλισε πάντας ('When he had heard this, Astyages armed all his Medes', Hdt. 1.127.2)

(363) <u>δυνατωτέρας</u> δὲ <u>γιγνομένης τῆς Ἑλλάδος</u> ... τὰ πολλὰ τυραννίδες ... καθίσταντο ('As Hellas became more powerful tyrannies were generally established', Th. 1.13.1)

(364) <u>Ἁρπάγῳ ἐπιόντι</u> σὺν τῷ στρατῷ ἀμαχητὶ σφέας αὐτοὺς παρέδοσαν ('When Harpagus came against them with his army they surrendered to him without resistance', Hdt. 1.174.6)

(365) ἐπαιάνιζον ... <u>ἅμα</u> ... <u>πλέοντες</u> ('They were singing a paean of victory while rowing', Th. 2.91.2)

(366) νῦν μὲν δειπνεῖτε παρ' ἡμῖν· <u>δειπνήσαντες</u> δὲ ἀπελαύνετε ὅποι ὑμῖν θυμός ('Now you must stay for dinner with us; after the dinner you are free to go wherever you wish', X. *Cyr.* 3.1.37;

observe that δειπνήσαντες is anterior to a future state of affairs
(ἀπελαύνετε))

(367) τοῦτον τὸν χρησμὸν οὐκ οἷοί τε ἦσαν γνῶναι οὔτε τότε ἰθὺς οὔτε
τῶν Σαμίων ἀπιγμένων ('They could not understand this oracle
either when it was spoken or at the time of the Samians' coming',
Hdt. 3.58.1; note the coordination with the temporal adverb τότε).

Note 1 Sometimes a circumstantial-causal nuance may be present, as in
(362), where the participle expresses the circumstances that led to Astyages'
action.

(ii)   *Causal* modifier (the participle often follows after the main verb):

(368) ὑπεδέξαντο τὴν τιμωρίαν, νομίζοντες ... ἑαυτῶν εἶναι τὴν
ἀποικίαν, ἅμα δὲ καὶ μίσει (causal dative) τῶν Κερκυραίων
('They took up the cause, because they considered the colony to be
their own, and also out of hatred for the Cercyrians', Th. 1.25.3)
(369) καὶ τῶνδε ὑμεῖς αἴτιοι, ... ἐάσαντες αὐτοὺς τὴν πόλιν ...
κρατῦναι ('And for this you are to blame, because you allowed
them to fortify their city', Th. 1.69.1)
(370) οὐδ' ἔτι ἐζήτησαν τὸ προσώτερω ... ἐκμαθεῖν, ἐστερημένοι τοῦ
ἡγεμόνος ('they made no endeavour ... to learn of the further parts,
now that they had been deprived of their guide, Hdt. 4.137.4)

ὡς and ἅτε + participle

Causal participles preceded by ὡς express that the onus of the reason is
left on the subject of the main verb (so-called 'subjective reason'); this
nuance may be made explicit by translating ὡς + participle by 'in the
conviction that', 'considering that', 'alleging that' etc. The participle does
not specify whether or not the state of affairs concerned is a fact. When,
on the other hand, ἅτε (also οἷον, οἷα, and in Herodotus ὥστε) precedes
the participle the onus of the reason is on the speaker/narrator, in which
case the reason is presented as an independent fact (objective reason; cp.
§ 27).
    Some examples:

(371) νῦν δέ, ὡς οὕτω ἐχόντων, στρατιὴν ... ἐκπέμπετε ('But now, considering that this is the way things stand, you must send out an army', Hdt. 8.144.4)

(372) Ἀρίστιππος ... αἰτεῖ αὐτὸν εἰς δισχιλίους ξένους καὶ τριῶν μηνῶν μισθόν, ὡς οὕτως περιγενόμενος ἂν τῶν ἀντιστασιωτῶν ('Aristippus asked him for three months' pay for two thousand mercenaries, alleging that in this way he should get the better of his opponents', X. An. 1.1.10; note participle + ἄν, having potential value)

(373) συμφορὴν ἐποιεῦντο τοὺς λόγους ὡς κακόν τι πεισομένης (' ... they were sorry for her words, thinking that the king would do her some hurt', Hdt. 8.69.1)

(374) αὐτοὶ ἐνταῦθ᾽ ἔμενον ὡς τὸ ἄκρον κατέχοντες· οἱ δ᾽ οὐ κατεῖχον ... ('They remained at the post themselves, supposing that they held the height; in fact, they were not holding it ...', X. An. 4.2.5)

(375) Κῦρος δὲ ἀπορίῃσι ἐνείχετο ἅτε χρόνου ... ἐγγινομένου συχνοῦ ... ('Cyrus knew not what to do because a lot of time was passing ...', Hdt. 1.190.2)

(376) ἀπῆγε τὴν στρατιὴν ὀπίσω ἅτε τῷ πεζῷ τε προσπταίσας πρὸς τοὺς Βρύγους καὶ τῷ ναυτικῷ μεγάλως περὶ ῎Αθων ('... he led his host away homewards since the Brygi had dealt a heavy blow to his army and Athos a blow yet heavier to his fleet', Hdt. 6.45.2)

Note 2 Not seldom an accusative absolute preceded by ὡς is found, with the same function as ὡς + genitive absolute (cp. ex. (373)), e.g. ἥδεσθε τοῦδ᾽ εἵνεκα ὡς περιεσομένους ἡμέας Ἑλλήνων ('... you may rejoice at the thought that we shall overcome the Greeks', Hdt. 9.42.4).

(iii) *Conditional* modifier (negative: μή):

(377) γενήσεται δὲ ὑμῖν πειθομένοις καλὴ ἡ ξυντυχία ('If you listen to us our joint enterprise will be a success', Th. 1.33.1; πειθομένοις = ἐὰν πείθησθε or εἰ πείσεσθε)

(378) ὃ νῦν ὑμεῖς μὴ πειθόμενοι ἡμῖν πάθοιτε ἄν ('That which might well happen to you if you do not listen to us', Th. 1.40.2; μὴ πειθόμενοι = εἰ μὴ πείθοισθε)

(iv)   *Concessive* modifier (often made explicit by καίπερ preceding the participle or by ὅμως with the main verb):

(379)   τοῦτον προθυμεόμενοι ἑλεῖν οὐ δυνάμεθα ('Though we strive to capture him we do not succeed', Hdt. 1.36.2)

(380)   τὸν ... Ἄδρηστον κατοικτίρει, καίπερ ἐὼν ἐν κακῷ ... τοσούτῳ ('He took pity on Adrastus, though his own sorrow was so great', Hdt. 1.45.2)

(381)   τὸ ... πλῆθος ἄμετρον ὁρῶντες, ὅμως ἐτολμήσατε ... ἰέναι εἰς αὐτούς ('Though you saw that their numbers were beyond counting, you nevertheless dared to charge upon them', X. *An.* 3.2.16)

(v)   Modifier of *manner*:

(382)   ληζόμενοι ζῶσι ('They live by plundering', X. *Cyr.* 3.2.25)

(383)   γράμματα γράφουσι .. Ἕλληνες ... ἀπὸ τῶν ἀριστερῶν ἐπὶ τὰ δεξιὰ φέροντες τὴν χεῖρα ('The Greeks write letters by moving the hand from left to right', Hdt. 2.36.4)

Also with the aorist participle:

(384)   ἀπώλεσέν μ' εἰποῦσα συμφορὰς ἐμάς ('She has destroyed me by speaking of my troubles', E. *Hipp.* 596)

This use of the aorist participle is called 'coincident', because the participle, while expressing a completed state of affairs, is not anterior to the main verb, but coincides with it. In our example the completion of the speaking coincides with the completion of the destroying. (Lit.: 'She has destroyed me by having spoken of my troubles').

(vi)   Modifier of *purpose* (only in the case of the future participle, especially after verbs of sending and going):

(385)   κήρυκα ... προύπεμψαν αὐτοῖς ... ἀπεροῦντα μὴ πλεῖν ('They sent a messenger forbidding them (who was to forbid them) to sail', Th. 1.29.3; for the infinitive with ἀπαγορεύω see § 33.1 (iv))

ὡς may, here too, precede the participle, in which case the future state of affairs is presented as a personal consideration of the subject of the main verb:

(386) παρεσκευάζοντο <u>ὡς πολεμήσοντες</u> ('They prepared themselves in order to wage war (considering that they would ...)', Th. 2.7.1)

(vii) *Comparative* modifier (ὥσπερ 'as if' always precedes the participle):

(387) ἐπιδεικνὺς ... τὴν εὐήθειαν τοῦ τὰ πλοῖα αἰτεῖν κελεύοντος, <u>ὥσπερ</u> πάλιν τὸν στόλον <u>Κύρου ποιουμένου</u> ('... pointing out the foolishness of the speaker who had urged them to ask for ships, just as if Cyrus were going home again', X. *An.* 1.3.16)

Note 3 When used absolutely, participles of impersonal verbs are expressed in the neuter accusative (*accusative absolute*). Thus, e.g.: ὄν, ἐξόν (: ἔστι, ἔξεστι 'it is possible'), δέον, χρεών (δεῖ, χρή 'it is necessary'), δόξαν (: ἔδοξεν 'it seemed right, it was decided'), ἀδύνατον ὄν (: ἀδύνατόν ἐστι 'it is impossible'). Passive participles of aorist and perfect are used in this way as well: δεδογμένον (: δέδοκται 'it has been decided'), etc. As to the interpretation, the same possibilities exist as in the case of the *participium coniunctum* and genitive absolute. Some examples: τί δὴ ὑμᾶς <u>ἐξὸν</u> ἀπολέσαι οὐκ ἐπὶ τοῦτο ἤλθομεν; ('Why, when it was possible for us to destroy you, did we not proceed to do so?', X. *An.* 2.5.22); ἐκβῆναι οὐκ <u>ὂν</u> ... ἀναγκαῖον ἦν ἐπ' ἀγκύρας ἀποσαλεύειν ('Since it was impossible to go ashore ... it was necessary to ride at anchor', D. 50.22). Also with 'subjective' ὡς (cp. above (ii) and Note 2): <u>ὡς ὢν μεταδεδογμένον</u> μοι μὴ στρατεύεσθαι ἐπὶ τὴν Ἑλλάδα ἥσυχοι ἔστε ('Take it therefore that my purpose of marching against Hellas is changed, and abide in peace', Hdt. 7.13.3).

§ 39 Periphrastic constructions

Outside the above uses the (predicative) participle is also used in so-called periphrastic constructions. The most important of these involve a participle plus a form of the verbs εἰμί or ἔχω, together forming an 'analytic' or complex verb phrase, with εἰμί and ἔχω as auxiliary verbs. These constructions are an alternative to a number of 'synthetic' or 'monolectic' verb forms, and are, generally speaking, considered to express the same meaning as the corresponding monolectic verb forms, but in a 'periphrastic' way. There is, however, much controversy about the precise nature of the periphrastic constructions, and, consequently, about their relationship with the monolectic forms.

Note 1 Other verbs may also form periphrastic constructions, notably those of going, e.g. εἰμι/ἔρχομαι with a future participle: ἐγὼ δὲ περὶ μὲν τούτων οὐκ ἔρχομαι ἐρέων ὡς ... ('For may part I am not going to say that ...', Hdt. 1.5.3. etc.). Cp. *I am going to say, je vais dire, ik ga zeggen.* For μέλλω + infinitive cp. § 9, Note 3, and § 33.1, Note 2.

The main periphrastic constructions of εἰμί and ἔχω in classical Greek are the following.

(i) εἰμί + participle

(a) + present participle

(388) δεινῶς ἀθυμῶ μὴ <u>βλέπων</u> ὁ μάντις <u>ᾖ</u> ('Dread misgivings have I that the seer can see', S. *OT* 747)

(389) τὰ δ᾽ ὄργι᾽ <u>ἐστὶ</u> τίν᾽ ἰδέαν <u>ἔχοντά</u> σοι; ('What form are these rites provided with in your view?', E. *Ba.* 471)

As in these two examples, the periphrastic construction is mostly a variant of a monolectic form of verbs expressing a state. This stative value may come to the fore more clearly in the periphrastic construction, the emphasis being put on the adjective-like participle, and thereby on the permanency of the characteristic in question. In (388) monolectic βλέπῃ would be rather a run-of-the-mill expression. Similarly, in (389), by choosing ἐστὶ ... ἔχοντα rather than ἔχει, Pentheus may stress, sarcastically no doubt, the permanency of the form of the rites.

Note 2 Example (388) illustrates the difficulties one may encounter in determining whether or not periphrasis is involved. For it might be argued that βλέπων is not 'adjective-like' but a full-fledged adjective, replacing the non-existing 'normal' adjective that would be the opposite of τυφλός, and that, as a result, ᾖ is a copula. Of course, in that case, too, we still have to explain the (dis)similarities with monolectic verb forms. Compare, by way of example, the difference between Engl. *The results were amazing* (not: **The results were amazing everybody*), as against *The results amazed everybody* (not: **The results amazed*). - In cases like the following, where a locative expression is present, we are not dealing with a periphrastic construction but with existential-locative εἰμί: ἦν δὲ περὶ Δαρεῖον ἀνὴρ Αἰγύπτιος φωνέων μέγιστον ἀνθρώπων ('There was with Darius an Egyptian whose voice was the loudest in the world', Hdt. 4.141; φωνέων is an appositive participle, see § 40); ... ἐπὶ τὴν Ποτείδαιαν, οὗ ἦν στράτευμα τῶν Ἀθηναίων πολιορκοῦν ('where an Athenian army was, continuing the siege', Th. 2.67.1; πολιορκοῦν appositive). However, in the latter example a periphrastic analysis is by no means excluded. (Cp. Engl. *Where John was, baptizing* with locative *was*, as against *Where John was baptizing*, with the past progressive of *baptize*). Commentators often hesitate, in fact, between a periphrastic and a locative analysis; a case in point is: ζῶν δ' ἔστ' ἐν οἴκοις ('Within he lives', E. *Pho.* 66; Loeb-transl.), where some interpret 'he is alive, in the palace' but others 'alive and well, he is in the palace'.

(b) + aorist participle

(390) οὐδέ τι νεώτερόν εἰμι ποιήσας νῦν ἢ καὶ ἐν εἰρήνῃ ἐώθεα ποιεῖν ('this that I have done is no stranger thing than I was wont to do in peace', Hdt. 4.127.1)

(391) οὔτε γὰρ θρασὺς / οὔτ' οὖν προδείσας εἰμὶ τῷ γε νῦν λόγῳ ('I am neither bold, nor thrown into fear beforehand by what you just said at least', S. *OT* 90)

In this puzzling (and rather rare) construction the participle can perhaps best be taken adjectivally; note, in (391), the coordination with θρασύς. Unlike adjectives, however, the participle has aspectual meaning, and this may be relevant here. Thus, προδείσας in (391) may exhibit the ingressive nuance of the aorist of verbs of emotion discussed in § 8.3.2: Oedipus is not one who began having fear while Creon spoke. Example (390) is more difficult; perhaps the combination of present εἰμί and anterior ποιήσας (the words are a reaction to a remark by Darius about the strange behaviour of Idanthyrsus, the Scythian king) stresses that Idanthyrsus is not of such a nature that he has now done something unusual, while semelfactive ἐποίησα would simply say that he has done nothing unusual, and stative-resultative πεποίηκα would suggest that Idanthyrsus has stopped behaving as he does.

(c) + perfect participle

(392) ἐς δὲ τὴν Σηστὸν ταύτην ... συνῆλθον ... καὶ δὴ καὶ ... Οἰόβαζος, ὃς τὰ ἐκ τῶν γεφυρέων ὅπλα ἐνθαῦτα ἦν κεκομικώς ('... they had

assembled at this same Sestos; among them ... Oiobazos, who had carried thither the tackle of the bridges', Hdt. 9.115)

(393) οἱ δὲ Αἰτωλοὶ (βεβοηθηκότες γὰρ ἤδη ἦσαν ἐπὶ τὸ Αἰγίτιον) προσέβαλλον τοῖς 'Αθηναίοις ('But the Aetolians (by this time they had come to the rescue of Aigition) attacked the Athenians', Th. 3.97.3)

(394) "Αριοι δὲ τόξοισι ... ἐσκευασμένοι ἦσαν Μηδικοῖσι ('The Arians were equipped with Median bows', Hdt. 7.66.1)

(395) κλαίων ὀθούνεχ' εἷς δυοῖν ἔσοιθ' ἅμα,
       πατρός τ' ἐκείνης τ', ὠρφανισμένος βίον
       ('weeping that he, being on his own, must now live bereaved of both alike - of mother and of sire', S. *Tr.* 941-2)

In this use the stative-confective value of the perfect stem is emphasized: it is expressed twice, so to speak, once by the perfect participle and a second time by the form of εἰμί. This point should not be pressed, though; thus, in (394) ἐσκευασμένοι ἦσαν may have been chosen instead of ἐσκευάδατο simply to vary the wording. (Monolectic ἐσκευάδατο occurs in the next chapter).

Note 3 That, semantically speaking, the periphrastic forms did not differ much from monolectic perfect and pluperfect forms may be inferred from the fact that in Attic Greek inscriptions, from the end of the 5th century onward, 3rd person plural middle-passive forms of verbs with a stem ending in a consonant (like σκευάζω) are always of the periphrastic type. They have, then, become part of the verbal paradigm, on a par both with the monolectic forms in the other persons and with the monolectic forms of other verbs (e.g. ἐσκευασμένοι εἰσί alongside ἐσκευάσμεθα, ἐσκεύασθε on the one hand, and corresponding to πεπαίδευνται, λέλυνται etc. on the other).

Note 4 The periphrastic perfect is mainly formed with the passive perfect participle, and, in the active, with participles of intransitive verbs. Example (392) is one of the few instances with an active participle of a fully transitive verb.

Note 5 As in the case of the present participle (cp. Note 2), there are instances of εἰμί + perfect participle where a non-periphrastic analysis is possible. Thus, in ἦσαν τῷ Φάνῃ παῖδες ἐν Αἰγύπτῳ καταλελειμμένοι (Hdt. 3.11.2), ἦσαν might be construed with the dative τῷ Φάνῃ, forming a possessive construction, with καταλελειμμένοι in apposition: 'Phanès avait des fils, qu'il avait laissés en Égypte' (Legrand, Budé-edition). But τῷ Φάνῃ might also be a *dativus auctoris*; in that case a periphrastic analysis imposes itself: 'Phanes had left sons in Egypt' (Godley, Loeb-edition).

(ii) ἔχω + participle

This is virtually confined to ἔχω + aorist participle

(396) νυκτὸς γὰρ ἡμᾶς τῆσδε πρᾶγος ἄσκοπον
       ἔχει περάνας, εἴπερ εἴργασται τάδε
       ('This night he hath done to us a thing which passes thought - if he
       is indeed the doer', S. *Ai.* 21-22; note neutral εἰ, with a slightly
       sceptical nuance, § 24.2)
(397)   τοὺς δὲ πρόσθεν εὐσεβεῖς
       κἀξ εὐσεβῶν βλαστόντας ἐκβαλοῦσ' ἔχεις
       ('thou hast cast out the earlier-born, the stainless offspring of a
       stainless marriage', S. *El.* 590)
(398) τὸν λόγον δέ σου πάλαι θαυμάσας ἔχω, ὅσῳ καλλίω τοῦ
       προτέρου ἀπηργάσω ('But all along I have been wondering at your
       discourse, you made it so much more beautiful than the first', Pl.
       Phdr. 257c)

This periphrastic construction, which is called σχῆμα 'Αττικόν or
Σοφόκλειον and is mainly found in Sophocles, Herodotus and Euripides,
is generally considered to have the same stative-confective value as the
monolectic perfect; one may point, in this connection, to the presence
of the perfect εἴργασται in (396), which refers to the same state as ἔχει
περάνας. It is often said that these periphrastic perfects, rather than being
alternatives to a monolectic form, with many verbs are the sole forms
available to express stative-confective meaning in the active voice, since
the monolectic perfects are not attested at all, or came into use after the
classical period (cp. also § 10.1, Note 4). The monolectic perfect of
περαίνω, πεπέραγκα, would, in fact, not seem to occur. On the other hand,
since forms of (ἐκ)βέβληκα are positively used by Sophocles (ἐκβεβλη-
κότων *OC* 646, cp. also ἐμβεβληκότα, *OC* 1392) and are, indeed, already
found in Homer (pluperfect βεβλήκει etc.), and since the same holds for
τεθαύμακα in Plato (τεθαύμακα, *Tht.* 161c), the 'non-availability' of
monolectic forms cannot be the only *raison d'être* of the periphrastic
construction. So in the end we have to reckon with the possiblity that this
periphrastic construction, too, like the other ones, has a value of its own;
with Moorhouse (1982: 206) we might say that 'the aor. part. here seems
to add a past notion to the continuing effect of ἔχω'.

Note 6 One might perhaps be tempted to take the presence of temporal modifiers like νυκτὸς τῆσδε (cp. (396)) and πάλαι (cp. (398)) as a factor favouring the aorist participle. However, such modifiers occur with the monolectic perfect as well (τέθνηχ' ὑμῖν πάλαι ('For you I have long been dead', S. *Ph.* 1030); γυνὴ τέθνηκ' ... ἄρτι ('the queen has died a moment ago', S. *Ant.* 1283)).

Note 7 Again, cp. Notes 2 and 5 above, one may waver between a periphrastic and a non-periphrastic analysis. Thus, in ἐπεὶ σὺ μὲν γῆν τήνδε διολέσας ἔχεις, / ὁ δ' ὠφελήσας ἀξίων οὐ τυγχάνει (E. *HF* 264-5), διολέσας ἔχεις might be 'You have ruined this country', but also 'You possess/occupy this country, although you have ruined it', as in the Loeb-translation ('You have destroyed this country and now you rule it'). Because of the parallel with ὠφελήσας ... οὐ τυγχάνει I prefer the latter analysis. Indeed, in quite a number of cases where both an aorist participle and ἔχω are present, to put it neutrally, ἔχω has possessive meaning, e.g. in τοὺς ἄλλους πάντας ὑπ' ἑωυτῷ εἶχε καταστρεψάμενος ὁ Κροῖσος ('the rest were subdued and became subjects of Kroisos', Hdt. 1.28), where the presence of ὑπ' ἑωυτῷ invites us, I think, to take εἶχε as 'had', and καταστρεψάμενος as 'having subdued', cp. τοὺς ... ἄλλους ἔχει ὑπ' ἑωυτῷ Θρήικας, Hdt. 4.118.5.

Note 8 There are a few cases of ἔχω + active perfect participle, e.g. S. *OT* 701 (οἷά μοι βεβουλευκὼς ἔχει 'because of the things he has devised against me'), X. *An.* 1.3.14 (οἱ Κίλικες ..., ὧν πολλοὺς καὶ πολλὰ χρήματα ἔχομεν ἀνηρπακότες ('... have taken away', but possibly rather: 'we have in our possession ... that we have seized as plunder' (Brownson, Loeb-edition). - The use of ἔχω + *passive* perfect participle is not attested for classical Greek.

§ 40 Attributive participle

Participles may also be used *attributively*, exclusively modifying the noun with which they agree. Syntactically, two types may be distinguished.

(i) The participle is placed in attributive position

When modifying a noun which has an article the participle is placed either between article and noun or after the noun, the article being repeated. Attributive participles are, therefore, fully comparable to attributively used adjectives. Examples: τὸ χρηστήριον τὸ τῷ Ἀλυάττῃ γενόμενον 'the oracular response given to Alyattes'; ἐν τῇ νῦν Ἑλλάδι καλεομένῃ χώρῃ 'in the country which is now called Hellas'; τῇ ἐπιγιγνομένῃ ἡμέρᾳ 'on the next day'; ἡ μάχη ἡ γενομένη ἐν Πτερίῃ 'the battle which has taken place at Pteria'; etc.

Like adjectives, participles are often used substantivally: οἱ παρὰ τὴν θάλατταν οἰκοῦντες 'those living along the sea'; οἱ φεύγοντες 'those who are fleeing'; τὰ νομιζόμενα 'the usual things'; τὸ δέον ('the necessary', often =) 'the right moment'; ἡ οἰκουμένη (sc. γῆ) 'the inhabited world'; τὰ προστεταγμένα 'the orders'. The aspectual differences between present and aorist stem are fully relevant for these participles, as appears from the following example:

(399)   κατὰ <u>τὸν γινόμενον</u> σφίσι καὶ <u>ἀπογινόμενον</u> ποιεῦσι τοιάδε· <u>τὸν μὲν γενόμενον</u> ... ὀλοφύρονται, <u>τὸν δ' ἀπογενόμενον</u> παίζοντές τε καὶ ἡδόμενοι γῇ κρύπτουσι ('(The Trausoi) do as I will show at the seasons of birth and death. When a child is born, the kinsfolk ... lament, but the dead they bury with jollity and gladness', Hdt. 5.4.1-2)

The present participles τὸν γινόμενον and ἀπογινόμενον refer to the newborn and dead people iteratively ('the people that again and again are born and die', = 'every time someone is born or dies'), while the aorist participles τὸν γενόμενον and τὸν ἀπογενόμενον rather refer to these persons in a semelfactive way, that is, as single individuals ('the one that is born', 'the one that has died').

Note 1 When an articular participle is negated by μή it has a generalizing value, when the negation is οὐ it refers to a particular entity; cp. τὸν μὴ εἰδότα ('anyone who does not know that ...', Pl. R. 406c), as against τῷ οὐκ εἰδότι ('he who has no knowledge', Pl. Men. 85c, referring to the slave who has been questioned by Socrates). Cp. also § 29.3 (ii), on μή and οὐ in relative clauses.
Note 2 Without an article, too, participles may be used substantively: (ἔπλει ...) ἐπὶ πολλὰς ναῦς κεκτημένους ('against men who owned many ships').

(ii) The participle stands in apposition

In this use, which syntactically is similar to the use of the participle as a satellite, the participle functions as a modifier of a noun only, much like a - digressive - relative clause, and unlike satellite participles, which modify rather a state of affairs. Like digressive relative clauses, these participles follow their noun; they usually mention a (semi-)permanent feature of the 'antecedent' noun. Some examples:

(400) Ἀστυάγεα ... τὸν Κυαξάρεω, <u>ἐόντα</u> Κροίσου μὲν γαμβρόν, Μήδων δὲ βασιλέα, Κῦρος ... καταστρεψάμενος εἶχε ('For Cyrus had subdued Astyages, son of Cyaxares, Croesus' brother-in-law and king of Media, and held him in subjection', Hdt. 1.73.2; for (periphrastic?) καταστρεψάμενος εἶχε see above)

(401) ... ὁρῶ / Τέκμησσαν, οἴκτῳ τῷδε <u>συγκεκραμένην</u> ('I see Tecmessa, steeped in the anguish of that wail', S. *Ai.* 895)

(402) μετὰ ταῦτα Κῦρος ἐξελαύνει ... ἐπὶ τὸν Χάλον ποταμόν, <u>ὄντα</u> τὸ εὖρος πλέθρου ... ('After this Cyrus marched to the Chalus river, which is a plethrum in width ...', X. *An.* 1.4.9)

The participle ὄντα etc. in (402) may be compared with the relative clause οὗ etc. in (403):

(403) Ἐντεῦθεν ἐξελαύνει ... ἐπὶ τὸν Ψάρον ποταμόν, <u>οὗ</u> ἦν τὸ εὖρος τρία πλέθρα ('Thence he marched ... to the Psarus river, the width of which was three plethra', X. *An.* 1.4.1)

Note 3 Sometimes a participle can be analysed both as an apposition and as a satellite: Πρόξενον δὲ τὸν Βοιώτιον <u>ξένον ὄντα</u> ἐκέλευσε ... παραγενέσθαι ('(Cyrus) directed Proxenus, the Boeotian, who was a friend of his (or 'because he was a friend of his') ... to come to him', X. *An.* 1.1.11).

V VOICE: ACTIVE, MIDDLE AND PASSIVE

§ 41 Introduction

41.1 Voice defined

As we have seen, the main function of the tense stems is, to put it briefly, to indicate the temporal relationship between two or more states of affairs. The moods, on the other hand, were seen to express the attitude of the language user towards his utterance; this involves notions like factuality, possibility, etc. The indicative, moreover, also serves to locate a state of affairs in time, with regard to the moment of utterance. The third important grammatical category of the Greek verbal system is *voice*. Voice involves differences like those between English *John opened the door* (active voice) versus *The door was opened by John* (passive voice). In the former case the subject of the state of affairs is *John*; this means that John is marked as the 'primary vantage point' for the presentation of the state of affairs. In the latter case, however, where the subject is *The door*, the same state of affairs has *the door* as its primary vantage point. Voice, then, enables the language user to vary the *perspective* from which persons and other entities involved in a given state of affairs are presented. As we will see presently, the Greek voices have a number of other uses, where the notions 'reflexivity' and 'causativity' are of special importance.

> *Note 1* For the terms 'primary vantage point' and 'perspective' cp. Dik (1997: 247ff.). Although the 'primary vantage point' often coincides with the pragmatic function 'Topic', the two should be kept distinct, see the discussion in Dik (1997: 254-59). See also Lyons (1977: 511).
>
> *Note 2* In discussions of the middle, besides 'voice' the term 'diathesis' is sometimes used, to distinguish formal from semantic properties. Thus, English *John dressed quickly* is said to be, formally, in the active voice, but to exhibit, semantically, middle diathesis, unlike e.g. *John ate the cheese*, which is both in the active voice and exhibits active diathesis. In the first example *John*, apart from being the Agent, in some way is also the Patient of the state of affairs, in the second example he is only the Agent (for these terms see below, § 41.3). In what follows I shall only use the traditional term 'voice', the semantic differences being discussed in other terms.

Greek has three voices: active, middle and passive. It should, however, be added immediately, that the middle and passive voices are not formally distinguished, except in the aorist and, to some extent, in the future tense stems. Henceforth, the terms 'middle' and 'passive' will be used only in connection with aorist and future. In all other cases I will use the term 'middle-passive'.

41.2   The morphological features of the Greek voices

The various morphological features of the voices may, for the majority of Greek verbs, be exemplified by table 1 (p. 136). It should be noted that 'active', 'middle' and 'passive' are used here in a strictly morphological sense. Unfortunately, they are traditionally also used in a semantic sense, particularly 'passive'. As we will see later in more detail, not all passive forms have passive meaning, cp. e.g. ἐπορεύθην (passive aorist): 'I marched'. When dealing with semantics, I will always speak of 'passive meaning'.

41.3   Survey of grammatical terms

In this chapter the following grammatical terms will be used:
– *Agent*: the person who has the power to decide whether or not a state of affairs will obtain. He is, in technical terms, the *controller* of the state of affairs. Verbs involving an Agent are called *agentive* verbs. Thus, in English, *look for* and *leave* are agentive verbs (cp. *John decided to look for the letter, John decided to leave*), whereas *find* and *wake up* are not (cp. **John decided to find the letter, *John decided to wake up*);
– *Experiencer*: the, normally animate, entity which is internally affected by the state of affairs (*John* was afraid/woke up). By extension also with non-animate entities (*the snow* melted).
– *Patient* (also called *Goal*): the entity at which the state of affairs is directed (e.g. John looked for/opened/found *the letter*); often, the Patient is brought about by the state of affairs (John wrote *a letter*);
– *Beneficiary*: the entity, usually a person, which in some way or other benefits from the state of affairs. Beneficiaries only occur with agentive verbs (cp. John looked for the letter, *for Bill's sake*, as against: *John found the letter, *for Bill's sake*).

Agent, Experiencer, Patient and Beneficiary are *semantic functions*.

Table 1: Morphology of the Greek voice system (indicative)

TENSE-STEM VOICE	PRESENT	FUTURE	AORIST	PERFECT	FUTURE PERFECT
ACTIVE	παιδεύω στέλλω βάλλω δίδωμι	παιδεύσω στελῶ βαλῶ δώσω	ἐπαίδευσα ἔστειλα ἔβαλον ἔδωκα	πεπαίδευκα ἔσταλκα βέβληκα δέδωκα	(-ξω) cp. §12
MIDDLE	παιδεύομαι στέλλομαι	παιδεύσομαι στελοῦμαι βαλοῦμαι δώσομαι	ἐπαιδευσάμην ἐστειλάμην ἐβαλόμην ἐδόμην	πεπαίδευμαι ἔσταλμαι	πεπαιδεύσομαι (not attested)
PASSIVE	βάλλομαι δίδομαι	παιδευθήσομαι σταλήσομαι βληθήσομαι δοθήσομαι	ἐπαιδεύθην ἐστάλην ἐβλήθην ἐδόθην	βέβλημαι δέδομαι	βεβλήσομαι (not attested)

- *transitive* verbs: verbs that have two *arguments*, i.e. two obligatory constituents, the second of which has the semantic function Patient, e.g. *look for, open, write, find* (cp. *John looked for/opened/wrote/found the letter*).
- *intransitive* verbs: verbs that have only one argument, i.e. one obligatory constituent. *Leave* is an agentive, *wake up* a non-agentive intransitive verb (cp. *John left; John woke up*).

- *subject*: the constituent that is marked as the 'primary vantage point' for the presentation of a given state of affairs (cp. § 41.1). As such, the subject triggers concord, i.e. determines the form of the verb (cp. Engl.: the letter *was* opened/the letter*s* *were* opened by John). In Greek, the subject typically appears in the nominative;
- *object*: the constituent that is marked as the 'secondary vantage point' in the presentation of a given state of affairs. In Greek, the object typically appears in the accusative.

Subject and object are *syntactic functions*. They are especially relevant in the case of transitive verbs, since with these verbs the point of view may be varied: either the first argument or the Patient may be marked as the subject.

Note 1 To avoid terminological overloading, I shall often use 'object' for 'Patient-object'. - Transitive verbs are part of an overall class of verbs with two arguments, so-called two-place (also: bivalent) verbs. Other members of this class are, for instance, verbs with a Manner or a Locative argument, cp. *behave* (*John behaves* well) and *live* (*John lives* in Amsterdam), respectively. - Intransitive verbs are also called one-place or monovalent verbs. For a discussion of the notion 'valency' see Lyons (1977: 481ff.).

Note 2 Besides the transitive verbs discussed above, there are also transitive verbs with three arguments (so-called three-place (or trivalent) verbs). These verbs have a Patient and a third argument which may have various semantic functions. English examples are: *give* (*John gave the book* to Mary (Recipient)), *teach* (*Mary teaches John* music/to play the piano (Complement)).

41.4   Survey of the contents of §§ 42-48

Not all verbs have all three voices. Some verbs only have active, others only middle-passive forms. A third group has active as well as middle-passive forms, in which case the interpretation of the middle-passive forms depends both on the meaning and the syntactic features of the active verb (the term 'active verb' is used as shorthand for 'verb used in the active voice'), and on the syntactic features of the middle-passive forms themselves. Because the third group is the most important in terms of the number of the verbs concerned and the semantic varieties, it will be dealt with first. The discussion involves, successively, middle-passive forms with passive meaning (§ 42), direct-reflexive meaning (§ 43), indirect-reflexive meaning (§ 44), pseudo-reflexive and pseudo-passive meaning (§ 45). Next verbs with active forms only will be treated (§ 46), followed by verbs with middle-passive forms only (§ 47). The chapter ends with a summary of the various uses of the middle-passive voice (§ 48).

§ 42   Middle-passive forms of transitive active verbs, with passive meaning

42.1   The principle

Consider a sentence such as

(404) οἱ ᾿Αθηναῖοι παρασκευάζουσι τὰς ναῦς ('The Athenians are preparing the ships')

The Agent (: οἱ ᾿Αθηναῖοι) is presented as the subject (: nominative), and the Patient (: τὰς ναῦς) as the object (: accusative). The passive counterpart

(405) αἱ νῆες παρασκευάζονται ὑπὸ τῶν ᾿Αθηναίων ('The ships are being prepared by the Athenians')

refers to the same state of affairs. However, the Patient is now presented as the subject (: αἱ νῆες), whereas the Agent is expressed by a prepositional phrase (: ὑπὸ τῶν ᾿Αθηναίων). Most transitive verbs have middle-passive forms with passive meaning, or, in short, may be passivized, as exemplified by παρασκευάζω above. The aorist is of the passive type (cp. table 1 on page 136).

In this case, the passive interpretation of παρασκευάζονται is co-determined by the nature of the subject (a non-animate entity) and the presence of the ὑπό-phrase. In other contexts παρασκευάζονται may get quite different interpretations (cp. below § 43.1 and § 44.1).

42.2 Particulars

(i) In the case of some transitive verbs passive meaning is not, or not always, expressed by passive forms, but by lexical means, i.e. by active verbs that may have passive meaning. This holds e.g. for ἀποκτείνω 'kill': 'be killed' = ἀποθνῄσκω (lit. 'die'), not *ἀποκτείνομαι. A prepositional Agent-phrase may occur with such verbs:

(406) ἀδελφεοῦ τοῦ ἐμοῦ Πολυκράτεος ὑπὸ 'Οροίτεω ἀποθανόντος ('Because my brother Polycrates has been killed by Oroites', Hdt. 3.140.5)

So, too, φεύγω (lit. 'flee') ὑπό = 'be prosecuted/expelled by', with διώκω 'chase, prosecute'; ἐκπίπτω (lit. 'fall out') ὑπό = 'be thrown out by, be banished by', with ἐκβάλλω 'throw out, banish'; and some others.

(ii) Whereas with most active verbs the second argument is a Patient, characterized by the accusative, there are also verbs with a second argument in the genitive or the dative. These verbs allow passivization, in which case the genitive or dative of the active construction appears as the subject, and thus in the nominative. Among these verbs are: ὀλιγωρῶ τινος 'neglect', καταγελῶ τινος 'laugh at', ἄρχω τινός 'rule', φθονῶ τινι 'be jealous of', πιστεύω τινί 'trust', ἐπιχειρῶ τινι 'attempt', πολεμῶ τινι 'fight against', ἐπιβουλεύω τινί 'plot against', and others.
Two examples:

(407) ... ἐπιβουλευόμενοι διάξουσι πάντα τὸν βίον ('... being plotted against they will pass their days', Pl. R. 417b)
(408) νικῶν μὲν γὰρ οὐκ ἂν θαυμάζοιο, ἀλλὰ φθονοῖο ('For by winning you will be hated rather then admired', X. Hier. 11.6)

Note 1 It is a matter of dispute whether there are semantic differences between (accusative) Patients and second arguments in the genitive or dative. I will not go into these problems here. For details I refer to Mulder (1987).

(iii) The future is usually of the passive type (-(θ)ήσομαι). Not seldom, however, the middle future is found, with passive meaning, e.g. ζημιώσομαι 'I will be punished', διδάξομαι 'I will be taught', καλοῦμαι 'I will be called', etc. Exceptionally a middle aorist is used with passive meaning: in classical Greek only the middle aorist of the compounds of ἔχω (ἐσχόμην) regularly occurs with this meaning, e.g. Hdt. 7.128.2 (ἐνέσχετο ἐν 'was caught by'), E. *Hipp.* 27 (κατέσχετο + dat. 'was seized by'); the regular passive aorist, ἐσχέθην, is post-classical.

(iv) Three-place active verbs meaning 'ask', 'demand', 'teach', 'deprive, rob', 'conceal', 'put on/off' have - besides an Agent - a Patient and a Complement that are both characterized by the accusative (the 'verbs with double object' of traditional grammar). When these verbs are passivized, the Patient-constituent appears as the subject (: nominative), while the Complement is, again, characterized by the accusative (cp. English: 'I am taught a lesson'), e.g.: ἐρωτῶμαι τὴν γνώμην (lit. 'I am asked my opinion') 'my opinion is asked', διδάσκομαι μουσικήν 'I am taught music', ἀποστεροῦμαι τὴν ἀρχήν 'I am robbed of my power', κρύπτομαι τὴν ἀλήθειαν 'the truth is concealed from me', etc.

42.3 Particulars, continued: the choice between active and middle-passive (passive meaning)

As we have seen (cp. § 42.1), the active and middle-passive voices allow the language user to present a given state of affairs in two ways. Nevertheless, the active occurs far more frequently. This especially applies to states of affairs where an Agent is involved: as a rule, the Agent appears as the subject and the Patient as the object. Sentences of type (405), where the Patient appears as the subject and the Agent in a prepositional phrase, are exceptional. Compare, by way of an illustration, the figures of the following table:

Table 2:   The distribution of active and middle-passive forms with passive meaning of transitive verbs in Herodotus 8.83-95 (= ca. 6 pages Oxf. Class. Texts) and Plato, *Laches* 178a-182d5 (= almost 6 pp. OCT). See also Note 5.

	Active	Middle-passive with passive meaning	
		Agent expressed	Agent not expressed
Herodotus	79	2	22
Plato	95	3	6

From this table it appears that, of transitive verbs, the active forms outnumber the middle-passive ones in a proportion of 77% : 23% for Herodotus, and 92% : 8% for Plato. It is also clear that an explicit Agent is, indeed, rare. The middle-passive with passive meaning is, in fact, predominantly used when there is no identifiable Agent, as in (407) and (408) ('by people', in general) or when the Agent is easily recoverable from the context. In the latter case, the passive presentation has the advantage of assuring 'topic continuity', as in:

(409) <u>οἱ Λακεδαιμόνιοι</u> ... ἐπὶ Τεγεήτας ἐστρατεύοντο ..., ὡς δὴ ἐξανδραποδιούμενοι τοὺς Τεγεήτας. <u>ἑσσωθέντες</u> δὲ τῇ συμβολῇ, ὅσοι αὐτῶν <u>ἐζωγρήθησαν</u> ... τὸ πεδίον τὸ Τεγεητέων ἐργάζοντο
('The Lacedaemonians ... marched against the men of Tegea, ... convinced that they would enslave the Tegeans. But they were worsted in the encounter, and those of them who were taken captive had to till the Tegean plain', Hdt. 1.66.3-4)

The Agents of the Spartan defeat (ἑσσωθέντες in the second sentence) are, of course, the Tegeans. To mention them explicitly, either by means of a prepositional phrase or through a presentation in the active voice, would be redundant, indeed pedantic. An 'active presentation' would, moreover, shift the attention of the reader to the Tegeans and thus completely mislead him as to the main point of the story, since it is the vicissitudes of the Spartans which are at stake.

Note 1 A number of active verbs, both transitive and intransitive, have a middle future. This phenomenon will be discussed in more detail in § 46.2.

Note 2 The passive is favoured especially with states of affairs in the *perfect* tense: it is the resulting state which counts, the preceding action and thus the Agent are of secondary importance. Cp. also § 43.2 (iii).

Note 3 In those cases where an Agent is expressed, he is, generally speaking, less important than the Patient-subject. If, in such a case, the Agent were to appear as the subject, the wrong element would be marked as the 'primary vantage point' (cp. § 41).

Note 4 Most Agent-phrases consist of ὑπό + genitive (pro-)nouns. Other prepositions used are ἐκ + genitive and πρός + genitive. (Pro-)nouns in the dative also occur, especially with the perfect. Natural forces may function as a 'pseudo-Agent' ('pseudo-', since they have no control over the state of affairs); they may appear in a ὑπό-phrase or in the dative. E.g. ὑπ' ἀνέμων ἀπενεχθείς ('having been carried away by the winds').

Note 5 Table 2 includes active constructions with accusative, genitive and dative second arguments, as well as active constructions with a Patient and a Complement ('double object'). Also, of course, their passive counterparts. Constructions with a dependent 'object'- or 'subject'-clause, e.g. of verbs of saying, are not included. - The totals for *all* active forms as opposed to middle-passive forms are shown in the following table:

	Active	Middle-passive		
Herodotus	181 (61%)	118 (39%)		
		passive meaning	direct-reflexive, indirect-refl., pseudo-refl. and pseudo-passive meaning	middle-passive forms only
		24 (20%)	40 (34%)	54 (46%)
Plato	170 (67%)	84 (33%)		
		9 (11%)	27 (32%)	48 (57%)

§ 42.4 *Excursus: verbal adjectives*

Passive meaning is also expressed by the so-called verbal adjectives, adjectives derived from verb stems. Two types may be distinguished: (a) adjectives in -τος, -τη, -τον; (b) adjectives in -τέος, -τέα, -τέον.

The adjectives in -τος etc. either express a passive state, comparable to the English perfect passive participle, e.g. κρυπτός 'hidden', ἀφύλακτος 'unguarded', or express that the state of affairs can or deserves to be done, comparable to Engl. adjectives in -able/-ible, e.g. διαβατός 'fordable', ἄρρητος 'not to be divulged', ἐπαινετός 'laudable'. Many adjectives have both meanings, e.g. διδακτός 'taught' and 'which can be taught'; ἄγνωστος 'unknown' and 'unknowable'. They are real adjectives, since (1) they form adverbs, (2) have degrees of comparison, and may be used (3) both attributively and (4) predicatively.

> Note 1 The meaning 'that which can be done' may have developed out of the passive state meaning 'that which has been done': the state has become an inherent property. Thus, an ἀνὴρ πιστός, a man that has been trusted, turns into a man that can be trusted. Compare, indeed, Engl. *trusted* 'reliable' etc.
>
> Note 2 Besides their passive meaning(s), some verbal adjectives in -τος have an active meaning, e.g. δυνατός 'which can be done, possible', but also 'capable, powerful', ἄπρακτος 'not done', 'against which nothing can be done', 'from which nothing can be gained', but also 'unsuccessful'.

The adjectives in -τέος, -τέα, -τέον express a (passive) necessity, comparable to the Latin gerundivum (*agenda* - 'the things that must be done'). The Agent usually appears in the dative (*dativus auctoris*). They are not adjectives in the full sense, since they lack the first three features mentioned above for adjectives in -τος, i.e., they are only used predicatively.

From two-place verbs (for this notion cp. § 41.3, Note 1) both a personal and an impersonal verbal adjective occur. An example of the former:

(410)   οὐκοῦν δῆλον ὅτι ... ὠφελητέα σοι ἡ πόλις ἐστίν (Lit.: 'Clearly, then, the city must be benefitted by you', X. *Mem.* 3.6.3; ἡ πόλις is Patient-subject, cp. ἡ πόλις ὠφελεῖται)

In the impersonal use the adjective appears in the neuter singular (-τέον) or, less often, in the neuter plural (-τέα). The copula ἐστί is often lacking. The Patient noun has the case form required by the corresponding verb, as in:

(411) εἴτε τοὺς θεοὺς ἵλεως εἶναί σοι βούλει, <u>θεραπευτέον τοὺς θεούς</u>
('If you want the favour of the gods, you must worship the gods',
X. *Mem.* 2.1.28; τοὺς θεούς is Patient-object, cp. θεραπεύω τινά)

(412) λόγος ... προείργαστο αὐτοῖς ὡς ... οὔτε <u>μεθεκτέον τῶν</u>
<u>πραγμάτων</u> πλέοσιν ἢ πεντακισχιλίοις (' ... a proposal had been
made that not more than five thousand should share in the
government', Th. 8.65.3; τῶν πραγμάτων is (partitive) Patient-
object, cp. μετέχω τινός)

> *Note 3* Not seldom the Agent appears in the accusative, on the analogy of
> constructions like δεῖ and χρή + accusative plus infinitive (cp. § 33.1); thus
> the οὔτε-clause quoted at (412) is preceded by οὔτε <u>μισθοφορητέον</u> εἴη
> <u>ἄλλους</u> ἢ τοὺς στρατευομένους λόγος ('(a proposal had been made that)
> no others ought to receive pay except those who were serving in the war').

From one-place (intransitive) verbs naturally only the impersonal use
occurs. An example:

(413) σοὶ <u>βαδιστέον</u> πάρος ('You must go first', S. *El.* 1502)

§ 43 Middle-passive forms of transitive active verbs, with direct-reflexive meaning

43.1   The principle

The middle-passive forms may indicate that the Agent applies the state of
affairs to himself; the Patient refers, then, to the same person as the Agent,
in other words, he is *co-referential* with the Agent (*direct-reflexive use*).
The Patient is not expressed lexically but is incorporated in the verb form.
The aorist and future are of the middle type.

This use is limited to a small group of agentive verbs, which have in
common that they denote a *habitual physical treatment*, i.e. a treatment
which forms part of the more or less normal practice of everyday life (also
called verbs of *grooming*). When the state of affairs is applied to an entity
other than the Agent, the active voice is used. Some examples of this
direct-reflexive use of the middle-passive voice are, notably: λοῦμαι/
λούομαι 'bathe (oneself)', ἀπονίζομαι 'wash oneself', particularly 'wash
one's hands', καθαίρομαι 'purify oneself', ζώννυμαι 'gird oneself',

ξυροῦμαι 'shave oneself'; κοσμοῦμαι 'adorn oneself'; κνῶμαι 'scratch oneself', δέφομαι 'rub oneself, masturbate', ἀλείφομαι 'anoint oneself', ἀπομύττομαι 'blow one's nose', ἀποψῶμαι 'wipe one's nose'; in the military sphere: παρασκευάζομαι 'prepare oneself', τάττομαι 'draw oneself up', γυμνάζομαι 'train (oneself)'; διατείνομαι 'exert oneself'; in the sphere of mourning rituals: κείρομαι 'cut off one's hair', κόπτομαι 'beat oneself'. Some instances of the direct-reflexive as opposed to the active use are:

(414) αἰσθόμενοι δὲ αὐτοὺς οἱ 'Αθηναῖοι ... παρασκευαζομένους ('When the Athenians perceived that they (sc. the enemy) were preparing themselves ...', Th. 3.16.1)

(415) ὕστερον δὲ ναυτικὸν παρεσκεύαζον ὅτι πέμψουσιν (cp. § 29.3 (viii)) ἐς τὴν Λέσβον ('Later, however, they prepared a fleet in order to send it to Lesbos', Th. 3.16.3)

(416) ὡς δὲ κατεῖδον ἀλλήλους, ἀντιπαρετάσσοντο ('When they saw one another, they drew themselves up in hostile array', Th. 1.48.3)

(417) ἐπὶ δ' αὐτῷ εἴκοσιν (sc. ναῦς) ἔταξαν τὰς ἄριστα πλεούσας ('Upon this (sc. wing) they placed their twenty best sailing ships', Th. 2.90.2)

(418) οὐκ ἐλούσατ' ἐξ ὅτουπερ ἐγένετο ('He has not bathed since he was born', Ar. Pl. 85)

(419) πρῶτον μὲν αὐτὸν ἐπὶ θάλατταν ἤγομεν, ἔπειτ' ἐλοῦμεν ('First we took him to the sea, then bathed him', Ar. Pl. 656-7)

43.2 Particulars

(i) To the verbs listed above also belongs ἀπάγχομαι 'hang oneself', apparently a common form of suicide.

(ii) With verbs other than those given above, e.g. with verbs denoting a state of affairs which the Agent does not normally apply to himself, reflexivity is expressed by the active verb and the reflexive pronoun. Two examples:

(420) ῥίπτει αὐτὸν εἰς τὴν θάλατταν ('He threw himself into the sea', D. 32.6)

(421) ἐπικατασφάζει τῷ τύμβῳ ἑωυτόν ('He slew himself by the sepulchre', Hdt. 1.45.3)

(iii) The only tense which unequivocally expresses a direct-reflexive state of affairs is the middle aorist (ἐλουσάμην, etc.). The middle-passive forms of the other tenses may also have passive meaning. Here the interpretation must be based on the context. Thus, λουόμενος has passive meaning in

(422) εὐδαίμων ἄρ᾽ ἦν / ... ψυχρᾷ θαλάττῃ <u>λουόμενος</u> ('O what a happy man, bathed in the cold sea', Ar. *Pl.* 657-8)

because we know from the preceding line that someone else was bathing him, cp. (419) above.

Sometimes the distinction between the two interpretations is irrelevant, especially in the case of passive perfects and pluperfects. Cp.

(423) τὸν υἱὸν ... εὑρὼν ἀπιόντ᾽ ἀπὸ γυμνασίου <u>λελουμένον</u> ('After meeting my son when he, having (been) bathed, returned from the baths', Ar. *Av.* 139-40)

(424) κατὰ μὲν δὴ ᾽Αθηναίους <u>ἐτετάχατο</u> Φοίνικες ('Opposite to the Athenians the Phoenicians were arrayed', Hdt. 8.85.1)

The Phoenicians may have arrayed themselves or they may have been arrayed (by the king or by their commanders); the important thing is that they stood there in array, while the Agent is of secondary importance. The same holds for (423).

The passive aorist and future (ἐλούθην, λουθήσομαι, etc.), of course, only have passive meaning.

Note 1 The verbs of § 43.1 take a reflexive pronoun and appear in the middle-passive or, more often, in the active voice, when the state of affairs is applied to the Agent himself as well as to others, e.g. ὁπότε <u>γυμνάσαι</u> βούλοιτο <u>ἑαυτόν τε καὶ τοὺς ἵππους</u> ('Whenever he wanted to train himself as well as his horses', X. *An.* 1.2.7). This occurs also in cases of contrast.

Note 2 To some of the verbs of § 43.1 a constituent may be added specifying the part of the body to which the state of affairs is applied. This constituent appears in the accusative (the so-called *accusative of respect*), e.g. ἀλειψαμένη <u>τὸ σῶμ᾽</u> ὅλον ('Having anointed my whole body', Ar. *Ec.* 63). Cp. French: *Je me lave les mains*, etc.

Note 3 When the subject of a middle-passive form is inanimate only a passive interpretation is, of course, possible: τὸ πλοῖον παρεσκευάζετο 'the ship was made ready'. Cp. § 42.1, end.

Note 4 Some of these middle-passives are also found with an external Patient, in which case they have indirect-reflexive meaning, e.g. κόπτομαι ξύλον 'I cut wood (in my own interest)'. See next section.

Note 5 The direct-reflexive meaning of the middle aorist of the verbs of grooming was recognized in antiquity, as appears from the following remark by the lexicographer Phrynichus (item 292 in Rutherford's edition): τὸ μὲν (viz. καρῆναι and ἐκάρην) ἐπὶ προβάτων τιθέασι, κείρασθαι δὲ ἐπὶ ἀνθρώπων ('"My hair was cut off" (lit. "I was shorn") is used for sheep, "to cut off one's hair" for people').

§ 44 Middle-passive forms of transitive active verbs, with indirect-reflexive meaning

44.1 The principle

In the case of many agentive transitive active verbs the middle-passive forms indicate that the Agent has a special interest in the state of affairs in which he is involved; frequently, he is the Beneficiary of that state of affairs (*indirect-reflexive use*). Syntactically, this use is characterized by the fact that, in principle, an object is present. Aorist and future are of the middle type (cp. table 1).

The corresponding active constructions do not indicate in whose interest the Agent is carrying out the state of affairs; usually, it is in the interest of others.

Some typical examples are:

(425) πλοῖα καὶ ἐπικούρους παρασκευασάμενοι διέβησαν ἐς τὴν νῆσον ('Having procured ships and allies they crossed over to the island', Th. 3.85.3)

(426) ναυτικὸν παρεσκεύαζον ὅτι πέμψουσιν ἐς τὴν Λέσβον ('They prepared a fleet in order to send it to Lesbos', Th. 3.16.3)

(427) ἀπὸ ὀλυρέων ποιεῦνται σιτία ('They make food from a coarse grain', Hdt. 2.36.2)

(428) οἱ ἀστοὶ ἄλευρά τε καὶ ἄλφιτα ἐποίευν ('The townsmen all prepared wheaten and barley meal', Hdt. 7.119.2)

In (425) the middle aorist indicates that the Agent has prepared the ships and the allies for his own benefit: he himself will have them at his disposal; in (426), on the other hand, the fleet is to support the Lesbians. Similarly, in (427), the Agent himself profits from the food he prepares, while in (428) the food is made for the Persian king.

44.2   Particulars

(i) The indirect-reflexive use is confined to verbs expressing a state of affairs which has no marked preference with regard to the person interested: it may be the Agent himself no less than some other person. On the other hand, verbs which express a state of affairs from which, normally speaking, only the Agent benefits do not form an indirect-reflexive middle-passive. This holds for, e.g.: πίνω 'drink', ἀνοίγω 'open (the door)', πολιορκῶ 'besiege', etc.

(ii) With the active forms the Beneficiary is usually implicitly present in the context. Sometimes, however, an explicit Beneficiary (appearing in the dative) is needed to avoid misunderstanding. This especially applies to infinitives with verbs of commanding, since in this case at least two persons are involved.

Cp. an example like:

(429)   ἀπέπεμπε κήρυκας ἐς τὴν Ἑλλάδα ... προερέοντας <u>δεῖπνα</u> <u>βασιλέϊ παρασκευάζειν</u> ('He sent heralds to Hellas ... to command the preparation of meals for the king', Hdt. 7.32)

Without βασιλέϊ the Beneficiary would be the heralds themselves (with παρασκευάζεσθαι it would be the persons receiving the order, i.e. the inhabitants of the various Greek cities).

(iii) When, for some reason or other, the Beneficiary is emphasized (e.g. in a case of contrast), the reflexive pronoun is added to the middle-passive forms, as in:

(430)   οὐκ ἄρα τυραννίδα χρὴ ... <u>παρασκευάζεσθαι</u> οὔθ' <u>ἑαυτῷ</u> οὔτε <u>τῇ πόλει</u> ('Then it is not despotic power that you ought to secure, either to yourself or to the state', Pl. Alc. I 135b)

The active voice + reflexive pronoun may also be used in this way.

(iv) The active voice may express professional activities, i.e. activities which inherently benefit others rather than the Agent himself (cp. also examples (427) - (428)). Thus in the following example the craftsmen are the Agents, for the benefit of the people:

(431) ... Καλλάτηβον πόλιν, ἐν τῇ ἄνδρες δημιοργοὶ <u>μέλι</u> ἐκ μυρίκης τε καὶ πυροῦ <u>ποιεῦσι</u> ('... the town of Callatebus, where craftsmen make honey out of wheat and tamarisks', Hdt. 7.31)

whereas in

(432) = (427) ... ἀπὸ ὀλυρέων <u>ποιεῦνται σιτία</u> ('... they make food from a coarse grain', Hdt. 2.36.2)

it is the people itself which is the Agent, for its own benefit.

(v) Verbal nouns (also called action nouns and *nomina actionis*), i.e. nouns which express a state of affairs, are often combined with the middle-passive voice of ποιῶ 'make' to form a periphrastic construction equivalent to the verb corresponding with the verbal noun.

Two examples:

(433) τότε μέν νυν οὐκ ἐξέχρησέ σφι ἡ ἡμέρη <u>ναυμαχίην ποιήσασθαι</u> ('That day there was not time enough left to offer (sea-)battle', Hdt. 8.70.1)

(434) ... τὰ Σοῦσα ταῦτα, ἔνθα βασιλεύς τε μέγας <u>δίαιταν ποιέεται</u> ('... that Susa, where the Great King resides', Hdt. 5.49.7)

ναυμαχίην ποιοῦμαι = ναυμαχῶ, δίαιταν ποιοῦμαι = διαιτῶμαι etc. In these cases, the Agent's interest in the state of affairs is one of active participation: he is the Agent of the state of affairs denoted by the noun rather than merely the Beneficiary. When, on the other hand, the active of ποιῶ is construed with a verbal noun the Agent need not be actively involved in the state of affairs denoted by that noun, as in:

(435) ... καὶ ὅστις μὴ τοῖς δεξαμένοις, εἰ σωφρονοῦσι, <u>πόλεμον</u> ἀντ' εἰρήνης <u>ποιήσει</u> ('... and anyone who to those who received him will not - if they are prudent - bring war instead of peace', Th. 1.40.2)

πόλεμον ποιῶ = 'to bring about war for others', 'to involve in war'. So, too, εἰρήνην ποιῶ 'bring about peace', between others; εἰρήνην ποιοῦμαι 'make peace', with an enemy. Cp. also ἄρχω : ἄρχω τοῦ λόγου 'to open a conversation' (e.g. X. *An.* 1.6.6) alongside ἄρχομαι τοῦ λόγου 'to begin one's speech' (e.g. X. *An.* 3.2.7); ἄρχω πολέμου 'to be the aggressor' (e.g. Th. 1.53.4): ἄρχομαι πολέμου 'begin one's operations' (e.g. X. *HG* 6.3.6).

(vi) In many cases the indirect-reflexive middle-passive has acquired a more or less specialized (idiomatic) meaning. Some examples:

ἀποδίδωμι 'give back'	:	ἀποδίδομαι 'sell'
γράφω τι 'write'	:	γράφομαί τινα 'indict'
συμβάλλω 'throw together'	:	συμβάλλομαι 'compare'
ἐπαγγέλλω 'proclaim'	:	ἐπαγγέλλομαι 'promise'; 'profess'
αἱρῶ 'take'	:	αἱροῦμαι 'choose'
φυλάττω 'guard'	:	φυλάττομαι 'be on one's guard'
ἅπτω 'fasten'	:	ἅπτομαι 'grasp (+ genit.)
ἀντιποιῶ 'do in return'	:	ἀντιποιοῦμαι 'seek after' (+ genit.)
γαμῶ γυναῖκα 'marry a woman'	:	γαμοῦμαι ἀνδρί 'marry a man'

From the last three examples it appears that the syntax may also change. Such middle-passives, whose meaning can not, or not easily, be derived from the active voice, belong to the lexicon rather than to the grammar.

Note 1 Sometimes the active and middle-passive voice have roughly the same meaning, e.g. βουλεύω τι and βουλεύομαί τι 'deliberate on', 'plan', 'devise'. Cp. δρησμὸν ἐβούλευον (v.l. -οντο; 'they planned flight', Hdt. 8.4.1) and δρησμὸν βουλεύονται ('they are planning flight', Hdt. 8.75.2).
Note 2 It testifies to the independence of some of the idiomatic middle-passives that they may have a passive aorist with passive meaning corresponding to the 'middle' meaning, e.g. ᾑρέθη 'he was chosen' (: εἵλοντο αὐτόν 'they chose him'), ἐγράφη 'he was indicted', etc. The perfect-tense forms may have a comparable passive meaning, e.g. ᾕρηται 'he has been chosen' (: 'middle' ᾕρηνται αὐτόν 'they have chosen him'), etc. Of course, these passive aorists may also correspond with the active forms (ᾑρέθη 'he was taken', cp. εἷλον αὐτόν 'they took him', etc.).

§ 45 Middle-passive forms of transitive active verbs, with pseudo-reflexive or pseudo-passive meaning

45.1 The principle

Greek has a large number of so-called *causative* verbs, i.e. verbs which denote a state of affairs by means of which an Agent-subject causes a change in the mental or physical situation of a Patient-object. The middle-passive forms of these verbs express either that the subject changes his own mental or physical situation - in this case he has the function Agent (*pseudo-reflexive use*) - or that a change comes about in his situation; in the latter case he is not the Agent, since he does not control the change, but rather an Experiencer (*pseudo-passive use*). In principle, these middle-passives have no second argument; they are, then, mostly used intransitively. Generally, they have an aorist and future of the passive type (cp. table 1). Verbs belonging to this category are, for instance:

agentive middle-passive

ἀπαλλάττω 'remove'	ἀπαλλάττομαι 'depart', 'go away'
ἀνάγω 'lead up to the high sea'	ἀνάγομαι 'put out to sea', 'set sail'
κλίνω 'cause to lean', 'make (someone) recline'	κλίνομαι 'lean', 'recline' (also used non-agentively)
κομίζω 'carry', 'convey'	κομίζομαι 'journey', 'travel'
ἀγείρω 'gather together'	ἀγείρομαι 'gather', 'assemble'
στέλλω 'dispatch', 'send'; 'make ready'	στέλλομαι 'set out', 'journey'; 'get ready'
στρέφω 'turn about'	στρέφομαι 'turn'
πορεύω 'make to go', 'convey'	πορεύομαι 'go', 'walk', 'march'
ἵστημι 'make to stand', 'set up'. So, too, the compound verbs: ἀφίστημι etc.	ἵσταμαι 'stand', 'get up', 'stand still'

non-agentive middle-passive

φοβῶ 'frighten', 'terrify'	φοβοῦμαι 'be seized by fear', 'be affrighted'

ἐκπλήττω 'astound', 'shock'	ἐκπλήττομαι 'be astounded', 'be shocked'
ἐγείρω 'awaken', 'rouse'	ἐγείρομαι 'wake up'
ῥήγνυμι 'break asunder', 'shatter'	ῥήγνυμαι 'break asunder', 'burst'
πείθω 'persuade', 'prevail upon'	πείθομαι 'be won over', 'listen', 'obey'
τρέφω 'cause to grow', 'bring up'	τρέφομαι 'grow up'
χέω 'pour out', 'let flow'	χέομαι 'become liquid', 'melt'
σήπω 'make rotten'	σήπομαι 'rot', 'moulder'

Some examples, both of the active and the middle-passive use:

(436) ἐτύγχανε ... <u>στρατιὰν</u> μέλλων ... <u>πορεύσειν</u> ὡς Βρασίδαν ('It happened that he was going to take an army to join Brasidas', Th. 4.132.2)

(437) Δαρεῖος ... <u>ἐπορεύετο</u> διὰ τῆς Θρηίκης ('Darius journeyed through Thrace', Hdt. 4.89.2)

(438) ἐκέλευε ... <u>τοὺς Πελοποννησίους ἀπαλλάξαι</u> ἐκ τῆς χώρας ('He ordered (him) to get the Spartans out of the country', Th. 8.46.4)

(439) οὗτος μέν νυν ὁ στόλος αἰσχρῶς ἀγωνισάμενος <u>ἀπηλλάχθη</u> ἐς τὴν 'Ασίην ('This expedition then after an inglorious adventure returned back to Asia', Hdt. 6.45.2)

(440) ... ὡς χρὴ ... <u>ἀποστῆσαι τὴν Λέσβον</u> ('... that it was necessary (for them) to bring about the revolt of Lesbos', Th. 8.32.3)

(441) Λεσβίων ἀφικνοῦνται πρέσβεις βουλόμενοι αὖθις <u>ἀποστῆναι</u> ('Envoys of the Lesbians arrived proposing to renew their revolt', Th. 8.32.1)

(442) πῶς δῆτ' ἂν ἥδιστ' <u>αὐτὸν ἐπεγείραιμ'</u>; ('Now how might I get him up in the nicest way?', Ar. Nu. 79)

(443) ἀλλ' οὐδ' ὁ χρηστὸς οὑτοσὶ νεανίας <u>ἐγείρεται</u> τῆς νυκτός ('But this fine young man here won't wake up during the night', Ar. Nu. 8-9)

(444) οἱ δὲ Πέρσαι <u>καταρρήξαντες τὴν κρυπτὴν γέφυραν</u> ἔθεον ἐς τὸ τεῖχος ('But the Persians broke down the hidden bridge and ran to the city', Hdt. 4.201.3)

(445) τὸ δὲ οἴκημα λαβὸν μεῖζον ἄχθος ἐξαπίνης <u>κατερράγη</u> ('But the house, being over-weighted, suddenly collapsed', Th. 4.115.3)

45.2   Particulars

(i) Whereas, in the active examples, it is the Agent who brings about the change, the Patient, too, may be actively involved in that change, at least if it refers to a human being. Thus, in (438), the removal of the Spartans by the Agent necessarily entails active participation on the part of the Spartans. In (444), on the other hand, no action is to be expected, of course, on the part of the Patient. The latter also holds for verbs like ἐγείρω 'wake', φοβῶ 'terrify', although they have a human Patient: the Patient cannot be expected to really 'do' something. All this has some consequences for the middle-passive forms: when the Patient of the active construction cannot possibly be actively involved in the change, the corresponding middle-passive forms are of the non-agentive type.

(ii) Above (p. 151) the semantic function of the subject with non-agentive middle-passives was called 'Experiencer' (for a definition cp. p. 135). In fact, most of these verbs (which have no object) express the idea that the state of affairs occurred all in the subject, cp. e.g. ἐγείρομαι 'wake up', σήπομαι 'rot', 'moulder'. (Cp. also Note 1 below.) However, to a few verbs that express an emotional affection an object may be added, e.g. φοβοῦμαι βρόμον 'fear the thunder'; ἐκπλήττομαί τινα 'be struck with panic fear of'.

(iii) Not all middle-passives have a passive aorist and future. Thus, ἵσταμαι has intransitive ἔστην, the passive aorist ἐστάθην usually having passive meaning; alongside ἠγέρθην (: ἐγείρομαι) we also find a thematic middle aorist ἠγρόμην, etc. The future is often of the middle type: πορεύσομαι, φοβήσομαι, etc.

(iv) The middle-passive and passive forms may also have *passive* meaning, most clearly when a ὑπό-phrase is present. Cp.:

(445a) ἐκ τῆς Αἰγύπτου <u>σταλέντες ὑπὸ</u> 'Αρυανδέω ('having been sent from Egypt by Aryandes', Hdt. 4.200.1)

(v) Many of the verbs listed above also have middle-passive forms with indirect-reflexive meaning, viz. when they are construed with a Patient-object. The aorist is, in this case, of the middle type. E.g.:

(446) τὸν ἀνδριάντα ... Θηβαῖοι ... ἐκομίσαντο ἐπὶ Δήλιον ('The Thebans ... brought the statue to Delium (in their own interest)', Hdt. 6.118.3)

Note 1 It will be clear from the above discussion that there are fundamental differences between direct-reflexive middle-passives, as discussed in § 43, and the middle-passives of causative verbs, although they are often treated on a par. To name only one important difference, with the first group the active voice never has the semantic feature 'cause to'. This may be illustrated by the different entailments of the active voice. Whereas e.g. ἀπήλλαξα αὐτόν 'I removed him' entails ἀπηλλάχθη 'he was removed' *or* 'he went off', ἔλουσα αὐτόν 'I bathed him' *only* entails ἐλούθη 'he was bathed', *not* ἐλούσατο 'he took a bath'. - The agentive middle-passive voice of causative verbs is said to have 'pseudo-reflexive' meaning for want of a better term, to simply distinguish it from 'direct-reflexive'. The notion 'reflexivity' would not seem to be wholly irrelevant, however, with this use. (Observe that 'direct-reflexive' meaning occurs only with agentive verbs (§ 43.1)). In the case of non-agentive middle-passives, where the subject is internally affected, I speak of 'pseudo-passive' meaning, since 'internal affection' and 'passive meaning' are related notions. Both imply that the subject undergoes a state of affairs, in the latter case with, in the former without, an Agent. In the linguistic literature non-agentive middle-passive verbs are sometimes called 'anti-causatives' or 'verbs of spontaneous events'.

Note 2 There are also syntactic differences between the two types. Whereas with direct-reflexive middle-passives an incorporated Patient-object is involved, this is not the case with pseudo-reflexives. This appears from the fact that with the first group the Patient-object may be expressed explicitly by means of the middle-passive or the active voice plus a reflexive pronoun in the accusative, e.g. in cases of contrasted objects; cp. ὁπότε γυμνάσαι βούλοιτο ἑαυτόν τε καὶ τοὺς ἵππους (X. *An.* 1.2.7, see § 43.2, Note 1). With pseudo-reflexives, however, contrast is effected by adding the oppositive adjective αὐτός in the *nominative* to the middle-passive forms, as in (from περαιῶ 'carry over'): διαπεραιοῦται αὐτός τε καὶ ἡ στρατιὰ ἐς Χίον ('He crossed over with his army to Chios', Th. 8.32.2).

Note 3 Greek grammars often mention another type of causative verbs, viz. the denominative verbs in -όω, e.g. δουλόω, ἐλευθερόω, also called 'factitive' verbs. The semantics of these verbs are quite different from the verbs discussed in the present section. While causative verbs like ἀπαλλάττω entail that the Patient-object is involved in a state of affairs (cp.

the entailment of ἀπήλλαξα αὐτόν mentioned in Note 1: as a result of my action someone is removed or goes off), the entailment of a verb like δουλόω is that the Patient-object is provided with the property denoted by (the nominal base of) the verb stem: ἐδούλωσα αὐτόν 'I made him a slave'; as a result of my action he is a slave. This means, in turn, that the middle-passive forms of these verbs are never used intransitively but only as passives. In terms of entailments: ἐδούλωσα αὐτόν only entails 'he was made a slave'. To avoid confusion the denominative verbs should perhaps exclusively be called 'factitive'.

Note 4 Some causative verbs are used intransitively in the active voice, with approximately the same meaning as the corresponding middle-passive. Thus, for instance, ἀπαλλάττω 'get off', especially 'escape'.

Note 5 Some middle-passive verbs differentiate in the aorist between a non-agentive passive aorist, and an agentive middle aorist. E.g. ψεύδομαι 'be mistaken' and 'cheat by lies': ἐψεύσθην 'be mistaken'; ἐψευσάμην 'lie', 'cheat'.

Note 6 With most verbs the change has a terminative value. In these cases the perfect expresses the result of the change: ἀπήλλαγμαι 'be gone', ἕστηκα (see next Note) 'stand', 'be stationary', ἐγρήγορα 'be awake', etc.

Note 7 A number of pseudo-reflexive and pseudo-passive middle-passives have an active perfect, e.g. φαίνομαι : πέφηνα; πήγνυμαι : πέπηγα; ἵσταμαι : ἕστηκα; ἐγείρομαι : ἐγρήγορα (besides ἐγήγερμαι), etc.

Note 8 The analysis of causative verbs presented above has a strictly synchronic basis. Historically things may have been different. The formation of active forms is probably a secondary development with respect to that of the middle-passive forms, since the active forms presuppose the existence of the middle-passive forms (cp. the entailment analysis presented in Note 1). Also, in many cases the middle-passive forms are attested (much) earlier and are more frequent than the active forms.

§ 46 Verbs with active forms only (so-called *activa tantum*)

46.1 *The principle*

Intransitive verbs (agentive or non-agentive), in principle, do not have middle-passive forms. This holds for e.g.: γελῶ 'laugh', νοσῶ 'be ill', νοστῶ 'return', πίπτω 'fall', μένω 'stay', βαίνω 'walk', γηθῶ 'rejoice', ὄζω 'smell', δακρύω 'weep', etc.

46.2   Particulars

Many intransitive active verbs, as well as a number of transitive ones, have, either exclusively or predominantly, a middle future. This group consists of verbs denoting essential functions of body and mind, e.g.

- verbs of sound such as ᾄδω : ᾄσομαι, βοῶ : βοήσομαι, γελῶ : γελάσομαι, κλαίω : κλαύσομαι, οἰμώζω : οἰμώξομαι, also their converse: σιγῶ : σιγήσομαι; to this group belongs perhaps also θαυμάζω : θαυμάσομαι;
- verbs of 'excretion' like ἐμῶ : ἐμοῦμαι, ἐρυγγάνω : ἐρεύξομαι, οὐρῶ : οὐρήσομαι, τίκτω : τεκοῦμαι, χέζω : χεσοῦμαι;
- verbs of grasping and taking (in), both mentally and physically, like ἀκούω : ἀκούσομαι, γιγνώσκω : γνώσομαι, μανθάνω : μαθήσομαι, οἶδα : εἴσομαι, ὁρῶ : ὄψομαι; δάκνω : δήξομαι, ἐσθίω : ἔδομαι, πίνω : πίομαι; λαγχάνω : λήξομαι, λαμβάνω : λήψομαι, τυγχάνω : τεύξομαι, also the converse of the latter: ἁμαρτάνω : ἁμαρτήσομαι;
- verbs of movement, e.g. βαδίζω : βαδιοῦμαι, βαίνω : βήσομαι, διώκω : διώξομαι, θέω : θεύσομαι, νέω : νεύσομαι, πίπτω : πεσοῦμαι, πλέω : πλεύσομαι, φεύγω : φεύξομαι;
- verbs of bodily affections, like γηράσκω : γηράσομαι, θνήσκω : θανοῦμαι, κάμνω : καμοῦμαι, πάσχω : πείσομαι; perhaps in this class also βιῶ : βιώσομαι, εἰμι : ἔσομαι, πνέω : πνεύσομαι.

This phenomenon is not easy to explain. Historically, the following may have happened (I owe this hypothesis to C.J. Ruijgh). The suffix -σε/σο- of these middle futures originally had a desiderative value (cp. English *will*). Being desiderative, these forms had a preference for middle endings, to emphasize the involvement of the subject in the state of affairs. When these desideratives entered into the verbal system, expressing future time, they were associated with middle-passive present forms. This, in turn, gave rise to active futures for the corresponding active present forms, but only with those verbs where a meaningful opposition between active and middle-passive voice was possible. In all other cases, the middle futures were connected with active present forms. This may be schematized as follows:

Table 3: The development of the middle future

Stage I

	Active		Middle-passive	
	'bring'	'laugh'	'bring'	'laugh'
Present	ἄγω	γελάω	ἄγομαι	–
Future	–	–	–	–
Aorist	ἤγαγον	ἐγέλασα	ἠγαγόμην	–
Desiderative	–	–	ἄξομαι	γελάσομαι

Stage II

	Active		Middle-passive	
	'bring'	'laugh'	'bring'	'laugh'
Present	ἄγω	γελάω	ἄγομαι	–
Future	ἄξω	–	ἄξομαι	γελάσομαι
Aorist	ἤγαγον	ἐγέλασα	ἠγαγόμην	–
Desiderative	–	–	–	–

Note 1 A small number of transitive active verbs do not have middle-passive forms either, e.g. φεύγω τι(νά) 'flee', 'avoid'. In English, the same phenomenon occurs with verbs like *have, lack, hold* and some others.

Note 2 There are also intransitive verbs with middle-passive forms only. See § 47.1 and § 47.2.1.

Note 3 Some verbs are used transitively as well as intransitively, e.g. δακρύω τι/τινά: 'weep for' besides δακρύω 'weep'. Middle-passive forms, with passive meaning, may occur of such verbs: ἥδε συμφορὰ δακρύεται (lit. 'this misfortune is (being) wept for', E. *Hel.* 1226).

Note 4 Many essentially transitive verbs are used intransitively, or rather pseudo-intransitively, viz. when the Patient is 'uniquely retrievable'. This means that the Patient is not expressed, because in the given context only one Patient can possibly be involved. Some examples: ὁ ποταμὸς ἐσβάλλει ἐς λίμνην ('The river empties (its water) into the lake', cp. Th. 1.46.4); Ἀλυάττης ἐς Κλαζομενὰς ἐσέβαλε '(King) Alyattes made an inroad into Clazomenae' ('threw (an army) into the territory of Clazomenae', Hdt.

1.16.2, cp. 1.14.4: ἐσέβαλε στρατιὴν ἐς Μίλητον); ἤλαυνον ἐς τὸ ἄστυ ('They drove (the chariot, horses) into the city', Hdt. 1.60.4); ἐπεὰν ἀπάρωσι ἀπὸ Σαλαμῖνος ('after they set sail from Salamis', Hdt. 8.60.1, cp. 8.57.2 ἦν ἀπάρωσι τὰς ναῦς ἀπὸ Σαλαμῖνος), etc. With some of these verbs the intransitive use is the rule, e.g., in the military sphere: ἄγω 'march', ἐλαύνω 'drive', φέρω 'rush upon', etc. Cp. ἐλαύνων ἵππῳ (instrumental) in X. An. 1.8.1.

Note 5 Of some intransitive verbs, notably those ending in -εύω, both active and middle-passive forms occur, without any discernible difference in meaning, e.g. στρατεύω, πολιτεύω, πρεσβεύω (cp. also § 44.2, Note 1). There may be individual preferences involved. Thus, of πολιτευ- 'be a citizen, act as a citizen', Plato uses only πολιτεύομαι, while in Thucydides only πολιτεύω occurs.

§ 47 Verbs with middle-passive forms only

47.1 Verbs with a middle aorist (so-called media tantum)

47.1.1 The principle

This group largely consists of verbs with a (pseudo-) sigmatic middle aorist; these verbs are all *agentive*. They may be intransitive, e.g. ἄλλομαι 'jump' or, more frequently, transitive, e.g. αἰτιῶμαι 'accuse'. A much smaller number of verbs has a thematic middle aorist; these may be agentive or non-agentive. Some important verbs with a (pseudo-) sigmatic middle aorist are: ἀγωνίζομαι 'contend for a prize', 'fight'; αἰτιῶμαι 'accuse'; ἀκροῶμαι 'listen'; ἄλλομαι 'jump'; ἀρῶμαι 'pray'; ἀσπάζομαι 'welcome', 'greet'; δέχομαι 'accept'; ἐργάζομαι 'work', 'make'; εὔχομαι 'pray'; ἡγοῦμαι 'lead the way', 'lead'; 'believe', 'hold'; θεῶμαι 'gaze at', 'contemplate'; ἰῶμαι 'heal', 'cure'; κτῶμαι 'acquire'; λογίζομαι 'count', 'reckon'; μαρτύρομαι 'call to witness'; μάχομαι 'fight'; μέμφομαι 'blame, censure' (but see also § 47.2.2 (ii)); μηχανῶμαι 'construct', 'contrive'; μιμοῦμαι 'imitate'; ὀλοφύρομαι 'lament, wail'; φείδομαι 'spare'; χαρίζομαι 'gratify', 'give graciously'; χρῶμαι 'use'.

Some verbs with a thematic aorist are:
(Agentive:) ἕπομαι 'follow'; πυνθάνομαι 'inquire' (present stem), also non-agentive 'learn', 'hear' (other stems); (Non-agentive:) γίγνομαι 'to be born', 'become', etc.; ἀπεχθάνομαι 'incur hatred'; ὀσφραίνομαι 'smell';

πέτομαι 'fly' (aor. ἐπτόμην, also ἐπτάμην and ἔπτην); ἀφικνοῦμαι 'arrive'; αἰσθάνομαι 'perceive'.

47.1.2 Particulars

(i) Observe that the fact that these agentive verbs have a middle aorist, mostly with the suffix -σα-, is in accordance with the - agentive - direct-reflexive and indirect-reflexive use of the middle-passive voice, as discussed in §§ 43-44: in the latter case, too, a middle aorist was involved. The suffix -σα-, when used in the middle-passive voice, always has agentive value.

(ii) The question arises, of course, whether these verbs have a 'middle' meaning, e.g. an indirect-reflexive one. The notion 'interest of the Agent' may, in fact, be involved with a number of verbs, e.g. ἐργάζομαι, δέχομαι, κτῶμαι. With other verbs the Agent-subject seems to be involved also in special ways. Thus, verbs like ἀγωνίζομαι, μάχομαι and ἀσπάζομαι express a reciprocal relationship. Of others, again, it can be argued that they imply a special mental or cognitive involvement of the Agent-subject, e.g. μηχανῶμαι, λογίζομαι, αἰσθάνομαι, θεῶμαι, ἀκροῶμαι. Related to the mental group are verbs of saying like αἰτιῶμαι, μέμφομαι, ὀλοφύρομαι, εὔχομαι, i.e. verbs that put various kinds of mental involvement into words, so to speak.

(iii) The transitive *media tantum* may have a passive aorist and future, with strictly passive meaning, e.g.

(447) ᾐτιάθη μέντοι ὑπό τινων προδοῦναι τὰς ναῦς ('He was charged, however, by some people with having betrayed the fleet', X. *HG* 2.1.32)

The perfect-stem forms often have passive meaning as well: ᾐτίαται 'he has been accused' (besides ᾐτίαμαι αὐτόν 'I have accused him'). So regularly τὰ εἰργασμένα 'the things done', 'deeds'. In the other tenses this is exceptional.

(iv) To express direct-reflexivity and indirect-reflexivity the reflexive pronoun must be used: ἑωυτὸν λωβησάμενος ('having mutilated himself',

Hdt. 3.154.2), ἑωυτῷ ἀρᾶσθαι ἀγαθά ('to pray for blessings for himself', Hdt. 1.132.2).

Note 1 Media tantum are also called (*verba*) *deponentia medii* 'deponent middle' verbs, because they may be considered to have 'laid down' (Latin *deponere*) the active voice.
Note 2 Some middle-passives, e.g. ἀποκρίνομαι 'answer' are considered *media tantum* in spite of the existence of active forms, because the meaning of the middle-passive does not derive directly from the active (ἀποκρίνω 'separate'). Cp. also § 44.2 (vi).
Note 3 Some middle-passive presents have active forms in one or more other tenses: πέρδομαι 'break wind', aor. ἔπαρδον, pf. πέπορδα. Also suppletive ἦλθον with ἔρχομαι 'go', 'come', etc.
Note 4 Semantically the non-agentive verbs with a thematic aorist belong to the *passiva tantum* rather than to the verbs discussed above. See next section.

47.2   Verbs with a passive aorist (so-called passiva tantum)

47.2.1   The principle

This group comprises verbs having a passive aorist with the suffix -θη- (and a future with -θη-σε/ο-). The verbs concerned are for the greater part intransitive, but to several of them an object can be added. (Other constructions of these verbs, e.g. with infinitive or participle, are ignored here.) Semantically, they are mostly non-agentive. These verbs resemble the non-agentive pseudo-passives of causative verbs, type φοβοῦμαι 'be affrighted', ἐκπλήττομαι 'be shocked', cp. § 45.1: the subject has the semantic function Experiencer. Among these non-agentive verbs we find, notably: ἄγαμαι (τινα/τι) 'wonder (at), admire'; αἰδοῦμαι (τι) 'be ashamed (of)'; ἄχθομαι 'be grieved'; βούλομαι 'want, will', 'wish'; δύναμαι 'be able'; ἐπίσταμαι (τι) 'know (something)', 'be able'; ἔραμαι 'love'; ἥδομαι 'enjoy oneself', 'take one's pleasure'; ἡττῶμαι 'be weaker than', 'be inferior to'; οἴομαι 'think', 'believe'.

There are, however, also a number of agentive *passiva tantum*. The most important are: ἁμιλλῶμαι 'compete'; ἀρνοῦμαι (τι) 'deny', 'refuse' (something), δέομαι 'beg' (also non-agentive 'be in want'); δημοκρατοῦμαι 'have a democratic constitution' (also non-agentive 'live under a democratic constitution'); διαλέγομαι 'hold converse with'; ἐνθυμοῦμαι (τι) 'ponder (something)' (also non-agentive 'take to heart', 'be angry'); διανοοῦμαι 'intend' (also non-agentive 'think'); ἐπιμέλομαι/-

οὖμαι 'take care of'; εὐλαβοῦμαι (τινα/τι) 'be cautious (of)'; προθυμοῦμαι 'be eager', 'show zeal'; φιλοτιμοῦμαι 'be ambitious', 'aspire' (also non-agentive 'be jealous'); πειρῶμαι 'endeavour', 'try'.

47.2.2 Particulars

(i) Often the future is of the middle type: αἰδέσομαι, δυνήσομαι, etc. Cp. the pseudo-passives, § 45.2 (iii).

(ii) Some verbs have a middle as well as a passive aorist, e.g., in Herodotus μέμφομαι: ἐμέμφθην/ἐμεμψάμην (the latter is normal in Attic; ἐμεμψάμην = 'censure' (agentive verb of saying, see § 47.1.2 (ii)), ἐμέμφθην 'be angry with'); πειρῶμαι 'try': ἐπειρήθην/ἐπειρησάμην (no discernible difference). Notice that in Homer far more middle-passives have both aorists, often with clear differences. In general, the -σα-aorist is more agentive; e.g. αἰδέομαι: ἠδεσάμην 'respect': ἠδέσθην 'to be ashamed'. Also, with pseudo-reflexives: κοιμάομαι: ἐκοιμησάμην 'go to bed': ἐκοιμήθην 'fall asleep'. So, too, in Attic: παύομαι: ἐπαυσάμην : ἐπαύσθην; ψεύδομαι: ἐψευσάμην : ἐψεύσθην. See § 45.2, Note 5.

Note 1 Passiva tantum are also called *deponentia passivi*; cp. § 47.1.2, Note 1.
Note 2 ἡττῶμαι has also passive meaning: 'to be defeated'; it functions as lexical passive to νικῶ. With the other verbs passsive meaning is extremely rare.
Note 3 Besides πειρῶμαι active πειρῶ also occurs, albeit far more seldom.

§ 48 Summary of the main uses of the middle-passive voice

48.1 Of verbs that are also used in the active voice

(i) Passive meaning
With transitive verbs. Middle-passive voice: the Patient has the syntactic function subject. A prepositional Agent-phrase is rare. The aorist is of the passive type. E.g.:

- αἱ νῆες παρεσκευάσθησαν (ὑπὸ τῶν ᾿Αθηναίων) 'The ships were prepared (by the Athenians)'; cp. οἱ ᾿Αθηναῖοι παρεσκεύασαν τὰς ναῦς;

Also with verbs governing the genitive or dative:

- οἱ ῞Ελληνες ἐπεβουλεύθησαν (ὑπὸ τῶν Περσῶν) 'The Greeks had plots formed against them (by the Persians)'; cp. οἱ Πέρσαι ἐπεβούλευσαν τοῖς ῞Ελλησιν.

(ii) *Direct-reflexive meaning*
With agentive transitive verbs that denote a habitual physical treatment. Middle-passive voice: the Agent applies the action to himself. The Patient is co-referential with the Agent, and incorporated in the verb form. The aorist is of the middle type. E.g.:

- ἐλουσάμην 'I took a bath'
- παρεσκευασάμην 'I prepared myself'

(iii) *Indirect-reflexive meaning*
With agentive transitive verbs which denote a state of affairs that may be in the interest of the Agent as well as of some other person. Middle-passive voice: the action is in the interest of the Agent. An object is usually present. The aorist is of the middle type. E.g.:

- παρεσκευασάμην τὰς ναῦς 'I prepared the ships in my own interest'

(iv) *Pseudo-reflexive and pseudo-passive meaning*
With transitive causative verbs, i.e. verbs that denote a state of affairs which causes a change in the situation of the Patient. Middle-passive voice: the subject changes his own situation (Agent: pseudo-reflexive) or is internally affected by the change (Experiencer: pseudo-passive). Rarely with object. The aorist is of the passive type. E.g.:

- ἀπηλλάχθην 'I went away' (Agent)
- ἐφοβήθην (τοῦτο) 'I got afraid (of this)' (Experiencer)

48.2   *Of verbs that are not used in the active voice*

(i) *Media tantum* (middle aorist)
Agentive verbs, mostly with a (pseudo-) sigmatic aorist. Both transitive and intransitive verbs occur. E.g.:

- ᾐτιασάμην αὐτόν 'I accused him'

– ἡλάμην 'I jumped'

(ii) *Passiva tantum* (passive aorist)
Agentive and non-agentive verbs. In het latter case, the subject is internally affected (Experiencer). With several verbs an object may be present. E.g.:
– ἠρνήθην (τοῦτο) 'I denied (this)' (agentive)
– ᾐδέσθην (τοῦτο) 'I got ashamed (of this)' (non-agentive)

> *Note 1* Surveying all uses of the middle-passive it is perhaps possible to assign a common semantic denominator to these uses. This denominator might well be 'subject-affectedness': in all uses the middle-passive explicitly indicates that the subject in one way or other is affected by the state of affairs concerned. The active voice, on the other hand, is neutral as regards the expression of subject-affectedness. The theoretical issues involved in dealing with the semantic relationship between the various uses of the middle-passive are studied in detail in Allan (forthcoming).

SELECT BIBLIOGRAPHY

(Further references may be found in the bibliographies of the works listed below; abbreviations are in accordance with *L'année philologique*, Paris: Les Belles Lettres)

A useful bibliographic tool on the internet, with links to other sites, is: M. Buijs, A bibliography of ancient Greek linguistics. At:

www.let.uu.nl/hist/goac/bgl/

General linguistic works

Comrie, B., *Aspect*. Cambridge 1976: CUP

Comrie, B., *Language universals and linguistic typology*. Oxford 1981: Blackwell

Comrie, B., *Tense*. Cambridge 1985: CUP

Dik, S.C., *Studies in Functional Grammar*. London & New York 1981: Academic Press

Dik, S.C., *The theory of Functional Grammar*. Part 1. Berlin-New York 1997[2]: Mouton de Gruyter

Kemmer, S., *The middle voice*. Amsterdam 1993: Benjamins

Klaiman, M.H., *Grammatical voice*. Cambridge 1991: CUP

Krisch, Th., *Konstruktionsmuster und Bedeutungswandel indogermanischer Verben*. Frankfurt/M etc. 1984: Peter Lang (investigates, among other things, the effects of an application of valency theory to a number of verbs in Greek and other languages)

Lehmann, Chr., *Der Relativsatz*. Tübingen 1984: Günter Narr

Levinson, S., *Pragmatics*. Cambridge 1983: CUP

Lyons, J., *Semantics*. Cambridge 1977: CUP

Lyons, J., *Linguistic semantics: an introduction*. Cambridge 1995: CUP

Palmer, F.R., *Mood and modality*. Cambridge 1986: CUP

Thelin, N.B., (ed.), *Verbal aspect in discourse*, Amsterdam 1990: Benjamins

Handbooks of Greek syntax

Adrados, F.R., *Nueva sintaxis del griego antiguo*. Madrid 1992: Gredos (contains an extensive bibliography)

Cooper III, G.L., *Attic Greek prose syntax after K.W. Krüger.* (2 vols). Ann Arbor 1998: The University of Michigan Press. - Enlarged English version of Krüger (see below). Makes Krüger's syntax far better accessible, but should be used with some caution, if only because Cooper wants us to believe that both after and before Krüger very little has been written on Greek syntax.

Gildersleeve, B.L., *Syntax of classical Greek, from Homer to Demosthenes*. New York 1900-1911 (reprinted, with an *Index of passages cited* by P. Stork. Groningen 1980: Bouma's Boekhuis). - Planned as a general syntax; the part on dependent clauses, infinitive and participle, however, never appeared. The moods and tenses in independent sentences are discussed extensively; many valuable and sober observations are to be found which are amply illustrated.

Goodwin, W.W., *Syntax of the moods and tenses of the Greek verb.* London 1889: MacMillan (reprinted several times). - Especially devoted to moods and tenses, including infinitive and participle. Many fine observations. Contains an index of passages discussed.

Krüger, K.W., *Griechische Sprachlehre für Schulen. I Über die gewöhnliche, vorzugsweise die attische Prosa.* Zweites Heft Syntax. 5. Auflage besorgt von W. Pökel. Leipzig 1875: K.W. Krügers Verlagsbuchhandlung. - Rather idiosyncratic handbook, but with many acute observations. Difficult to consult due to its layout and system of abbreviations.

Kühner, R. and B. Gerth, *Ausführliche Grammatik der griechischen Sprache. Satzlehre.* 2 volumes. Hannover 1898-1904[3]: Hahnsche Buchhandlung (reprinted several times) + W.M. Calder III, *Index locorum zu Kühner-Gerth.* Darmstadt 1965: Wiss. Buchgesellschaft). - Excellent descriptive syntax, with a very extensive collection of examples, taken from a wide range of authors. Indispensable.

Meier-Brügger, M., *Griechische Sprachwissenschaft.* 2 Bände. Berlin: 1992: de Gruyter (Sammlung Göschen; up-to-date survey of the history of the study of Greek, with extensive bibliography)

Ruijgh, C.J., *Autour de 'τε épique'. Etudes sur la syntaxe grecque.* Amsterdam 1971: Hakkert. – Contains an extensive general discussion of the use of moods and tenses (Ch. VII), as well as of relative clauses and the use of the moods therein (Ch. VIII).

Schwyzer, Ed. and A. Debrunner, *Griechische Grammatik. 2. Band: Syntax und syntaktische Stilistik.* München 1950: Beck. plus: F. Radt and S. Radt, *Stellenregister.* München 1971: Beck. – Extensive syntax, with many diachronic observations. Offers, however, little news, when compared with Kühner-Gerth.

Smyth, H.W., *Greek Grammar.* Revised by G.M. Messing. Cambridge (Mass.) 1956: Harvard Univ. Press. – Contains a useful syntax.

Stahl, J.M., *Kritisch-historische Syntax des griechischen Verbums.* Heidelberg 1907: Winter. – Extensive handbook of the use of the verb. Often shrewd; at times, however, the formulations are rather abstruse. Many examples. With index of passages discussed.

Monographs and articles on the syntax of the Greek verb

Aerts, W.J., *Periphrastica.* Amsterdam 1965: Hakkert

Allan, R.J., *The middle voice in Ancient Greek. A study in polysemy.* Amsterdam 2003: Gieben

Amigues, S., *Les subordonnées finales par ὅπως en attique classique.* Paris 1977: Klincksieck

Amigues, S., 'Les temps de l'impératif'. *REG* 90 (1977) 223-238

Amigues, S., 'Remarques sur la syntaxe de πρίν'. *LEC* 48 (1980) 193-210

Armstrong, D., 'The Ancient Greek aorist as the aspect of countable action'. In: Ph.J. Tedeschi and A. Zaenen (eds.), *Tense and aspect.* New York etc. 1981: Academic Press (= Syntax and semantics, vol. 14, pp. 1-12)

Bakker, E.J. (ed.), *Grammar as interpretation. Greek literature in its linguistic contexts.* Leiden etc. 1996: Brill

Bakker, S.J., 'Futura zonder toekomst.' *Lampas* 35 (2002) 199–214

Bakker, W.F., *The Greek imperative.* Amsterdam 1966: Hakkert

Basset, L., *Les emplois periphrastiques du verbe grec* μέλλειν. Lyon 1979: Maison de l'orient

Boel de, G., 'Towards a theory of the meaning of complementizers in classical Attic'. *Lingua* 52 (1980) 285-304

Chanet, A.-M., 'ἕως et πρίν en grec classique'. *REG* 92 (1979) 166-207

Cock, A.J.C.M., 'ποιεῖσθαι : ποιεῖν. Sur les critères déterminant le choix entre l'actif ποιεῖν et le moyen ποιεῖσθαι.' *Mnemosyne* 34 (1981) 1-62

Crespo, E., 'On the system of substantive clauses in ancient Greek'. *Glotta* 62 (1984) 1-16

Delaunois, M., 'Contribution à l'étude de la proposition circonstancielle consécutive en grec classique'. *AC* 41 (1972) 78-93

Dietrich, W., 'Der periphrastische Verbalaspekt im Griechischen und Lateinischen'. *Glotta* 51 (1973) 188-228 (does not discuss constructions with ἔχω)

Duhoux, Y., *Le verbe grec ancien. Éléments de morphologie et de syntaxe historiques.* Louvain-la-Neuve 2002²: Peeters

Fanning, B.M., *Verbal aspect in New Testament Greek.* Oxford 1990: Clarendon Press

García Gual, C., *El sistema diatético en el verbo griego.* Madrid 1970: Instituto 'Antonio de Nebrija'

Hettrich, H., *Kontext und Aspekt in der altgriechischen Prosa Herodots.* Göttingen 1976: Vandenhoeck und Ruprecht

Jacquinod, B. (ed.), *Les complétives en grec ancien.* Saint-Étienne 1999: Publications de l'Université de Saint-Étienne

Jacquinod, B. (ed.), *Études sur l'aspect verbal chez Platon.* Saint-Étienne 2000: Publications de l'Université de Saint-Étienne

Kahn, Ch.H., *The verb 'be' in Ancient Greek.* Dordrecht/Boston 1973: Reidel

Kurzová, H., *Zur syntaktischen Struktur des Griechischen: Infinitiv und Nebensatz.* Amsterdam/Prag 1968: Hakkert

Lloyd, M., 'The tragic aorist.' *CQ* 49 (1999) 24-45

McKay, K.L., 'On the perfect and other aspects in the Greek non-literary papyri'. *BICS* 27 (1980) 23-50

McKay, K.L., 'The use of the Greek perfect down to the second century A.D.'. *BICS* 12 (1965) 1-21

Monteil, P., *La phrase relative en grec ancien*. Paris 1963: Klincksieck

Moorhouse, A.C., *The syntax of Sophocles*. Leiden 1982: Brill

Oguse, A., *Recherches sur le participe circonstantiel en grec ancien*. Paris 1962

Rijksbaron, A., *Temporal and causal conjunctions in ancient Greek*. Amsterdam 1976: Hakkert

Rijksbaron, A., Review article of Hettrich 1976. *Lingua* 48 (1979) 223-257

Rijksbaron, A., 'The discourse function of the imperfect'. In: A. Rijksbaron et al. (eds), *In the footsteps of Raphaël Kühner*. Amsterdam 1988: Gieben, pp. 237-254

Rijksbaron, A., *Aristotle, verb meaning and Functional Grammar. Towards a new typology of States of Affairs*. Amsterdam 1989: Gieben

Rijksbaron, A., *Grammatical observations on Euripides' Bacchae*. Amsterdam 1991: Gieben

Rijksbaron, A., 'Sur les emplois de ἐάν et ἐπεάν.' *Lalies* 12 (1993) 131-144

Ruijgh, C.J., Review article of García Gual 1970. *Lingua* 36 (1975) 359-370

Ruijgh, C.J., 'L'emploi "inceptif" du thème du présent du verbe grec'. *Mnemosyne* 38 (1985) 1-61

Ruipérez, M.S., *Structure du système des aspects et des temps du verbe en grec ancien*. Paris 1982: Les Belles Lettres

Sauge, A., *Les degrés du verbe. Sens et formation du parfait en grec ancien*. Bern 2000: Peter Lang

Sicking, C.M.J., 'The distribution of aorist and present stem forms in Greek, especially in the imperative'. *Glotta* 69 (1991) 14-43; 154-174

Sicking, C.M.J. & P. Stork, *Two studies in the semantics of the verb in Classical Greek. Part I Aspect choice. Time reference or discourse function?; Part II The synthetic perfect in Classical Greek.* Leiden etc. 1996: Brill

Stork, P., *The aspectual usage of the dynamic infinitive in Herodotus.* Groningen 1982: Bouma's Boekhuis

Strunk, K., 'Historische und deskriptive Linguistik bei der Textinterpretation'. *Glotta* 49 (1971) 191-216

Wakker, G.C., *Conditions and conditionals. An investigation of Ancient Greek.* Amsterdam 1994: Gieben

Additions to the Bibliography

Buijs, M., *Clause combining in Ancient Greek narrative discourse. The distribution of subclauses and participial clauses in Xenophon's Hellenica and Anabasis.* Leiden 2005: Brill

De Jong, I.J.F. & A. Rijksbaron, *Sophocles and the Greek language. Aspects of diction, syntax and pragmatics.* Leiden 2006: Brill

Crespo, E. et al., *Sintaxis del griego clásico.* Madrid 2003: Editorial Gredos

INDEX OF TERMS

(: is to be read as 'as opposed to'; the references are to the pages)

INDEX OF GREEK WORDS

οὐ μή
- + future indicative   34
- + subjunctive   59n3

παύω (-ομαι) + participle   120

πείθω
- + accusative plus infinitive   100
- + acc. with supplementary inf.   100, 106

περιορῶ + participle   120

ποιῶ/ποιοῦμαι + verbal noun   149

πρίν
- + indicative   76, 78
- + infinitive   78

πρὶν ἄν   82

πυνθάνομαι
- + accusative plus infinitive   96
- + indirect question   56
- + participle   117

σκοπῶ
- + indirect question   56
- + μή-clause   58
- + ὅπως-clause   59

σχῆμα Ἀττικόν, Σοφόκλειον   130

τί οὐ in questions with iussive force   9, 31

τολμῶ   98n3

τοῦ (μή) + infinitive   115n2

τυγχάνω + participle   120

ὑπισχνοῦμαι + infinitive   109

φαίνομαι   117
- + infinitive or participle   121n6

φθάνω + participle   120

φυλάττομαι
- + μή-clause   58
- + μή + infinitive   104

χαίρω
- + ὅτι/ὡς-clause   50, 54
- + participle   119

χρῆν   25f.

ὡς
- conjunction

INDEX LOCORUM

(The numbers between (...) refer to the examples, all other numbers to the pages)

ESSENTIALS OF *SYNTAX AND SEMANTICS*

Note   This survey differs in some respects from the main text, in that the various uses of a tense or mood may be grouped together under one heading

I   TENSE/ASPECT STEMS (§§ 1-4)

Common values of all forms of

- present stem: expresses incompletion: state of affairs is being carried out; can be interrupted
- aorist stem: expresses completion; state of affairs cannot be interrupted
- perfect stem: expresses completion + resulting state
- future stem: indifferent as to completion; temporal value only: state of affairs will be carried out after a given orientation point.

II   THE MOODS AND TENSES IN INDEPENDENT SENTENCES (§§ 5-16)

INDICATIVE

Present indicative (§ 5)

- *Locates ongoing state of affairs at the moment of utterance*

(5)   ὁ δ' ὦμος οὑτοσὶ <u>πιέζεται</u> ('My shoulder here is stuck', Ar. *Ra.* 30)

- *Expresses habitual (iterative) state of affairs (generic present)*

(8)   <u>συσσιτοῦμεν</u> γὰρ δὴ ἐγώ τε καὶ Μελησίας ὅδε, καὶ ἡμῖν τα μειράκια <u>παρα-σιτεῖ</u> ('Melesias here and I dine together, and the boys dine with us', Pl. *La.* 179b)

- *Expresses omnitemporal/timeless state of affairs*

(9)   τῶν δὲ κροκοδείλων φύσις <u>ἐστὶ</u> τοιήδε ('The nature of the crocodile is as follows:', Hdt. 2.68.1)

- *Marks decisive state of affairs in a narrative (historic present)* (§ 7)

(48)   ... ὑπεκδὺς ἐχώρεε ἔξω. καὶ ἡ γυνὴ <u>ἐπορᾷ</u> μιν ἐξιόντα ('... he slipped away and went out. And the woman saw (sees) him leave', Hdt. 1.10.1-2)

- *Punctuates a narrative*

(49a)   Κῦρος ... ὡρμᾶτο ἀπὸ Σαρδέων· καὶ <u>ἐξελαύνει</u> διὰ τῆς Λυδίας ('Cyrus was setting forth from Sardis; and he marched through Lydia ...', X. *An.* 1.2.5)

Imperfect

NARRATIVE USE (§ 6)

- *Locates ongoing state of affairs in the past, creating framework for other states of affairs*

(11)   ἐβουλεύοντο ... περὶ τῶν παρόντων ...παρελθὼν δὲ Ἀρχίδαμος ... ἔλεξε τοιάδε ... παρελθὼν δὲ Σθενελαΐδας ... ἔλεξεν ὧδε ('.. they discussed the situation. Archidamos, their king, came forward and made the following speech: (...); Sthenelaïdas came forward and spoke as follows', Th. 1.79-85)

(14)   ... Καμβύσης ... ἐπὶ ... Αἴγυπτον ἐποιέετο στρατηλασίην ('... Cambyses prepared an expedition against Egypt', Hdt. 2.1.2)

- *Expresses a habitual (repeated) state of affairs*

(18)   ἐπειδὴ δὲ τὸ παιδίον ἐγένετο, ἡ μήτηρ αὐτὸ ἐθήλαζεν ('When our child had been born his mother suckled it', Lys. 1.9)

- *Expresses an attempted state of affairs (conative use)*

(25)   ἄγγελοι ἔπειθον ἀποτρέπεσθαι· οἱ δ' οὐχ ὑπήκουον ('Messengers tried to persuade them to turn back, but they would not listen', X. *An.* 7.3.7)

(29)   βάρβαρον λέχος / πρὸς γῆρας οὐκ εὔδοξον ἐξέβαινέ σοι ('... your marriage with a foreign woman was likely to end in an inglorious old age', E. *Med.* 591-2; imperfect of likelihood)

- *Expresses that a state of affairs follows immediately upon another state of affairs (immediative use)*

(34)   διαλαβόντες δὲ τὰς οἰκίας ἐβάδιζον ('They apportioned the houses amongst them, and were on their way', Lys. 12.8)

- *Expresses a completed state of affairs, mostly with verbs of saying; seeks a reaction*

(39)   ὁ μὲν δή σφι τὰ ἐντεταλμένα ἀπήγγελλε, τοῖσι δὲ ἔαδε μὲν βοηθέειν Ἀθηναίοισι ('Thus he gave the message with which he was charged, and they resolved to send help to the Athenians ...', Hdt. 6.106.3)

NON-NARRATIVE USE (§ 8)

- *Of modal verbs; opposed to existing state of affairs*

(52)   εἰέν, τί σιγᾷς; οὐκ ἐχρῆν σιγᾶν, τέκνον ('Why are you silent? You shouldn't be silent, my child', E. *Hipp.* 297)

- In unrealizable wishes

(60)   εἰ γὰρ τοσαύτην δύναμιν εἶχον ('Would that I had such power ...', E. *Alc.*
        1072)

Aorist indicative

NARRATIVE USE (§ 6)

- Locates completed state of affairs in the past

(11)   ἐβουλεύοντο ... περὶ τῶν παρόντων ... παρελθὼν δὲ Ἀρχίδαμος ... ἔλεξε
        τοιάδε ... παρελθὼν δὲ Σθενελαΐδας ... ἔλεξεν ὧδε ('... they discussed the
        situation. Archidamos, their king, came forward and made the following
        speech: (...); Sthenelaïdas came forward and spoke as follows', Th. 1.79-85)

- Expresses past-in-the-past

(42)   τούς τε Ἱμεραίους ἔπεισαν ... τοῖς ναύταις ... ὅπλα παρασχεῖν (τὰς γὰρ ναῦς
        ἀνείλκυσαν ἐν Ἱμέρᾳ) ('They persuaded the Himeraeans to supply arms for
        the crews (for their ships they had beached at Himera)', Th. 7.1.3)

- Ingressive use (with stative verbs)

(43)   μετὰ δὲ ... ἐνόσησε ὁ Ἀλυάττης. μακροτέρης δέ οἱ γινομένης τῆς νούσου
        ('But presently Alyattes fell sick; and, his sickness lasting longer and longer
        ...', Hdt. 1.19.2)

NON-NARRATIVE USE (§ 8)

- In unrealizable wishes

(59)   εἴθε σοι, ὦ Περικλεῖς, τότε συνεγενόμην ('If only, Pericles, I had met you
        then', X. *Mem.* 1.2.46)

- Constative use

(61)   διὸ ὑμέας ἐγὼ συνέλεξα, ἵνα ... ('For this reason I have called you together,
        to ...', Hdt. 7.8α.2)

- Of performative verbs ('tragic aorist')

(65)   ἐπήνεσ', ἀλλὰ στεῖχε δωμάτων ἔσω ('Thanks, but come on, go into the
        house', E. *IA* 440; matter-of-fact reaction)

- Gnomic (generic) use (in descriptions)

(70)   ἐς ἔχθεα μεγάλα ἀλλήλοισι ἀπικνέονται, ἐξ ὧν στάσιες ἐγγίνονται, ἐκ δὲ
        τῶν στασίων φόνος, ἐκ δὲ τοῦ φόνου ἀπέβη ἐς μουναρχίην ('They get into

serious personal quarrels, which lead to party-strife; this leads to bloodshed, and that situation (inevitably) results in monarchy', Hdt. 3.82.3)

Future indicative (§ 9)

(72d) ἀλλ᾽ εἰς ἀγορὰν <u>ἄπειμ᾽</u> ('But I'm off to the agora', Ar. *Th.* 457; announcement)

Perfect indicative (§ 10)

- Expresses completion + state (with terminative verbs)

(75) <u>γέγραφε</u> δὲ καὶ ταῦτα ὁ αὐτὸς Θουκυδίδης Ἀθηναῖος ('Of this too the same Thucydides from Athens is the author', Th. 5.26.1)

- Expresses state (with stative verbs)

ἥγημαι be firmly convinced, from ἡγοῦμαι etc.

Pluperfect (§ 11)

Expresses completion + state (with terminative verbs) in the past

(77) ταῦτα μέν νυν ὁ Σικυώνιος Κλεισθένης <u>ἐπεποιήκεε</u>,... ('This, then, Cleisthenes from Sikyon had done', Hdt. 5.69.1; cp. perfect indicative)

SUBJUNCTIVE (§ 13, § 16)

- Adhortative (directive, iussive) use

(82) ἐπίσχες· <u>ἐμβάλωμεν</u> εἰς ἄλλον λόγον ('Stop, let us change the subject', E. *El.* 962)

(83) ἀλλὰ <u>μή</u> μ᾽ <u>ἀφῆς</u> ἔρημον ('But dont leave me all by myself', S. *Ph.* 486; prohibitive use)

- Deliberative use (in questions)

(86) οἴμοι, <u>τί δράσω</u>; <u>ποῖ φύγω</u> μητρὸς χέρας; ('Ah me, what should I do? Whither should I flee, to escape from my mothers hands?', E. *Med.* 1271)

OPTATIVE (§ 14, § 16)

- Without ἄν (realizable wishes; cupitive use)

(88) <u>μὴ</u> πλείω κακὰ <u>πάθοιεν</u> ('May they be grieved no more', S. *Ant.* 928)

- With ἄν (potential use)

(117) ἔγωγε πολὺ <u>ἄν</u> ἥδιον μετὰ σοῦ <u>σκοποίμην</u> εἴθ' ἀληθὲς εἴτε μὴ τὸ λεχθέν ('For my part I would greatly prefer to have you as partner in the inquiry as to whether what was said is true or not', Pl. *Chrm.* 162e; present optative: open discussion)

(118) ἀλλ' ἔγωγε ἐκεῖνο <u>ἄν</u> ἥδιστα, ὅπερ ἠρόμην τὸ πρῶτον, καὶ <u>σκεψαίμην</u> καὶ <u>ἀκούσαιμι</u> ('But for my part I would like best of all to examine that question I asked at first, and hear your view', Pl. *Men.* 86c; aorist optative: discussion concerns one single question)

IMPERATIVE (§§ 15-16)

(102) ὅθεν οὖν ἀπέλιπες <u>ἀποκρίνου</u> ('So go on answering where you left off', Pl. *Grg.* 497c; present imperative: request to continue an interrupted state of affairs)

(107) καὶ νῦν δὴ τούτων ὁπότερον βούλει <u>ποίει</u>, <u>ἐρώτα</u> ἢ <u>ἀποκρίνου</u> ('So now, take whichever course you like: either put questions or answer them', Pl. *Grg.* 462b; present imperative: request to start an open discussion)

(108) βούλομαι πυθέσθαι ἀπ' αὐτοῦ τίς ... :: <u>ἐροῦ</u> αὐτόν ('I want to find out from the man what ... :: Ask him', Pl. *Grg.* 447c; aorist imperative: request to deal with one single issue)

III   THE MOODS AND TENSES IN DEPENDENT (SUBORDINATE) CLAUSES (§§ 17 - 29)

A. *IN OBJECT AND SUBJECT CLAUSES (OBLIGATORY CLAUSES)* (§§ 18ff.)

- With verbs of perception and emotion; conjunctions: ὅτι and ὡς; negative: οὐ (§ 18.1)

(121) ὁρῶντες <u>ὅτι</u> μόνος <u>ἐφρόνει</u> οἷα δεῖ τὸν ἄρχοντα ('... because they saw that he alone possessed the wisdom which a commander should have', X. *An.* 2.2.5)

- With verbs of saying (verba dicendi); conjunctions: ὅτι and ὡς; negative: οὐ (§ 18.2)

(131) ὑπειπὼν ... <u>ὅτι</u> αὐτὸς τἀκεῖ <u>πράξοι</u> ᾤχετο ('After adding that he would himself look after matters there, he departed', Th. 1.90.4; oblique future optative, direct speech: τἀκεῖ πράξω)

(133a) οὗτοι ἔλεγον <u>ὅτι</u> Κῦρος μὲν <u>τέθνηκεν</u>, Ἀριαῖος δὲ ... ἐν τῷ σταθμῷ <u>εἴη</u> ('They told that Cyrus was dead, and that Ariaeus ... was now at the stopping-place', X. *An.* 2.1.3; tense/mood of direct speech combined with oblique optative; former is in the context more relevant)

- *Indirect speech with verbs of perception* (§ 18.3)

(135) ἠπιστάμην <u>ὅτι οὐ</u> περὶ τῶν μειρακίων ὁ λόγος <u>ἔσοιτο</u> ('I knew that our discussion would not be about the boys', Pl. *La.* 188b; oblique optative; direct speech: οὐκ ... ἔσται)

- *Indirect questions; conjunctions:* τίς/ὅστις, πῶς/ὅπως *etc.; (yes/no-questions:)* εἰ, πότερον ... ἤ, εἰ ... εἴτε (§ 19.2)

(147) ᾔδει δ' οὐδεὶς <u>ὅποι στρατεύουσιν</u> ('No one knew whither they were marching', Th. 5.54.1; direct question: ποῖ στρατεύομεν;)

(149) ἡ μήτηρ διηρώτα τὸν Κῦρον <u>πότερον βούλοιτο</u> μένειν ἢ ἀπιέναι ('His mother asked Cyrus whether he wished to stay or go', X. *Cyr.* 1.3.15; oblique optative; direct question: πότερον βούλει μένειν ἢ ἀπιέναι;)

- *With verbs of fearing; conjunction:* μή; *negated:* μὴ οὐ (§ 20)

(151) δέδοικα <u>μὴ</u> ... <u>ἐπιλαθώμεθα</u> τῆς οἴκαδε ὁδοῦ ('I fear that we may forget the way home', X. *An.* 3.2.25)

(155) ἐφοβεῖτο ... <u>μὴ οὐ δύναιτο</u> ... ἐξελθεῖν ('He was afraid that he would not be able to get away', X. *An.* 3.1.12; oblique optative)

- *With verbs of contriving; conjunctions:* ὅπως, *negated:* ὅπως μή (§ 21)

(158) ἐσκοπούμην ... <u>ὅπως</u> αὐτὸς <u>ἀπολυθήσομαι</u> τῆς ἐγγύης ('I set about considering how I might get myself free from my pledge', D. 33.10)

B. IN SATELLITE CLAUSES (ADVERBIAL CLAUSES) (§§ 22ff.)

- *Purpose clauses; conjunctions:* ἵνα, ὡς, ὅπως; *negative:* ἵνα (ὡς, ὅπως) μή, μή *alone* (§ 22)

(161) ἐγὼ δ' ἄπειμι, <u>μὴ κατοπτευθῶ</u> παρών ('But I will go away, lest I be seen here', S. *Ph.* 124)

(162) ἀπεκάλει ... (τὸν Κῦρον), <u>ὅπως</u> τὰ ἐν Πέρσαις ἐπιχώρια <u>τελοίη</u> ('He called Cyrus back to complete the regular curriculum in Persia', X. *Cyr.* 1.4.25; oblique optative)

- *Consecutive clauses; conjunction:* ὥστε (§ 23)

ὥστε + *indicative; negative:* οὐ

(165) ἐπιπίπτει χιὼν ἄπλετος, <u>ὥστε ἀπέκρυψε</u> καὶ τὰ ὅπλα καὶ τοὺς ἀνθρώπους ('But there came such a tremendous fall of snow that it completely covered both the arms and the men', X. *An.* 4.4.11; result is a fact)

ὥστε + infinitive; negative: μή

(169) κραυγὴν πολλὴν ἐποίουν καλοῦντες ἀλλήλους, <u>ὥστε</u> καὶ τοὺς πολεμίους <u>ἀκούειν</u> ('They made a great uproar with calling one another, so that the enemy could also hear it', X. *An.* 2.2.17; possible fact)

- *Conditional clauses; conjunction: εἰ; negative: μή* (§ 24)

εἰ + indicative: neutral condition: the condition may or may not be fulfilled; in the apodosis (main clause): *any tense or mood* (§ 24.2)

(177) <u>εἰ ψεύδομαι</u>, ἐξέλεγχε ('If I am lying, refute me', Pl. *Smp.* 217b)

ἐάν (ἤν, ἄν) + subjunctive (§ 24.3)

* *Prospective* condition: chances are that the condition will be fulfilled; in the apodosis: *future indicative* or other form with future reference

(183) τοὺς ξυμμάχους, <u>ἢν σωφρονῶμεν</u>, οὐ περιοψόμεθα ἀδικουμένους ('If we are in our right minds, we shall not permit our allies to be wronged', Th. 1.86.2; prospective subjunctive)

* Condition is *repeatedly fulfilled*; in the apodosis: *generic present indicative*

(186) <u>ἐὰν</u> οὖν τις <u>αἰσχύνηται</u> καὶ <u>μὴ τολμᾶ</u> λέγειν ἅπερ νοεῖ, ἀναγκάζεται ἐναντία λέγειν ('If a man is ashamed and dares not say what he thinks, he is forced to contradict himself', Pl. *Grg.* 482e; every time when, iterative subjunctive)

εἰ + optative (§ 24.4)

* *Potential* condition: fulfilment of the condition is merely possible; in the apodosis: *optative + ἄν*

(187) <u>εἰ</u> δ' ὡς μάλιστ' <u>ἀπεχοίμεθ'</u> οὗ σὺ δὴ λέγεις,
ὃ μὴ γένοιτο, μᾶλλον ἂν διὰ τουτογὶ
γένοιτ' ἂν εἰρήνη;
('But if we would abstain as much as possible from what you say, which I wish may not happen, would there be peace because of that?', Ar. *Lys.* 146-48)

* Condition is *repeatedly fulfilled in the past*; in the apodosis: *imperfect*

(191) <u>εἰ</u> μὲν <u>ἐπίοιεν</u> οἱ Ἀθηναῖοι, ὑπεχώρουν, <u>εἰ</u> δ' <u>ἀναχωροῖεν</u>, ἐπέκειντο ('If the Athenians attacked they retreated, but if they retreated they charged', Th. 7.79.5; iterative optative)

εἰ + past tense: counterfactual condition: fulfilment of the condition is no longer possible; in the apodosis: *past tense + ἄν* (§ 24.5)

206   ESSENTIALS

(193) εἰ δ' ἐκεῖνά γε <u>προσέθηκεν</u>, οὐδεὶς ἀντεχειροτόνησεν ἄν ('And if he had added this, no one would have voted against him', Ar. *Ec.* 422-3)

- *Concessive clauses; conjunctions: εἰ καί* and *καὶ εἰ*; express an *exceptional* or *unlikely* condition (§ 25)

(200) <u>καὶ</u> γὰρ <u>εἰ</u> μυθώδης ὁ λόγος <u>γέγονεν</u>, ὅμως αὐτῷ καὶ νῦν ῥηθῆναι προσήκει ('For even if the story has taken the form of a myth, yet it deserves to be told again', Isoc. 4.28; καὶ εἰ+ indicative: neutral condition)

- *Temporal clauses* (§ 26)

Conjunctions: ἐπεί, ἐπειδή, ὡς, ὅτε; ἕως, ἐν ᾧ; πρίν + imperfect or aorist indicative: when, after; express *single* past states of affairs. *Negative: οὐ.* Main clause: *any past tense* (§ 26.1)

(201) <u>ἐπεὶ</u> ὦν ὁ βουκόλος ... <u>ἀπίκετο</u>, ἔλεγε ὁ Ἅρπαγος τάδε ('So when the cowherd had come, Harpagus said the following', Hdt. 1.110.3; ἐπεί (ἐπειδή, ὡς, ὅτε) + aorist indicative: the state of affairs is *anterior to* that of the main clause)

(202) καὶ <u>ὅτε</u> δὴ <u>ἦν</u> δεκαέτης ὁ παῖς, πρῆγμα ... τοιόνδε ... ἐξέφηνέ μιν ('And when the boy was ten years old, the following occurrence revealed his identity', Hdt. 1.114.1; (ἐπεί, ἐπειδή, ὡς) ὅτε + imperfect: the state of affairs is *simultaneous* with that of the main clause)

ἕως + imperfect: as long as; ἐν ᾧ + imperfect: while (§ 26.1 and 2)

(203) καὶ <u>ἕως</u> μὲν <u>ἐτιμᾶτο</u>, πιστὸν ἑαυτὸν παρεῖχεν· ἐπειδὴ δὲ ... ('So long as he found favour, he showed himself loyal; but when ...', Lys. 12.66-7; ἕως + imperfect: simultaneous state of affairs; the state of affairs of the main clause lasts *as long as* that of the subordinate clause (conditional nuance))

(204) <u>ἐν ᾧ</u> δὲ <u>ὡπλίζοντο</u> ἧκον ... οἱ ... σκοποί ('While they were arming themselves, however, the scouts returned ...', X. *An.* 2.2.14-5; ἐν ᾧ + imperfect: simultaneous state of affairs; the state of affairs of the main clause occurs *at some time* during that of the subordinate clause)

ἕως + aorist indicative: until; πρίν + aorist indicative: before (§ 26.1 and 2)

(205) αὕτη δὲ ἐφύλαττεν (αὐτόν), <u>ἕως ἐξηῦρεν</u> ὅτι εἴη τὸ αἴτιον ('And she kept a close watch on him, until she discovered what was the cause', Lys. 1.15; ἕως + aorist indicative: the state of affairs of the subordinate clause is *posterior to* that of the main clause and marks the end of that of the main clause)

(206) παραπλήσια δὲ καὶ οἱ ἐπὶ τῶν νεῶν αὐτοῖς ἔπασχον, <u>πρίν</u> γε δὴ οἱ Συρακόσιοι ... <u>ἔτρεψαν</u> τοὺς Ἀθηναίους ('The men aboard the ships were affected in a similar way, at least before the Syracusans routed the Athenians', Th. 7.71.5; πρίν + aorist indicative: the state of affairs of the

subordinate clause is *posterior to* that of the main clause and marks the end
of that of the main clause)

πρίν + infinitive: before (§ 26.2)

(210) ὀλίγον δὲ <u>πρὶν</u> ἡμᾶς <u>ἀπιέναι</u>, μάχη ἐγεγόνει ἐν Ποτειδαίᾳ ('And shortly
before we left there had been a battle at Potidaea', Pl. *Chrm.*
153b; the state
of affairs of the subordinate clause is simply *posterior to* that of the main
clause)

Conjunctions: ἐπήν, ἐπειδάν, ὅταν; ἕως ἄν; πρὶν ἄν + subjunctive; negative: μή.

* Express *single future* states of affairs; in the main clause: *form with future reference*
(§ 26.4-5)

(215) τάφος δὲ ποῖος δέξεταί μ', <u>ὅταν θάνω</u>; ('And what tomb shall receive me, after
I have died?', E. *IT* 625; aorist subjunctive: anterior state of affairs)

(216) <u>ἕωσπερ ἂν ἐμπνέω</u> καὶ <u>οἷός τ' ὦ</u> , οὐ μὴ παύσωμαι φιλοσοφῶν ('So long as I
live and am able to continue, I shall never give up philosophy', Pl. *Ap.* 29d;
ἕως ἄν + *present* subjunctive: so long as)

(217) δεῖ μὴ περιμένειν <u>ἕως ἂν ἐπιστῶσιν</u> ('You must not wait until they are upon
you', Isoc. 4.165; ἕως ἄν + *aorist* subjunctive: until)

(220) μὴ ἀπέλθητε <u>πρὶν ἂν ἀκούσητε</u> ('Do not go away before you have heard ...',
X. *An.* 5.7.12; πρὶν ἄν + aorist subjunctive *(only after negative main clause):*
before)

* Express *habitual* states of affairs (iterative subjunctive); in the main clause:
(generic) present indicative, or *gnomic aorist* (§ 26.6)

(225) τότε γὰρ πλεῖστα κερδαίνουσιν, <u>ὅταν</u> ... τίμιον τὸν σῖτον <u>πωλῶσιν</u> ('For
they make most profit when ... they sell their corn at a high price', Lys.
22.14; every time when)

(226) <u>ἕως ἂν σώζηται</u> τὸ σκάφος, τότε χρὴ ... προθύμους εἶναι ('So long as the
vessel is safe, you must be willing', D. 9.69; ἕως ἄν + *present* subjunctive: so
long as)

(227) ποιοῦμεν ταῦθ' ἑκάστοθ' ... <u>ἕως ἂν</u> αὐτὸν <u>ἐμβάλωμεν</u> ἐς κακόν ('We do this
every time ... until we have driven him into misery', Ar. *Nu.* 1458-60)

Conjunctions: ἐπεί, ἐπειδή, ὡς, ὅτε; ἕως, ἐν ᾧ + (iterative) optative; negative: μή.
Express *habitual past* states of affairs; in the main clause: *imperfect* (§ 26.7)

(231) περιεμένομεν οὖν ἑκάστοτε, <u>ἕως ἀνοιχθείη</u> τὸ δεσμωτήριον· ... <u>ἐπειδὴ</u> δὲ
<u>ἀνοιχθείη</u>, εἰσῆμεν παρὰ τὸν Σωκράτη ('Every day we used to wait about,

until the prison was opened; and when it was opened, we went in to Socrates',
Pl. *Phd.* 59d)

- *Causal clauses; conjunctions:* ὅτι, διότι; ἐπεί + *present indicative* in direct speech;
negative: οὐ (§ 27, § 26.3)

(233) οἱ Ἀθηναῖοι ἐνόμιζον ἡσσᾶσθαι, ὅτι οὐ πολὺ ἐνίκων ('The Athenians
thought they were defeated, because they were not signally victorious', Th.
7.34.7)

(212) ἐπεὶ ... οὐ δύναμαί σε πείθειν ..., σὺ δὲ ὧδε ποίησον ('Now that I cannot
convince you ..., you must act as follows: ...', Hdt. 1.112.2)

C. IN RELATIVE CLAUSES (§ 29)

Introduced by *relative pronouns:* ὅς, indefinite ὅστις; *relative adjectives:* οἷος, ὅσος,
indefinite ὁποῖος, ὁπόσος; *relative adverbs, e.g.* οὗ, ὡς, indefinite ὅπου, ὅπως etc.
For the negative see the main text.

- *Anaphoric clauses* (§ 29.1)

* Anaphoric *determinative clauses*: the relative clause is indispensable for identifying the antecedent; e.g.:

(238) τῷ ἀνδρὶ ὃν ἂν ἕλησθε πείσομαι ('I shall obey the man whom you choose
(lit. will have chosen)', X. *An.* 1.3.15; prospective subjunctive; future indicative in main clause)

(239) ... ἀποτίνει ζημίην τὴν ἂν οἱ ἱρέες τάξωνται ('... he pays whatever penalty
the priests appoint', Hdt. 2.65.5; iterative subjunctive; generic present in
main clause)

Other moods used: indicative, secondary indicative + ἄν, optative + ἄν, cupitive optative, optative of potential condition, iterative optative.

The relative pronoun of a determinative clause may be *attracted* into the caseform of
the antecedent:

(254) ... σὺν τοῖς θησαυροῖς οἷς (for οὓς) ὁ πατὴρ κατέλιπεν ('... with the treasures
that my father left me', X. *Cyr.* 3.1.33)

The antecedent may be *incorporated* into the relative clause:

(256) εἰ δέ τινα ὁρῴη ... κατασκευάζοντα ... ἧς ἄρχοι χώρας ('Whenever he saw
that a man was organizing well the country over which he ruled ...', X. *An.*
1.9.19; the relative clause functions as object of κατασκευάζοντα)

* Anaphoric *digressive clauses*: the relative clause is not necessary for identifying the antecedent; e.g.:

(243) ἥξετε ἐπὶ ... Ἅλυν, ὃν οὐκ ἂν δύναισθε ἄνευ πλοίων διαβῆναι ('You will come to ... the Halys, which you could not cross without boats', X. *An.* 5.6.9; optative + ἄν)

Other moods used: indicative, secondary indicative + ἄν, cupitive optative, imperative, adhortative subjunctive

- *Autonomous clauses* (§ 29.2); moods as in anaphoric determinative clauses, e.g.:

(246) ὁρᾷς ἃ ποιεῖς ('Do you see what you are doing?', Ar. *Pl.* 932; indicative, the clause functions as object)

(249) καὶ οὓς μὲν ἴδοι εὐτάκτως ... ἰόντας, ... τίνες εἶεν ἠρώτα ('And those whom he saw marching in good order ... he asked who they were', X. *Cyr.* 5.3.55; iterative optative, the clause functions as object; NB εἶεν = oblique optative)

IVA INFINITIVE (§ 31-35)

Dynamic infinitive

Present or aorist infinitive; after verbs and adjectives expressing a desire, request, ability, necessity etc. *Is always posterior to the main verb. Negative: μή. Cannot be modified by ἄν.*

(266) αἰσχύνομαι οὖν ὑμῖν εἰπεῖν ... τἀληθῆ ('Now I'm ashamed to tell you the truth', Pl. *Ap.* 22b; nominative plus infinitive)

(269) ἐδέοντο αὐτοῦ παντὶ τρόπῳ ἀπελθεῖν Ἀθήνηθεν ('They asked him to leave Athens at all costs', Lys. 13.25; genitive plus supplementary infinitive)

(288) κεῖνον ... ἐκέλευον ἀναβάντα ἐπὶ πύργον ἀγορεῦσαι ὡς ... ('They orderded him te go up on a tower and declare that ...', Hdt. 3.74.3; (accusative plus) supplementary infinitive: κεῖνον governed by ἐκέλευε; ἀγορεῦσαι: order as such)

(289) ἀνεβίβασαν αὐτὸν ἐπὶ πύργον καὶ ἀγορεύειν ἐκέλευον ('They brought him up on a tower and ordered him to speak', Hdt. 3.75.1; ἀγορεύειν: actual execution of the order, cp. ex. (288))

Verbs of forbidding etc. are followed by μή + infinitive (§ 33.1 (iv)):

(293) τοῖς ... νέοις ἀπαγορευόντων αὐτῶν μὴ διαλέγεσθαι ('When they forbade him to talk with the young people', X. *Mem.* 4.4.3)

Declarative infinitive

Present, future or aorist infinitive; after verbs of saying and thinking. *Present* infinitive: *simultaneous* with main verb, *aorist* infinitive: *anterior* to main verb, *future* infinitive: *posterior* to main verb. *Negative: οὐ. Can be modified by ἄν.*

(274) ὑπώπτευον γὰρ ἤδη ἐπὶ βασιλέα ἰέναι ('For they suspected by this time that they were going against the king', X. *An.* 1.3.1; nominative plus infinitive)

(276) οὕτω ... Ἰοῦν ἐς Αἴγυπτον ἀπικέσθαι λέγουσι Πέρσαι ('The Persians say that Io came to Egypt in this way', Hdt. 1.2.1; accusative plus infinitive)

(277) ἥξειν νομίζεις παῖδα σὸν γαίας ὕπο; ('Do you think your son will return from beneath the earth?', E. *HF* 296; accusative plus infinitive)

(316) εἰ μὲν ὅσιά σοι δοκῶ παθεῖν ('If you think the treatment I have received is such as the gods approve', E. *Hec.* 788; nominative plus infinitive)

Verbs of denying are followed by μή + *infinitive* (§ 33.2 (iii)):

(305) ὁ Πρεξάσπης ἔξαρνος ἦν (= ἐξηρνέετο) μὴ .... ἀποκτεῖναι Σμέρδιν ('Prexaspes denied that he had killed Smerdis', Hdt. 3.67.1; nominative plus infinitive)

Articular infinitive (§ 35)

nominative, as subject:
(327) οὐκ ἄρα τὸ χαίρειν ἐστὶν εὖ πράττειν ('So to enjoy oneself is not to fare well', Pl. *Grg.* 497a3; dynamic; does not refer to any particular time-sphere)

genitive, with a phrase governing the genitive:
(331) πρὸς τὴν πόλιν προσβαλόντες ἐς ἐλπίδα μὲν ἦλθον τοῦ ἑλεῖν ('... having attacked the city they at first had hopes of taking it', Th. 2.56.4; dynamic)

dative of instrument/cause; articular accusative plus infinitive:
(335) ἦν ... ἡ βασίλεως ἀρχὴ ... τῷ διεσπάσθαι τὰς δυνάμεις ἀσθενής ('The king's power was weakened because of the scattered condition of the forces', X. *An.* 1.5.9; non-dynamic, the infinitive refers to an independent fact)

IVB   PARTICIPLE (§§ 36-40)

As an obligatory constituent; always with factive value (§ 37)

- With verbs of *perceiving, knowing; emotion; enduring* etc.

(344) ἤκουσε Κῦρον ἐν Κιλικίᾳ ὄντα ('He heard that Cyrus was in Cilicia', X. *An.* 1.4.5; accusative plus participle; factive value: Cyrus *was* in Cilicia. ἤκουσε Κῦρον ἐν Κιλικίᾳ εἶναι = it is not certain that Cyrus was in Cilicia)

(347) οἱ δ' ὡς ἔγνωσαν ἐξηπατημένοι... ('When they found that they had been deceived ...', Th. 2.4.1; nominative plus participle; factive value: they *had been deceived*)

(353) τοῦτο μὲν οὐκ αἰσχύνομαι λέγων ('My saying this does not make me feel ashamed', X. *Cyr.* 5.1.21; nominative plus participle; factive value: I *am saying this*)

- With *phasal* verbs (e.g. ἄρχομαι, διατελέω, παύω/παύομαι); e.g.

(356) ἄρξομαι ... ἀπὸ τῆς ἰατρικῆς λέγων ('I shall begin (by) speaking about medicine', Pl. *Smp.* 186b)

- With τυγχάνω, λανθάνω, φθάνω; e.g.

(360) ἔτυχον ... ἐν τῇ ἀγορᾷ ὁπλῖται εὕδοντες ('Hoplites happened to be sleeping in the market-place', Th. 4.113.2)

As an optional constituent (use as satellite; both participium coniunctum and genitive absolute) (§ 38)

- *Temporal* modifier

(362) ἀκούσας δὲ ταῦτα ὁ Ἀστυάγης Μήδους ... ὥπλισε πάντας ('When he had heard this, Astyages armed all his Medes', Hdt. 1.127.2; aorist participle: anterior state of affairs)

- *Causal* modifier

(368) ὑπεδέξαντο τὴν τιμωρίαν, νομίζοντες ... ἑαυτῶν εἶναι τὴν ἀποικίαν ('They took up the cause, because they considered the colony to be their own', Th. 1.25.3)

ὡς + *participle: subjective reason* (onus of the reason is on the subject of main verb)

(373) συμφορὴν ἐποιεῦντο τοὺς λόγους ὡς κακόν τι πεισομένης (' ... they were sorry for her words, thinking that the king would do her some hurt', Hdt. 8.69.1)

ἅτε + *participle: objective reason* (onus of the reason is on the narrator)

(376) ἀπῆγε τὴν στρατιὴν ὀπίσω ἅτε τῷ πεζῷ ... προσπταίσας πρὸς τοὺς Βρύγους ... ('... he led his host away homewards since the Brygi had dealt a heavy blow to his army ...', Hdt. 6.45.2)

- *Conditional* modifier

(378) ὃ νῦν ὑμεῖς <u>μὴ πειθόμενοι</u> ἡμῖν πάθοιτε ἄν ('That which might well happen to you if you do not listen to us', Th. 1.40.2; μὴ πειθόμενοι = εἰ μὴ πείθοισθε)

- *Concessive* modifier (often preceded by καίπερ)

(380) τὸν ... Ἄδρηστον κατοικτίρει, <u>καίπερ ἐὼν</u> ἐν κακῷ ... τοσούτῳ ('He took pity on Adrastus, though his own sorrow was so great', Hdt. 1.45.2)

- Modifier of *manner*

(384) ἀπώλεσέν μ' <u>εἰποῦσα</u> συμφορὰς ἐμάς ('She has destroyed me by speaking of my troubles', E. *Hipp.* 596)

- *Comparative* modifier (always preceded by ὥσπερ)

(387) ἐπιδεικνὺς ... τὴν εὐήθειαν τοῦ τὰ πλοῖα αἰτεῖν κελεύοντος, <u>ὥσπερ</u> πάλιν τὸν στόλον <u>Κύρου ποιουμένου</u> ('... pointing out the foolishness of the speaker who had urged them to ask for ships, just as if Cyrus were going home again', X. *An.* 1.3.16)

PERIPHRASTIC CONSTRUCTIONS (§ 39)

- *εἰμί + participle*

(389) τὰ δ' ὄργι' <u>ἐστὶ</u> τίν' ἰδέαν <u>ἔχοντά</u> σοι; ('What form are these rites provided with in your view?', E. *Ba.* 471)

(393) οἱ δὲ Αἰτωλοὶ (<u>βεβοηθηκότες</u> γὰρ ἤδη <u>ἦσαν</u> ἐπὶ τὸ Αἰγίτιον) προσέβαλλον τοῖς Ἀθηναίοις ('But the Aetolians (by this time they had come to the rescue of Aigition) attacked the Athenians', Th. 3.97.3)

- *ἔχω + participle*

(398) τὸν λόγον δέ σου πάλαι <u>θαυμάσας ἔχω</u>, ὅσῳ καλλίω τοῦ προτέρου ἀπηργάσω ('But all along I have been wondering at your discourse, you made it so much more beautiful than the first', Pl. *Phdr.* 257c)

ATTRIBUTIVE PARTICIPLE (§ 40)

- In *attributive* position (i.e. with article)

τὸ χρηστήριον τὸ τῷ Ἀλυάττῃ γενόμενον the oracular response given to Alyattes, τῇ ἐπιγιγνεμένῃ ἡμέρᾳ on the next day, etc. Used substantively: οἱ παρὰ τὴν θάλατταν οἰκοῦντες those living along the sea, etc.

- As *apposition*

(402) μετὰ ταῦτα Κῦρος ἐξελαύνει ... ἐπὶ τὸν Χάλον ποταμόν, <u>ὄντα</u> τὸ εὖρος πλέθρου ('After this Cyrus marched to the Chalus river, which is a plethrum in width ...', X. *An.* 1.4.9)

V   VOICE (DIATHESIS) (§§ 41-48)

PASSIVE MEANING (§ 42)

- With *transitive* verbs governing an accusative. The Patient has the syntactic function subject. Also with a number of verbs governing a *genitive* or *dative*. A prepositional Agent-phrase is rare. The aorist is of the passive type (-θη-/-η-). E.g.:

(405) αἱ νῆες <u>παρασκευάζονται</u> (ὑπὸ τῶν Ἀθηναίων) ('The ships (Patient-subject) are being prepared (by the Athenians)); cp. οἱ Ἀθηναῖοι παρασκευάζουσι τὰς ναῦς (Patient-object))

(407) <u>ἐπιβουλευόμενοι</u> διάξουσι πάντα τὸν βίον ('... being plotted against they will pass their days', Pl. *R.* 417b; cp. ἐπιβουλεύω τινί)

- *Verbal adjectives* (§ 42.4)

The adjectives in -τος, -η, -ον either express a passive state e.g. κρυπτός hidden, ἀφύλακτος unguarded, or express that the state of affairs can or deserves to be done, e.g. διαβατός fordable, ἄρρητος not to be divulged, ἐπαινετός laudable.

The adjectives in -τέος, -τέα, -τέον express a (passive) necessity. The Agent usually appears in the dative (*dativus auctoris*)

(410) οὐκοῦν δῆλον ὅτι ... <u>ὠφελητέα</u> σοι ἡ πόλις ἐστίν ('Liter.: Clearly, then, the city must be benefitted by you', X. *Mem.* 3.6.3; ἡ πόλις is Patient-Subject, cp. ἡ πόλις ὠφελεῖται)

There is also an impersonal use, -τέον (ἐστί) or -τέα (ἐστί)

(413) σοὶ <u>βαδιστέον</u> πάρος ('You must go first', S. *El.* 1502)

DIRECT-REFLEXIVE USE (§ 43)

With *agentive transitive* verbs that denote a *habitual physical treatment*. The middle-passive voice expresses that the Agent applies the state of affairs to himself: the Patient is co-referential with the Agent and is incorporated into the verb form. The aorist is of the middle type (-σάμην). E.g.:

(414) αἰσθόμενοι δὲ αὐτοὺς οἱ Ἀθηναῖοι ... <u>παρασκευαζομένους</u> ... ('When the Athenians perceived that they (sc. the enemy) were preparing themselves ...', Th. 3.16.1; παρασκευάζομαι without object = direct-reflexive)

INDIRECT-REFLEXIVE USE (§ 44)

With *agentive transitive* verbs that denote a state of affairs that *may be in the interest of the Agent as well as of some other person*. Middle-passive voice: the state of affairs is in the interest of the Agent. An object is usually present. The aorist is of the middle type (-σάμην). E.g.:

(427) ἀπὸ ὀλυρέων <u>ποιεῦνται</u> σιτία ('They make food from a coarse grain', Hdt. 2.36.2; for themselves; ποιεῦσι = for someone else)

PSEUDO-REFLEXIVE AND PSEUDO-PASSIVE USE (§ 45)

With *transitive causative* verbs, i.e. verbs that denote a state of affairs which causes a change in the situation of the Patient. The middle-passive voice expresses that the subject changes his own situation (: Agent; pseudo-reflexive) or is internally affected by a change (: Experiencer; pseudo-passive). Mostly used intransitively, i.e. without object. The aorist is of the passive type (-θη-/-η-). E.g.:

(437) Δαρεῖος ... <u>ἐπορεύετο</u> διὰ τῆς Θρηίκης ('Darius journeyed through Thrace', Hdt. 4.89.2; pseudo-reflexive use; active πορεύω τινά = make to go, convey)

(443) ἀλλ᾽ οὐδ᾽ ὁ χρηστὸς οὑτοσὶ νεανίας <u>ἐγείρεται</u> τῆς νυκτός ('But this fine young man here won't wake up during the night', Ar. *Nu.* 8-9; pseudo-passive use; active ἐγείρω τινά = wake up someone)

MEDIA TANTUM (MIDDLE AORIST, -ΣΑΜΗΝ OR -ΟΜΗΝ (§ 47.1))

With aorist in -σάμην: agentive verbs. E.g.:

αἰτιῶμαι + acc. accuse, aor. ᾐτιασάμην; passive aor. with passive meaning: ᾐτιάθην
ἅλλομαι jump, aor. ἡλάμην

With aorist in -όμην: agentive and, more often, non-agentive verbs. E.g.:

πυνθάνομαι + acc. inquire (agentive), aorist ἐπυθόμην learn, be told (non-agentive)
ἀφικνοῦμαι arrive, aor. ἀφικόμην (non-agentive)

PASSIVA TANTUM (PASSIVE AORIST, -ΘΗ-/-Η- (§ 47.2))

Agentive and non-agentive verbs. In het latter case, the subject is Experiencer (= internally affected). E.g.:

ἐπιμελοῦμαι + gen. take care of, aor. ἐπεμελήθην (agentive)
δέομαι + gen. need, be in want (non-agentive); beg, request (agentive), aor. ἐδεήθην
δύναμαι be able (non-agentive), aor. ἐδυνήθην
βούλομαι want (non-agentive), aor. ἐβουλήθην

Made in the USA
San Bernardino, CA
13 September 2016